# A Universal Second Language

## By

## Elmer Joseph Hankes

## PRELIMINARY EDITION

FOR RESEARCH PURPOSES ONLY

**Persons wishing to learn this language and communication system should obtain a copy of the first edition due in 1993/4**

THE HANKES FOUNDATION

MINNEAPOLIS MINNESOTA 55403-3001 U S A

This Preliminary Edition of 10,000 copies was manufactured in The United States of America.



**Library of Congress Cataloging in Publication Data**

Hankes, Elmer Joseph, 1913–

⊧⅃Γ2x Ehmay ghee chah — A Universal Second Language

1. Languages, Artificial. 2. Languages, Universal.

I. Title.

PM8088.H34 1992 — 499′.99 — 81–71727

AACR2

English Preliminary Edition (for research and development).

ISBN 0–925837–10–5



**THE HANKES FOUNDATION**

1768 Colfax Ave. S. Minneapolis, Minnesota 55403–3001 U.S.A.

# NOTICE TO ALL RECIPIENTS OF THIS PRELIMINARY EDITION

This work was distributed on a complimentary basis to about 6000 professional people concerned with the development, dissemination and preservation of knowledge, in the hope and expectation that they would expose their colleagues and students to its possibilities. It is also hoped that many of you will organize experimental learning and discussion centers. To facilitate such activities, Elmer Hankes and the Hankes Foundation, do hereby permit xeroxing parts of this preliminary edition, in such quantities as may be needed to properly and expeditiously conduct experimental studies on universal languages and the universal numerical nomenclature. This permission is limited to professional circles and not to the general public; nor shall any copies be offered for sale in whole or in part to anyone. Permission to override the copyright restrictions applies only to this preliminary edition and ceases December 31, 1993. Newspapers, magazines, newsletters, other media and professional journals must comply with the usual copyright restrictions. The Hankes Foundation has a limited number of copies for cash sale to identified professionals, organizations and serious amateurs. The price is a modest five U.S. dollars per copy (prepaid by you —we are not a business per se.), including surface postage to any 'not-for-profit' institution, school, or library anywhere in the world that subscribes to the international postal convention. If you want air shipment you must prepay the entire air mail cost because we encounter additional non-standard handling costs. (The shipping weight is 15 oz. or 450 gr.) The five dollar price applies only to the institutions mentioned and members of their staffs. All others must pay the listed price of fifteen dollars.

Of course we want to hear from you but we ask that all of your correspondence be in English because we cannot afford to pay for translations. In a few years when we all use ⊧⅃Γ2ₓ that will be no problem. As you form study groups please let us know so that we can put you in touch with other groups.

Our address is 1768 Colfax Avenue South; Minneapolis, Minnesota U.S.A. 55403-3001.

# AUTHOR'S PREFACE

In 1982 "Enterprises of Great Pith and Moment ⊧⅃ˉΓ (*EmSighAy*)" was issued by the Camilla Publishing Company. Although the rules and format for the vocabulary were defined, a vocabulary was not formulated at that time. During the intervening years attempts to do so using scholars in Calcutta and other Indian cities met with little success, so early in 1990 I took it upon myself to do so. This activity generated many changes including the name of the language which is now called ⊧⅃Γ2ₓ (*EhmayGheeChah*) or 'second language' to emphasize the fact that it is meant to be a universal utility language. Although it is more comprehensive than any other invented language, it is not designed to replace existing languages but just to give everyone a common tongue.

I do not argue the pros and cons of, or the need for, a lingua franca. Many have and still others will continue to do so. That there is some need is attested to by the many attempts at it, even though none have been successful. Then too, English because of its inherent flexibility and tremendous literature plus the post war economic and scientific dominance of the United States, has assumed that role. Ethnic, religious and nationalistic biases and the long time that it takes to learn mitigate against its general acceptance, so it tends to be elitist. In countries where it is used a lot, even where it is the dominant tongue, it changes in ways that are puzzling to its other users. Rather than argue the point, I herewith present a viable solution, which is part of a total package of human communications, and invite you to participate in this noble enterprise.

Elmer Hankes May 1992

FOR WORLD PEACE NOW AND FOREVER

## ACKNOWLEDGEMENTS, SALUTES and Γ⅂Γ·


To the most marvelous age in the history of mankind.

To the most wonderful nation for freedom and opportunity.

To scientists and scholars.

To our schools and teachers.

To the people.

To Roget, Chapman et.al.

To BASIC English, Esperanto, and the many other attempts;
their authors and adherents.

To Amiga, TEX, Max, Bob, Dick, Dwayne, Steve et.al.

To persistence.

To PEACE.

To you.

To a future full of promise and peril
that is yours to build and master.

**and may I take a bow too?**

# TABLE of CONTENTS

To

EVAN,

my grandson

# ⊦ ┘ Γ 2×

The graphemes in the above title are individually pronounced *Eh, Muh, Ay, Ghee, and Chah*; all together—*Ehmay ghee chah* with a slight accent on the first letter. As you will later discover, all words that begin ⊦┘ have to do with language. You will also learn that all of our core words are triads (three letters long). I say "all cores" even though there may be four to ten monads or words of only one letter; and combinations of cores yielding words of six, nine or twelve letters with or without intervening *linkages*, the punctuational graphemes which are unique to ⊦┘Γ2×. If ultimately used (as of now they are optional) six of the monads will be personal pronouns and four will be the very important amenities *please, excuse me, thank you* and *you're welcome.* Indeed, our very first word is Γ (*Ay*) meaning please. Because this is the most important word in all languages as regards harmonious human interrelationships I appended the letter Γ to ⊦┘ to give the implication of "polite language" and 'decreed' that ⊦┘Γ2× should be regarded as always being in the polite mode, countered only by the addition of the imperative ! or !! (! *Sweefeh* or !! in ⊦┘Γ2×). The saltire × *CHah* is a punctuational grapheme that when used before a numeral indicates a cardinal number and when after, an ordinal number; thus ×6 *CHahGah* is number 6; but 6× *GahCHah* is 6th; and 2× *GheeCHah* is 2nd.

It is important to note that ⊦┘Γ2× is the key part of a major communicational concept geared to human capabilities, needs and limitations as well as the marvels of modern technology with their great future potential. In fact, ⊦┘Γ2× is designed to facilitate the realization of some of that potential, particularly with regard to the interface of man and machine and the integration of the handicapped into the mainstream of the general population. With ⊦┘Γ2×, people are able to communicate even if blind, deaf and mute. It sounds like a tall order but stay the course and watch it unfold.

The alphabet has 20 vowels, 20 consonants and 16 POTENTS. These characters have a dual binary basis. Each has one to three short horizontal bars sticking out from either side of a vertical stem or spine, but never from both sides. The bars are evenly spaced with one at the top of the spine, one at the bottom, and the other in the middle. In the binary scheme of things the top bar is considered to have a value of one unit, the middle bar two units and the bottom bar four units. At least one of the bars is always present so there is no 'zero'. The top bar is ONE; middle bar alone gives TWO; top and middle together give THREE; bottom alone is FOUR; middle and bottom together give us SIX; and all three bars together yield SEVEN. The dots appear only on the same side as the bars. The upper dot is located between the positions occupied by bars one and two and the lower dot appears between the positions occupied by bars two and four. Otherwise the bars and dots are independent of each other; that's why we can refer to the system as a dual binary. The dots yield counts of ZERO, ONE, TWO and THREE. Now refer to the chart on page 5. Notice that when the bars (and dots) are to the right of the stem the character is a vowel (V), and when they are to the left of the stem it is a consonant (C). In the upper left-hand corner of each box of the chart you will see a two numeral number. There are 100 numbers from 00 to 99. The first numeral represents the digital total of the dots for that particular character and the second numeral is the digital total of its bars. This is exactly true for the vowels but for the consonants a count of four has been added to the initial numeral. In the chart the alphabet occupies a space seven blocks horizontally by eight blocks vertically. That leaves 44 blocks which are taken up by punctuational characters or operational functions. We'll get to them in due course.

I've taken some pains to describe the two digit code because it figures very importantly in the development of the vocabulary and the typesetting of this book. I devised this code so that the ⊦JΓ2x characters could be entered from the same keyboard used to enter the roman alphabet and arabic numerals without the dreadfully laborious procedure of switching back and forth between several keyboard configurations or using three or four keystrokes for each character and being constrained to using the codes specified for each particular computer and program. I was confident that the ⊦JΓ2x characters could be entered through the 10 key numerical key pad which is a part of all computer keyboards but it took two discouraging years before I finally convinced an experienced professional programmer that it could be done. Once convinced he produced very versatile programs based on the Amiga computer and the TEX program. This has so greatly simplified and expedited the compilation of the vocabulary that I can truly say that I could not otherwise have brought ⊦JΓ2x to its present state in my alloted days. These programs may be made available to those who wish to make a serious contribution to ⊦JΓ2x. See page 148 for details.

The TEX programs permitted me to make an initial listing of nearly 12,000 words from various sources including "Roget's International Thesaurus" (Fourth Edition ©1979 Harper & Row Ltd.). Then by using the very fast index generator and analytical spreadsheets those 12,000 entries were reduced in several stages over a period of time to about 6,000. Despite the indispensable help of the TEX program this is very arduous and intensive work for a person working alone. In the spreadsheets I can still see many places for improvement in word location and arrangement by categories but it's necessary to publish now so that the manuscript can be given a wide distribution to get the benefit of widespread cultural input. There are many words that can be deleted; some that are unneeded in a utility language and others that can be reasonably compounded from the remaining cores. I would guess that even with the expected addition of words of importance from other cultures and the discovery of inadvertent omissions, that the final total of cores would not exceed 5,000. The final selection is a proper job for the editorial staffs of the publishers, that may elect to issue this work, working together with linguistic institutions, scholars and other interested parties. The computer programs are a big help, but specialized human knowledge is the deciding factor because the establishment of a viable vocabulary requires one judgmental decision after the other!

The nations and peoples of the world are in ferment as never before. A unifying project like ⊦JΓ2x may be just the thing to promote peace because it has no national, ethnic, or overt linguistic parentage. It just does the communicational thing that mankind has developed over the ages but does it in a comprehensive, up-to-date and logically organized way. As a foreign language to everyone it is less liable to alteration and abuse than one's native language and because everyone starts from the same base, the learner's confidence is improved because there is no sense of being patronized or ridiculed by other users. Learning it will not overburden local educational facilities. All one needs to know is contained in this book. Its many features stimulate interest and its logic adds immeasurably to the learner's mental development.

Traditional alphabets have innumerable combinations of arcs that defy resolution except by very sophisticated (and expensive) devices. Some systems require that the documents being read must have been created with a special type size and format. The ⊦JΓ2x characters are already of that nature. Except for the ten arabic numerals there are only straight lines and dots in designated positions. Only the diagonal lines of the virgules and saltires offer any difficulty. ⊦JΓ2x reduces the number of options that a scanning system must consider by several orders of magnitude. Even neatly handwritten ⊦JΓ2x letters would be machine readable. Other considerations in the design are ease of learning, retention and recall. Instant recognition which involves instant response to viewing or hearing a letter by visualizing it when it is heard, and by being able to voice it when it is seen requires practice and takes time, so a set of flashcards is included. Because of my advanced age I am a rather slow reader of ⊦JΓ2x. When this book is finished and has been distributed I will get someone to help me practice with the flash cards.

Although system and logic are more elusive when we seek to apply some phonetic order to the letters you will see that a fairly good solution has been achieved. The consonants follow a consistent pattern but the vowels have minor irregularities. The ⊦JΓ2x alphabet has 56 characters each with its own distinct and discrete sound, but even including all of the punctuation, numbers and operational commands there are only thirty separate phonemes. In our situation discreetness is a measure of the phonic separation between sounds that ensures reliability in audition and in voice operated devices. The reduction in the number of phonemes and their discreetness reduces the burden on audio devices to the same degree that our graphics do for scanners.

The chart on page 5 is complete and explicit. It is the heart of ⊦JΓ2x. When you have mastered everything in it you will be half way home as far as ⊦JΓ2x is concerned. Write and voice these letters. If you use the tape you will learn the numbers in just a few days at most. Then from the same tape you can learn the alphabetic sounds. Voice the sounds as closely as you can to those on the audio tape. In fact close isn't good enough. You must achieve perfection. The key to a successful international language is standardization of the phonics from both a vocal and auditory standpoint. It is because of this that each of the letter sounds must always be distinct, unaffected by adjacent letters as in other languages. This feature of ⊦JΓ2x eliminates the "marzidoats" syndrome, aids audition and facilitates machine speech, dictation and computer operation by vocal commands. Keeping phonic clarity and discreetness at a high level provides a basis for the use of ⊦JΓ2x as a communication system for the handicapped and in emergency or stressful situations. You may find the sounds odd or funny, but to some degree that's always the case when you study a foreign language. Just remember that everyone studying ⊦JΓ2x is starting out from the same base. After you have really learned the phonics, go for instant recognition by getting someone to help you with the flashcards. In two to four weeks you should be ready to study word formation and the discipline of the categories as expressed in the spreadsheets.

In speech you must develop a certain cadence to give the listener a clear signal of word separation. It helps that all core words are 3 letters long. The most important way that you can define your words is to stress the first letter and to give a slight pause at the end of each word.

Some things are discussed in the appendix because ⊧JΓ2x has several important aspects. There is the general utility language; then special vocabularies; computers; global locations and physical features; name development for devices, procedures, and other man made things; Participation, education, control and related activities; and the further development and implementation of ⊧JΓ2x' benefits for the handicapped. This last item should be thoroughly investigated by those institutions, individuals, schools and governmental agencies that are already active in that field. I shall seek to obtain their cooperation and active involvement. The items in the appendix are not to be regarded as of lesser importance, it's just that the general language is enough to deal with at the outset. All of the other things depend on its success.

⊧JΓ2x doesn't have an upper and lower case. The letters have only one form.. For signs or dramatic effects the letters may be in a horizontal mode, slanted. adorned etc. but for the most part they will be in the vertical mode as shown in the chart. Punctuation can only be in the vertical mode. There being no cursive or connected characters, handwriting becomes hand-printing, resulting in vastly improved legibility.

> This chapter ended at this point until March 26, just two weeks before going to press when, while recording the numbers on the tape, it came upon me with great force that the ⊧JΓ2x numerical nomenclature by itself alone, could be the greatest boon of the twenty-first century! Just think of how many different ways there are to say each of the commonly used numbers and that no other language has the logical orderliness of ⊧JΓ2x. With that revelation I changed the back cover to emphasize the G-J-Z names. Think how splendid it would be to create a universally beneficial grass-roots revolution by everyone learning the G-J-Z nomenclature. It's incredibly easy; you can have it firmly implanted in less than a week. Try it, and get others to do so, too. We don't have to wait for governmental action for this one. Get it going. It doesn't cost anything and takes so very little time and effort. Nor does it take anything away from anyone or anything. It can live in harmony with the existing systems. I think that the advantages will be so apparent that everyone will be happy to cooperate, especially those persons that have to work with foreign telephone operators.

Γ ⊧⊣⊧ ▪

*Ay WihPingWye Swee* or in English, "please help."
(▪ *Swee* is the ⊧JΓ2x period)

| | | | | | | | | | |
|---|---|---|---|---|---|---|---|---|---|
| 01 *Ay* | 02 *Ee* | 03 *I* | 04 *Aw* | 05 *Ow* | 06 *ŌŌ* | 07 *Oi* | 08 kern ← *Fuh* | 09 alien *Shuh* | 00 space → *Suh* |
| 11 *wAy* | 12 *wEe* | 13 *wYe* | 14 *wAw* | 15 *wOw* | 16 *woo* | 17 *wOi* | 18 *Saw* | 19 *Sow* | 10 *See* |
| 21 *Ah* | 22 *Eh* | 23 *Ih* | 24 *ă* | 25 *Oh* | 26 *who* | 27 *hOi* | 28 *Swaw* | 29 *Swow* | 20 *Swee* |
| 31 *wAh* | 32 *wEh* | 33 *wIh* | 34 *wă* | 35 *wOe* | 36 *you* | 37 *yOi* | 38 *CHwah* | 39 *CHwih* | 30 *Sweefee* |
| 41 *K* | 42 *T* | 43 *P* | 44 *M* | 45 *L* | 46 *D* | 47 *N* | 48 *Să* | 49 *Soh* | 40 *Seh* |
| 51 *sK* | 52 *sT* | 53 *sP* | 54 *sM* | 55 *sL* | 56 *sD* | 57 *sN* | | | 50 *Seefeh* |
| 61 *King* | 62 *Ting* | 63 *Ping* | 64 *Ming* | 65 *Ling* | 66 *Ding* | 67 *Ning* | | | 60 *Sweefeh* |
| 71 *sKing* | 72 *sTing* | 73 *sPing* | 74 *sMing* | 75 *sLing* | 76 *sDing* | 77 *sNing* | 78 *Swă* | 79 *Swoe* | 70 *Sweh* |
| 81 *Say* | 82 *Sway* | 83 *Swayfay* | 84 *Sah* | 85 *Sayfah* | 86 *Swayfah* | 87 *Swah* | 88 *CHay* | 89 *CHway* | 80 *CHah* |
| 91 *Sigh* | 92 *Swye* | 93 *Swyefie* | 94 *Sih* | 95 *Sighfih* | 96 *Swyefih* | 97 *Swih* | 98 *CHigh* | 99 *CHwye* | 90 *CHih* |

*Soo* is the decimal point *Soi* is the comma for pointing off 1,000's \chuh is 1/2 kern

## PUNCTUATION NOT SHOWN IN THE CHART

| Grapheme | Phoneme | TeX Macro | Keypad Codes |
|---|---|---|---|
| | *SwawFaw* | \aw3 | 18-08-28 |
| | *SawFă* | \aw5 | 18-08-48 |
| | *SwawFă* | \aw6 | 28-08-48 |
| | *SwowFow* | \ow3 | 19-08-29 |
| | *SowFoh* | \ow5 | 19-08-49 |
| | *SwowFoh* | \ow6 | 29-08-49 |
| | *CHwayVay* | \cha3 | 88-08-89 |
| | *CHayVah* | \cha5 | 88-08-80 |
| | *CHwayVah* | \cha6 | 89-08-80 |
| | *CHwyeVigh* | \chi3 | 98-08-99 |
| | *CHighVih* | \chi5 | 98-08-90 |
| | *CHwyeVih* | \chi6 | 99-08-90 |

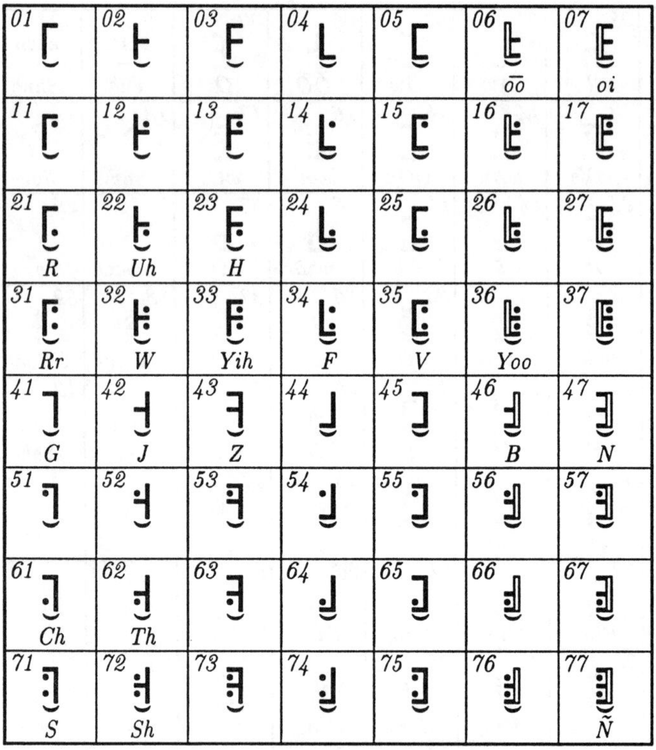

| 01 | 02 | 03 | 04 | 05 | 06 $\overline{oo}$ | 07 oi |
|---|---|---|---|---|---|---|
| 11 | 12 | 13 | 14 | 15 | 16 | 17 |
| 21 R | 22 Uh | 23 H | 24 | 25 | 26 | 27 |
| 31 Rr | 32 W | 33 Yih | 34 F | 35 V | 36 Yoo | 37 |
| 41 G | 42 J | 43 Z | 44 | 45 | 46 B | 47 N |
| 51 | 52 | 53 | 54 | 55 | 56 | 57 |
| 61 Ch | 62 Th | 63 | 64 | 65 | 66 | 67 |
| 71 S | 72 Sh | 73 | 74 | 75 | 76 | 77 Ñ |

Note: The tape codes for the alien characters are formed by adding 100 to the code numbers in the chart.

We cannot expect people to give up their names and the names of things and places, so for the most part such items will be in their usual form in their native alphabet. But we do need to provide a phonetic equivalent, in our codes, to permit universal voicing and machine dictation. That is the reason for the alien characters. Also, to assure proper interpretation of names and to prevent their being misinterpreted as ⊧JΓ2x words, five of the POTENTS (p.11) are devoted to various aspects of this problem. They need not be attached to words that are in native languages, but they are prefixed to all ⊧JΓ2x names. Their presence prevents that particular collection of letters from being interpreted as an ⊧JΓ2x word. Names can be of any length and can have both regular and alien characters. The punctuational protocols of ⊧JΓ2x regarding reflexive, possessive and plural will be observed. In conversation the name POTENT will be silent except when the failure to voice it could lead to serious misunderstanding or confusion. There are, or will be, ⊧JΓ2x names beginning with CC or VV for places and things that will not use the name POTENTS because their initial letters give them categorical identification and their first three letters are important functional identifiers. VV and CC ⊧JΓ2x words are in the higher level vocabulary. See p.150.

Company names may be registered for protection with an ⊧JΓ2x central agency. No other names can. All ⊧JΓ2x letters and other graphics are copyrighted and registered as the property of the Hankes Foundation. Combinations of graphics and compilations and publication of the resultant ⊧JΓ2x words will be under the sole control of the central agency to be established by the Foundation and its publisher-licensees.

Two major aspects of human communication have already been universally standardized. Arabic numerals including that greatest and simplest of inventions, the zero and its offspring, the decimal system are used and understood in their written form in all countries. If only their names could have been standardized too! The French development of the metric system came into being during the first flowering of the scientific revolution. It was not universally accepted until its superiority became evident as the industrial age matured. Now it is accepted in its entirety including nomenclature everywhere. The only holdout is the United States where its implementation has lagged despite its enactment by Congress. There is no doubt that this omission has a negative affect on our unfavorable trade balance and we should do more to join the world community in this regard. ⊦JΓ2x uses the metric system in all of its elegant orderliness as prescribed by the International Bureau of Weights and Measures without any changes in nomenclature whatsoever, but must make concessions to local customs. This all falls into the category of names and alien characters.

⊦JΓ2x gives patterned names to the numerals and decimal categories both greater or less than zero. As we did in the punctuational phonemes we will use the vowels of the five letters Γ, ⊦, F, L, [, Γ·, ⊦·, ⊧, L·, and [·. But in this case the identifying phonemes will be G for the units; J for the decades (10s) and Z for the higher orders. In ⊦JΓ2x we never write out the names of numbers but always use the Arabic form.

| | UNITS | | DECADES | HIGHER ORDERS | | |
|---|---|---|---|---|---|---|
| 1 | *Gay* | 10 | *Jay* | 1,000 | *Zay* | or 1ˣ3 |
| 2 | *Ghee* | 20 | *Jhee* | 1,000,000 | *Zee* | or 1ˣ6 |
| 3 | *Guy* | 30 | *Jigh* | 1,000,000,000 | *Zigh* | or 1ˣ9 |
| 4 | *Gaw* | 40 | *Jaw* | 1,000,000,000,000 | *Zaw* | or 1ˣ12 |
| 5 | *Gow* | 50 | *Jow* | 2,000,000,000,000,000 | *Zow* | or 2ˣ15 |
| 6 | *Gah* | 60 | *Jah* | 3,000,000,000,000,000,000 | *Zah* | or 3ˣ18 |
| 7 | *Geh* | 70 | *Jeh* | 1,000,000,000,000,000,000,000 | *Zeh* | or 1ˣ21 |
| 8 | *Gih* | 80 | *Jih* | | *Zih* | or 1ˣ24 |
| 9 | *Gă* | 90 | *Jă* | | *Ză* | or 1ˣ27 |
| 0 | *Go* | 100 | *Jo* | INFINITY | *Zo* | or ∞ |

In ⊦JΓ2x The decimal point is voiced as *Soo.* Thousands may be pointed off with a comma called *Soi.*

1ˣ3 *Gay CHwayVay Guy* is 1 times 10 to the third power or 1,000, but 1ˣ-3 *Gay CHwayVay Swye Guy* (note the minus sign) is 0.001 .

Numbers less than zero should always begin with zero decimal point (0.) *Go Soo* as a matter of accuracy and emphasis. Therefore .25 should be 0.25 *Go Soo ghee Gow*

Fractions are simply stated as one number divided by another, e.g., 3⁄8 *Guy Swow Gih*, or 7⁄16 *Geh Swow JayGah; Swow* is 'divided by'. Reciprocals can be stated as ∃2 *Nuh Ghee*, (1/2). ∃ is the antonym POTENT *Nuh*, so 7∃16 *Geh Nuh JayGah* is another way of saying 7/16.

Other examples are; 0.00125 is *Go Soo GoGoGayGheeGow*, 1.25 is *GaySooGhee Gow*, and 60,379 is *JahZay GuyJo JehGă.*

For clock time see page 11.

The purpose of the ⊧JΓ2x audio-tape is to establish the phonic value of the vowels and consonants so that spoken ⊧JΓ2x will be universally understood. It starts as I say "⊧JΓ2x by Elmer Hankes". After a pause I'll repeat that to give you a chance to say it yourself. Everything on the tape will be repeated. Keep talking along with me and rerun each section of the tape until you are letter perfect before going on to the next section. You will be guided by the charts on the next page and coordinated by the sound of a drum, bell, whistle, musical notes and cymbal in various combinations as printed in the left margin of each line of the charts. After each phonic identifier I will carefully recite and repeat the items in that line so that you can do the same. Work with a friend so that you will not only master ⊧JΓ2x speech but also become accustomed to hearing its unique sounds. Remember, you must be exact. Unlike native languages ⊧JΓ2x does not tolerate regional variations. Only 14 phonemes are needed for the ⊧JΓ2x numbers, which we will call 2x. They are G, J, Z, Soo (for the decimal point) and ten vowels. The ten vowels will be learned in a particular order because they are the decimal 'names' of the units, decades and higher orders. They also are the basis of the punctuational nomenclature. G is the units identifier; J is for decades and Z for the higher orders. G, J, and Z have no other function in ⊧JΓ2x itself. Their only other use is in foreign names in which case they may be presented in their native alphabets or by an *alien* character. After you have completed the numbers on the next page We'll come back to this page for some numerical exercises before going on to the alpabetic chart. The bells, whistles etc. will keep us synchronized. LET'S GO TO PAGE 9! ⟶

---

<u>DRUM4</u> NOW WE'RE BACK!

| 10 | 11 | 12 | 13 | 14 | 15 | 16 | 17 | 18 | 19 |
|---|---|---|---|---|---|---|---|---|---|
| *Jay* | *JayGay* | *JayGhee* | *JayGuy* | *JayGaw* | *JayGow* | *JayGah* | *JayGeh* | *JayGih* | *JayGă* |
| 20 | 21 | 22 | 23 | 24 | 25 | 26 | 27 | 28 | 29 |
| *Jhee* | *JheeGay* | *JheeGhee* | *JheeGuy* | *JheeGaw* | *JheeGow* | *JheeGah* | *JheeGeh* | *JheeGih* | *JheeGă* |
| 30 | 31 | 32 | 33 | 34 | 35 | 36 | 37 | 38 | 39 |
| *Jigh* | *JighGay* | *JighGhee* | *JighGuy* | *JighGaw* | *JighGow* | *JighGah* | *JighGeh* | *JighGih* | *JighGă* |
| 40 | 41 | (you can see the perfect regularity of these sequences and | | | | | | | |
| *Jaw* | *JawGay* | have no trouble completing the count to 100.) | | | | | | | |
| 90 | 91 | 92 | 93 | 94 | 95 | 96 | 97 | 98 | 99 |
| *Jă* | *JăGay* | *JăGhee* | *JăGuy* | *JăGaw* | *JăGow* | *JăGah* | *JăGeh* | *JăGih* | *JăGă* |

| | | |
|---|---|---|
| Drum1-Bell1 | 4,675.89 | *GawZayGahJoJihGowSooGihGă* |
| Drum1-Bell2 | 34,574.32 | *JighGawZayGowJoJehGawSooGuyGhee* |
| Drum1-Bell3 | 243,687.91 | *GheeJoJawGuyZayGahJoJihGehSooGăGuy* |
| Drum1-Hi note1 | 8,000,432 | *GihZheeGawJoJighGhee* |
| Drum1-Hi note2 | 1,584,000,000 | *GayZighGowJoJihGawZay* |
| Drum1-Lo note1 | 0.134 | *GoSooGayGuyGaw* |
| Drum1-Lo note2 | 0.0054 | *GoSooGoGoGowGaw* |
| Drum1-Lo note3 | 2.0763 | *GheeSooGoGehGahGuy* |

BACK TO PAGE 9 →

---

An optional way to speak the numbers is to read the numerals in order, one at a time giving voice to the commas and decimal point too. That is the way that numbers less than one are spoken. For instance .87 is 0.87 *Go Soo Gih Geh* and 468.35 would be *Gaw Jo Jah Gih Soo Guy Gow*. Always put 0. *Go Soo* (zero decimal point) before numbers less than one.

| | | | | | | | | | | |
|---|---|---|---|---|---|---|---|---|---|---|
| Drum1 | 1 Gay | 2 Ghee | 3 Guy | 4 Gaw | 5 Gow | 6 Gah | 7 Geh | 8 Gih | 9 Ga(t) | 0 Goh |
| Drum2 | 10 Jay | 20 Jhee | 30 Jigh | 40 Jaw | 50 Jow | 60 Jah | 70 Jeh | 80 Jih | 90 Ja(t) | 100 Joh |
| Drum3 | 1,000 Zay | Million Zhee | Billion Zigh | Trillion Zaw | (in Zow | order Zah | by Zeh | 1,000's) Zih | Za(t) | ∞ Zoh |

Drum4 RETURN TO PAGE 7 FOR NUMERICAL EXERCISES

| | | | | | | | |
|---|---|---|---|---|---|---|---|
| Bell1 | 01 *Ay* | 02 *Ee* | 03 *I* | 04 *Aw* | 05 *Ow* | 06 *o͞o* | 07 *Oi* |
| Bell2 | 11 *wAy* | 12 *wEe* | 13 *wYe* | 14 *wAw* | 15 *wOw* | 16 *woo* | 17 *wOi* |
| Bell3 | 21 *Ah* | 22 *Eh* | 23 *Ih* | 24 *a* | 25 *Oh* | 26 *who* | 27 *hOi* |
| Bell4 | 31 *wAh* | 32 *wEh* | 33 *wIh* | 34 *wa* | 35 *wOe* | 36 *you* | 37 *yOi* |
| Whistle1 | 41 *K* | 42 *T* | 43 *P* | 44 *M* | 45 *L* | 46 *D* | 47 *N* |
| Whistle2 | 51 *sK* | 52 *sT* | 53 *sP* | 54 *sM* | 55 *sL* | 56 *sD* | 57 *sN* |
| Whistle3 | 61 *King* | 62 *Ting* | 63 *Ping* | 64 *Ming* | 65 *Ling* | 66 *Ding* | 67 *Ning* |
| Whistle4 | 71 *sKing* | 72 *sTing* | 73 *sPing* | 74 *sMing* | 75 *sLing* | 76 *sDing* | 77 *sNing* |
| Hi note1 | 81 *Say* | 82 *Sway* | 83 *Swayfay* | 84 *Sah* | 85 *Sayfah* | 86 *Swayfah* | 87 *Swah* |
| Hi note2 | 91 *Sigh* | 92 *Swye* | 93 *Swyefie* | 94 *Sih* | 95 *Sighfih* | 96 *Swyefih* | 97 *Swih* |
| Hi note3 | 10 *See* | 20 *Swee* | 30 *Sweefee* | 40 *Seh* | 50 *Seefeh* | 60 *Sweefeh* | 70 *Sweh* |
| Hi note4 | 18 *Saw* | 28 *Swaw* | 318 *SwawFaw* | 48 *Sa* | 518 *SawFa* | 618 *SwawFa* | 78 *Swa* |
| Lo note1 | 19 *Sow* | 29 *Swow* | 319 *SwowFow* | 49 *Soh* | 519 *SowFoh* | 619 *SwowFoh* | 79 *Swoe* |
| Lo note2 | 88 *CHay* | 89 *CHway* | 388 *CHwayVay* | 80 *CHah* | 588 *CHayVah* | 688 *CHwayVah* | 38 *CHwah* |
| Lo note3 | 98 *CHigh* | 99 *CHwye* | 398 *CHwyeVigh* | 90 *CHih* | 598 *CHighVih* | 698 *CHwyeVih* | 39 *CHwih* |
| Lo note4 | decimal point *Soo* | comma *Soi* | | 1/2 kern ⟵ *Chuh* | 08 kern ⟵ *Fuh* | 09 alien *Shuh* | 00 space ⟶ *Suh* |

Keep these charts in view so that you can correlate what we're saying with the graphics. When a particular phonic identifier is sounded I will speak the characters in that line. The words in italics at the bottom of each box express the intended phoneme in English, but they are subject to misinterpretation. The tape will reduce the possible variations in pronunciation. It is important that you learn from the tape and not from other persons. In the future there may be other learning devices but for now the most practical means is the tape. Please observe that five of the vowel sounds in the bell1 (first) and bell3 (third) lines are the ones we used for the numbers. Later you'll discover that they are also used for the punctuation by changing the lead phoneme to *S* or *CH* instead of *G, J or Z*. The sounds in the first and third lines are inflected by a leading *W* to produce the sounds in the bell2 (second) and bell4 (fourth) lines, except for 26–36 and 27–37. These inflections are signaled by the dots. Upper dot for the leading *W* of lines two and four and lower dot for the lagging *H* of lines three and four. It's quite clear on the chart. The consonants use *S* and *ing* in a like manner. Listen for the phonic identifier of each line and you will have no trouble with the alphabet. Go at your best pace. Don't hurry. Learn each section really well before you go on to another. Just keep rewinding the tape and reciting along with me. Try writing the graphemes as you say them. Then go for instant recognition by using the flash cards with a friend but go no further until the alphabet is mastered.

When a binary-two punctuational element is combined with a binary-one or binary-four we pronounce the binary-two element first and preface the other element with *V* for the 88 and 98 families and with *F* for the others. This is to tell the computer or the listener that all of the elements are to be grouped together as a single member of the family. You'll hear this as we voice the pronunciation.

The last thing we will do on the tape is voice the alien characters.

| | | | | | | | | | | | |
|---|---|---|---|---|---|---|---|---|---|---|---|
| Cymbal1 | 106 *o͞o* | 107 *oi* | 121 *R* | 122 *Uh* | 123 *H* | 131 *Rr* | 132 *W* | 146 *B* | 147 *N* | 161 *Ch* | 162 *Th* |
| Cymbal2 | 133 *Yih* | 134 *F* | 135 *V* | 136 *Yoo* | 141 *G* | 142 *J* | 143 *Z* | 171 *S* | 172 *Sh* | 177 *Ñ* | |

⊧JΓ2x is designed for simplicity.

No two words sound alike.

No word has more than one meaning.

All of the core words are triads.

There are no spelling or pronunciational irregularities (or peculiarities).

Plurals, possessives, reflexives and any combination thereof are created by affixing a well defined set of voiced punctuation marks.

Everything is gender neutral except when either of the gender POTENTS E or E is affixed.

Words are readily compounded by following a strict protocol (p.18) so that new concoctions are accurately interpreted by others.

Core words fall into categories identified by their initial letters (see the Chart of Charts p 18). Words in the general vocabulary begin with VC or CV. For instance LC words have to do with government; L̇C with police and military; L.C with law and economics; L:C with business and finance; ⁊V with flora; JV with fauna; J̇V with foods and nutrition; and ]V with sensation. Affixes are ]V or ]C.

All communication involves some action either stated or implied. To a large extent syntax, a word with Greek roots meaning *putting together in an orderly fashion* is dependent on the clear identification of that action or of the word or words that define the action. In complex sentences this may be difficult or become obscure. Our solution, since ⊧JΓ2x is a utility language, is to try to keep all sentences reasonably simple and to put a tag on the action word. This puts more of a burden on the speaker or writer but makes for greater clarity. It also sharpens the ideative process. With the need to label the verb the speaker or writer is more apt to deal in simple sentences. As a rule extemporaneous speakers, but not orators, do keep their statements short because of the feedback or interplay between persons in face to face situations. Direct conversation is either plagued or enhanced by interruptions, incomplete sentences, non-specific but expressive vocalizations, facial expressions, body language, gestures, emotions, tonal variations, etc. So syntax is hardly a problem. Writing is another matter. There is no feedback. Writers must rely on a strict adherence to the rules and at the same time keep shifting into the role of the reader to make sure that the message is going to be understood as intended. Telephonic conversation, especially between strangers, has limited feed back and is more like writing in its need for more formality. Mutual syntactical understanding is assured by the unique features of ⊧JΓ2x.

The features noted above are properly included under syntax because their *labels* give positive identification to many parts of speech. The most important of these labels and the key element in our grammar is the verbal POTENT Ŀ which together with its 'C' consort defines the verb in a sentence. This feature not only helps the reader/auditor but also trains the speaker/writer into simpler more definitive sentences and sharpens the ideative process..

As the name implies, POTENTS (⊦⅃L• *ehmaw sway* in ⊦⅃Γ2x) have special powers. They look like letters (of bar binary-count six or seven) but they are not to be considered as letters but as super affixes. They are not included in the letter count of a triad even if more than one is used on the same word as in EΓ⅃⊦E *woo aimee oo* (aunt paternally related). You will note that spines of the POTENTS in this book are doubled to make them stand out. That's just a font characteristic and need not be done when writing by hand. A POTENT affects only the core that it's attached to. Mostly they appear as prefixes to alert the reader or auditor, but the verbal POTENT is always a suffix because it usually has a C consort.

L VERBALS, *pronounced 'oo' as in woo.* Fully detailed on page 12.

L TIME, *pronounced 'woo'.* Gives a temporal aspect to any core to which it is affixed. Seven time periods are identified by L plus a linkage and numbers. L92 or L1992 is '92 or 1992; L92¯2_14 is Feb. 14, 1992. L‗15⁼36∶24 is 15 hours 36 minutes and 24 seconds or 3:36:24pm; L¯5 is May; L⁝1 is Sunday. Together with L and an appropriate number; ¯ designates months (1 to 12 at present; 21 to 33 for a thirteen month calendar); ⁼ minutes; _ days of the month; ‗ hours of the day (always in the 24 hour mode); ∶ seconds; ⁝ days of the week. - is not used to avoid confusion because of its employment as the minus sign in math. The linkages identify time periods only when numbers are used and L is present.

L MASS ?, *pronounced 'who'.* Since CGS (Centimeter-Gram-Seconds) units are the basis of all physical measurements, might we make something of this? If not consider ⅃ and ⅃ as unassigned.

L SIZE ?, *pronounced 'you'.* L1 is lineal; L2 is areal; L3 is volumetric.

E MASCULINE, *pronounced 'oi' as in oil.*

E FEMININE, *pronounced 'woi'.*

E EXTENDER, *pronounced 'hoi'.* Has potential use in special vocabularies. See appendix p. 131.

E PLACE NAME, *pronounced 'yoi'.* This and the next four items may be prefixed to any string of ⊦⅃Γ2x letters including *aliens* and when any of these five POTENTS appear, the contiguous letter combinations(including other POTENTS) lose all meaning and have phonetic value only. See page 6.

⅃ GIVEN NAME, *pronounced 'duh'.* Usually without the gender POTENTS E or E, which may be used as prefixes to proclaim the sex of that individual; or as affixes to indicate filial relationship to the person or family whose name appears next in the series and are linked together by ∶ *Swyefie* (of).

⅃ FAMILY NAME, *pronounced 'zduh'.* The gender POTENTS may be suffixed to a family name to indicate a matronymic or patronymic.

⅃ NAMES OF DEVICES, *pronounced 'ding'.* See appendix page 150 for classification of devices by words beginning with CC.

⅃ COMPANY NAMES, *pronounced 'zding'.*

Ǝ ANTONYM, *pronounced 'nuh'.*

Ǝ Un-, De-, *pronounced 'snuh'.*

Ǝ NO, Non-, NOT, *pronounced 'ning'.*

Ǝ BAD, Dys-, Mal-, *pronounced 'sning'.*

In ⊧JΓ2ₓ the POTENT Ŀ is used to designate a verb. Originally all four members of the Ŀ family were to have been used for this purpose but by restricting ourselves to PAST, PRESENT, FUTURE and the INFINITIVE each varied by the PROGRESSIVE, PERFECT and the PERFECT PROGRESSIVE, plus the PARTICIPLES varied in a similar manner, only one POTENT Ŀ together with its consonantal consort (C) is needed to give a totally satisfactory verb affix. The complete list is given at the right. Each variant of the affix is explicit in itself.

When used, auxiliary verbs are appended to the verbal core as prefixes using the ˉ linkage *Sigh* which states that the following core is dominant and the action and temporal factors reside in that core and its ĿC suffix.

The auxiliaries would, could, do, etc. when used as linked CORES are in their nominative form and not in their verb form in the past or present tense, as for instance can - could, shall - should, will - would, and may - might. Agreement is not a factor in ⊧JΓ2ₓ so some other aspects of the verb do not change it as in English usage. Voice, mood, person, and number are determined by punctuation or sentence format. Voice is set by format but if a refinement is needed a punctuational item can be assigned to indicate the passive voice as noted in the section on pronouns. The indicative mood is the norm and it is modified by punctuation to the interrogatory, imperative or subjunctive. Sentence format takes care of the various aspects of the subjunctive. There is no need to change the verb for person or number because those matters are established by other sentence elements. In general people use language without knowing the names of its various components. It's only after-the-fact that grammarians delve into usage to analyze what we're doing, tell us the why and wherefore, give names to the components, and try to be helpful by setting the rules.

Any action word (for instance Γ⅂Γ "change") without the verb POTENT Ŀ becomes the noun designating that action. Adding the POTENT Ŀ (without a C consort) creates a verbal noun which is called a gerund.

In ⊧JΓ2ₓ there are no irregular, weak or strong verbs. There is only one schedule to memorize and you will have noticed that you don't have to use the auxiliaries 'have' and 'be' as in the English equivalents cited above, because they are implicit in the verb addend. Memorizing this schedule is aided by the fact that, except for the participles, the upper dot in the consonantal consort is the progressive tense and the lower dot is the perfect tense. Although not really necessary, especially in a utility language, passive and reflexive forms can be indicated by affixing the punctuational possessive ˙ for the passive and the punctuational reflexive . for the reflexive form.

ANY ⊧JΓ2x word takes a verbal form when the POTENT Ŀ is affixed and NO ⊧JΓ2x word is a verbal without it. Just put any appropriate ⊧JΓ2x word before these affixes and you will instantly have a completely conjugated verb. Then you may enhance it by prefixing any auxiliary using the linkage *sigh* ( ˉ ). The examples on the next page use the first person I in the English equivalents as a matter of form but of course the ⊧JΓ2x first person is not present. Any pronoun; you, he, they, it, or any animate or inanimate object could be applied without altering the verbal suffix because ⊧JΓ2x has no requirements in the matter of 'agreement' You'll also discover that it pays no attention to other niceties such as euphony. Because we limit our words to just three letters and try hard to keep them together in categories; it's a matter of letting the chips fall where they may. Our words may sound funny-peculiar but then so do many foreign tongues.

nominative

Ŀ gerund

Ŀ˥ present
Ŀ˥˙ present progressive
Ŀ.˥ present perfect
Ŀ:˥ present perfect progressive

Ŀ⊣ past
Ŀ˙⊣ past progressive
Ŀ.⊣ past perfect
Ŀ:⊣ past perfect progressive

Ŀ∃ future
Ŀ∃˙ future progressive
Ŀ.∃ future perfect
Ŀ:∃ future perfect progressive

ĿJ infinitive, present
Ŀ˙J inf. present progressive
Ŀ.J inf. perfect
Ŀ:J inf. past progressive

Ŀ] adverb?? consider this possibility.
Ŀ˙] present participle
Ŀ.] perfect participle
Ŀ:] past participle

__ nominative; be

__ gerund; being

__ present; I am

present progressive;
__ I am being

present perfect;
__ I have been

present perfect progressive;
__ I have been

__ past; I was

past progressive;
__ I was being

__ past perfect; I had been

past perfect progressive;
__ I had been

__ future; I will

future progressive;
__ I will be

future perfect;
__ I will have been

future perfect progressive;
__ I will have been

__ infinitive present; to be

inf. present progressive;
__ to be being

__ inf. perfect; to have been

inf. past progressive;
__ to have been

__

__ present participle; being

perfect participle;
__ having been

__ past participle; been

__ nominative; do

__ gerund; doing

__ present; I do

present progressive;
__ I am doing

present perfect;
__ I have done

present perfect progressive;
__ I have been doing

__ past; I did

past progressive;
__ I was doing

__ past perfect; I had done

past perfect progressive;
__ I had been doing

__ future; I will do

future progressive;
__ I will be doing

future perfect;
__ I will have been doing

future perfect progressive;
__ I will have been doing

__ infinitive present; to do

inf. present progressive;
__ to be doing

__ inf. perfect; to have done

inf. past progressive;
__ to have been doing

__

__ present participle; doing

perfect participle;
__ having done

__ past participle; done

__ nominative; write

__ gerund; writing

__ present; I write

present progressive;
__ I am writing

present perfect;
__ I have written

present perfect progressive;
__ I have been writing

__ past; I wrote

past progressive;
__ I was writing

__ past perfect; I had written

past perfect progressive;
__ I had been writing

__ future; I will write

future progressive;
__ I will be writing

future perfect;
__ I will have written

future perfect progressive;
__ I will have been writing

__ infinitive present; to write

inf. present progressive;
__ to be writing

inf. perfect;
__ to have written

inf. past progressive;
__ to have been writing

__

__ present participle; writing

perfect participle;
__ having written

__ past participle; wrote

__ nominative; think

__ gerund; thinking

__ present; I think

present progressive;
__ I am thinking

present perfect;
__ I have thought

present perfect progressive;
__ I have been thinking

__ past; I thought

past progressive;
__ I was thinking

past perfect;
__ I had thought

past perfect progressive;
__ I had been thinking

__ future; I will think

future progressive;
__ I will be thinking

future perfect;
__ I will have thought

future perfect progressive;
__ I will have been thinking

__ infinitive present; to think

inf. present progressive;
__ to be thinking

inf. perfect;
__ to have thought

inf. past progressive;
__ to have been thinking

__

__ present participle; thinking

perfect participle;
__ having thought

__ past participle; thought

__ nominative; persist

__ gerund; persisting

__ present; I persist

present progressive;
__ I am persiting

present perfect;
__ I have persisted

present perfect progressive;
__ I have been persisting

__ past; I persisted

past progressive;
__ I was persisting

past perfect;
__ I had persisted

past perfect progressive;
__ I had been persisting

__ future; I will persist

future progressive;
__ I will be persisting

future perfect;
__ I will have persisted

future perfect progressive;
__ I will have been persisting

__ inf. present; to persist

inf. present progressive;
__ to be persisting

inf. perfect;
__ to have persisted

inf. past progressive;
__ to have been persiting

__

present participle;
__ persisting

perfect participle;
__ having persisted

__ past participle; persisted

__ nominative; change

__ gerund; having changed

__ present; I change

present progressive;
__ I am changing

present perfect;
__ I have changed

present perfect progressive;
__ I have been changing

__ past; I changed

past progressive;
__ I was changing

past perfect;
__ I had changed

past perfect progressive;
__ I had been changing

__ future; I will change

future progressive;
__ I will be changing

future perfect;
__ I will have changed

future perfect progressive;
__ I will have been changing

__ inf. present; to change

inf. present progressive;
__ to be changing

inf. perfect;
__ to have changed

inf. past progressive;
__ to have been changing

__

present participle;
__ changing

perfect participle;
__ having changed

__ past participle; changed

The facing page has the seven families of punctuation. Each family has three elements that combine into seven characters that are arranged in a binary order somewhat like the letters. The seventh character which combines the three elements gives rise to the family name. They were created to give greater flexibility and accuracy to ⊧JΓ2× and by giving them a logical pattern of phonemes, to permit total machine dictation. Although they are all useful, only two of the families are essential to ⊧JΓ2×. One is ˙ *Swah* (81 to 87 inclusive). These are the suffixes that give us the possessive, plural and reflexive. The other is the ¯ *Swih* family (91 to 97 inclusive) of linkages which assure us that compounded cores will be universally understood. As for the rest, they can be ignored and local grammatical customs observed. They are kept in this compilation to illustrate their possibilities.

The ˙ family completely eliminates separate dictionary listings for plural, possessive and reflexive forms and any combinations thereof. (The verbal POTENT ŁC has the same effect regarding verb forms.)

The chart on page 5 and the audio tape (p.8), give the pronunciation of these punctuational graphemes. Because of computer restrictions the ˋ , ˊ , × , and ⁎ families are different from the others. Three members of each of those families are created by using the back kern *Fuh* 08. The phonemes follow the same pattern as for the others, except that 'F' is replaced by 'V' in the × and ⁎ families. These differences are noted in the listing below. Notice that in the two items of each family that pair binary-two bar with either binary-one bar or binary-four bar, the nomen always begins with the phoneme for the binary-two bar. Thus; ⁚ is *SwayFay* and ⁑ is *CHwayVay.*

The ˋ and ˊ families are innovative. They perform the functions of quotation marks, parentheses or brackets but they do not have a left-hand counterpart to mark the termination of the 'set-off', which in ⊧JΓ2× continues until the initiating mark is repeated.

The pairing 'and' was created to avoid the awkwardness of too many 'ands' at the end of a listing. The pairing 'and' is used to tie together items that are meant to be considered as one.

As the ⊧JΓ2× punctuational system evolved it became apparent that it was possible to make innumerable combinations of the various marks for mathematical, chemical or other purposes; even to replace words or phrases. A small amount of this was done as is demonstrated in the last two columns on the facing page. More can be done as needed but strict control must be maintained.

*say*
__ POssessive

*sway*
__ PLural

*swayfay*
__ PL-PO

*sah*
__ REflexive

*sayfah*
__ PO-RE

*swayfah*
__ PL-RE

*swah*
__ PL-PO-RE

*sigh*
__ following core is dominant, used between cores and AFTER prefixes

*swie*
__ links cores of equal importance; minus in math; as a dash with full spaces fore and aft

__ For the purpose of

__ preceeding core is dominant, used between cores and BEFORE suffixes

__ WITH, Can stand alone. Equals in math

__ OF, made of. Can stand alone

__ what follows is arbitrary i.e., uncategorized, expands meaning by rote

__ 2nd sub-quote, or a 'set-off' if not in a standing quotation

__ true quotation of speech or writing

__ 'sounds like' or 'rhymes with'

__ 1st sub-quote

__ attribution, not an exact quotation

__ Sic, as spoken or written

__ Gist, conclusion or emphasis

__ parenthesis; ellipsis when empty

__ ellipsis

__ Fraction 1/2; PER; divided by, in math

__ 3rd bracket

__ 2nd bracket

*sowfoh*
__ metanym

__ special import; is followed by other marks to indicate jest, sarcasm, fantasy etc.

__ 1st bracket

__ colon

__ period

__ question

__ comma

__ semi-colon

__ exclamation

__ disbelief, incredulity

__ asterisk; with numerals for footnotes or with single letters for instructions; also an aside

9×3
__ cube of 9

9×-3
__ cube root of 9

__ multiply by, in math; also percent, ×.06 is six percent

__ powers of ten, both positive and negative; (*CHwayVay*)

4 3
__ is 4000

4 -3
__ is .004

×6
__ cardinal; number 6

6×
__ ordinal; sixth

__ money, followed by three letter national designation

__ YET

__ ERGO

__ AND

__ DITTO

__ pairing AND; plus in math

__ et.al.

__ OR

__ and/or

__ either/or

__ etc.

__ equal to or more than

__ equal to or less than

__ not equal to

__ plus or minus

__ more than

__ less than

The ⊧JΓ2x core words were culled from word usage frequency lists, personal experience, traveler's guides, BASIC English, current practice and to the greatest extent from Roget's Thesaurus. None were created, just adopted. Some important ones may have been overlooked and there must be many more from other languages and cultures that should be added. Some that were selected should be dropped if inappropriate for a utility language or if they can be readily compounded out of existing cores and other graphic elements. It is mostly a matter of judgement as to what should be done. For instance, the word ⊧˥F (lullaby) could also be ⊧˥Γ·⁻Γ⅂Γ· (song for baby) or ƎE⅂⊧˥Γ· (cradle song). In this case, a separate triad for lullaby is selected because it is frequently and universally used. That there is ample space for it the ⊧˥ line of the spreadsheet is also a factor. Had this line been crowded it would have been expedient to use one of the alternatives. In the first alternative a linkage is used to separate the cores while in the second alternative the cores run together. Since everyone knows that ⊧JΓ2x cores are always triads and that the last core is dominant unless linkages are used to indicate otherwise they read or hear it as a compound word.

The linkages came from my early experiences with German engineers arguing amongst themselves about the exact meaning of some particularly long and involved German technical word. A rational system of inter-element notation such as the ⊧JΓ2x linkages would have made the intended meaning obvious. Latin scholars are often at odds regarding the meaning of some words or phrases but those differences stem from other causes such as the exactness of that language and its antiquity.

Affixes in English are usually derived from Latin or Greek word elements. Euphony probably plays a part in determining which root will be appended and whether it should be a prefix or suffix or in rare cases an infix. Laurence Urdang lists 4400 affixes in his 1982 and 1984 compilations published by Gale Research Company. One of the reasons that Greek and Latin are favored as affixes is simply that their alien nature sets them off from the native language to which they are appended even though a great deal of that language is made up of adopted words. At first the ⊧JΓ2x word elements that would serve as affixes were scattered throughout the vocabulary in harmony with the categories. This didn't set them apart in that they lacked the desireable distinctiveness. To obtain that quality, a class of two letter words for use with the ‾ or - linkages was established. But then categorization conflicts arose and a distinctive way to bring them back into the fold as triads was sought. This was achieved as the process of categorization wound down and it became apparent that there were 800 possibilities for ƎCV and ƎCC words. The two letter words were then abandoned and reconstituted as ƎCC/V. They obtained a distinct identity so that they could be used fore or aft without linkages; or stand alone as cores in their own right. Partly as a result of being moved around so much the affixes are not in good order and are especially in need of a kind and knowing hand to set them to rights.

Most of the items in a long list of medical prefixes were dropped as inappropriate. They will appear in the special vocabulary devoted to health sciences; possibly as ƎCV/C cores, in which case space will have to be reserved for them. This may also be true for other special vocabularies.

Very early on in the development of ⊢JΓ2x I had determined to try to put its words into groups based on their meaning. In January of 1980 when I bought a copy of Roget's 4th edition I was delighted to see that their "Synopsis of Categories" divided the vocabulary into eight classes. Based on my plan to 'tag' the words and the ten families of letters I needed ten categories, so I created the two additional categories that I named "Control" and "Animalics". Categorization is an ancient ideal. The Publisher's Preface to Roget's International Thesaurus (fourth edition) states in part "...Roget himself knew about the thousand-year-old *Amarakosha* ("treasury of Amara"), which was a crude arrangement of words according to subjects, by the Sanskrit grammarian Amara Sinh. Roget also knew about a *Pasigraphie*, published in Paris in 1797, which tried to classify language so that it could be understood universally without translation. But Dr. Roget, this erudite physician with a flair for invention, developed a superb and revolutionary principle: the grouping of words according to ideas ...".

⊢JΓ2x goes much further along these lines in that it puts a tag or label on every word. The first two letters of a word tell the reader just where that word fits into ⊢JΓ2x schema. VC and CV words make up the general vocabulary whose categories are listed on page 20 and indexed on page 21. VV words are arranged into special vocabularies of words not in the general vocabulary but which are important in our various professional or scientific endeavors, page 150, and CC words are concerned with computer operation, tangible and intangible things, tools, devices etc. and global locations and features. The VV and CC words are part of the higher level ⊢JΓ2x vocabulary so they are noted in the appendix. Only if ⊢JΓ2x achieves a reasonable degree of acceptance will the VV and CC categories be fully developed.

Absolute and total categorization is not possible but this work is proof that enough can be done to make the effort worthwhile. In fact, placing words in categories as is done in ⊢JΓ2x prevents a word from having more than one meaning or any two words from sounding alike. The most careful consideration should be given to the VCV and CVC words. I know that fresh minds can correct my errors and improve the placement and arrangement of our words in the spreadsheets. It may seem strange to think of beloved words in such a mechanical framework but these schematic arrangements are really another form of dictionary that gives us the kind of overview that permits us to visualize the relationship of the words. It's a new venture in linguistics only possible in an ⊢JΓ2x triad format.

The general objective is to be somewhat chary when selecting words to be included in the general vocabulary and to stay as close as we can to our guidelines so that tomorrow's students will have an easier time of it. Although the spreadsheets have plenty of space we are not out to fill all of them. The total possible number of triads is 64,000. At present we only use half of that number because we stay to a VCV or CVC format even though we could use VCC or CVV. 32,000 is more than we need. The 5,000 or more cores we will end up with will readily expand into a comprehendible vocabulary of several hundred thousand words.

POTENTS are another form of categorization, dominating all others.

*Everyone interested in working on ⊢JΓ2x vocabulary should have a copy of Roget's Fourth Edition handy.*

SECTION 1A
*ABSTRACT RELATIONS*

__ PERSONAL PRONOUNS
__ AMENITIES 1
__ AGE AND STATUS
__ PERSONALITY
__ VOCATION
__ AVOCATION
__ RELATIONSHIPS
__ PHRASES
__ ABBREVIATIONS

SECTION 1B

__ BEING
__ NUMBER
__ MATHEMATICS
__ ARTICLES, CONNECTIVES
__ RELATIVE ADJECTIVES
__ AUXILIARIES
__ ACTIONS

SECTION 1C

__ TIME

SECTION 1D

__ POWER

SECTION 2A
*INTELLECT*

__ INTELLECT

SECTION 2B

__ ART
__ PUBLICATION
__ THEATER
__ DANCE

SECTION 2C

__ MUSIC
__ MUSICAL INSTRUMENTS
__ AMUSEMENT
__ SPORTS
__ TEAM SPORTS
__ LANGUAGE
__ GRAMMAR
__ SPEECH

SECTION 2D

__ COMMUNICATION
__ EDUCATION

SECTION 3
*VOLITION*

__ VOLITION

SECTION 4A
*CONTROL*

__ GOVERNMENT

SECTION 4B

__ POLICE AND MILITARY

SECTION 4C

__ LAW AND ECONOMICS

SECTION 4D

__ BUSINESS AND FINANCE

SECTION 5A
*AFFECTIONS*

__ EMOTION

SECTION 5B

__ SOCIABILITY

SECTION 5C

__ MORALITY

SECTION 5D

__ RELIGION

SECTION 6A
*SPACE*

__ SPACE

SECTION 6B

__ DIMENSIONS

SECTION 6C

__ STRUCTURE

SECTION 6D

__ MOTION

SECTION 7A
*PHYSICS*

__ PHYSICAL SCIENCES

SECTION 7B

__ LIGHT
__ ELECTRICITY
__ TECHNOLOGY

SECTION 7C

__ CHARACTERISTICS
__ COLOR

SECTION 7D

__ MATERIALS

SECTION 8A
*MATTER*

__ COSMOS

SECTION 8B

__ INORGANIC
__ GEOLOGY
__ WEATHER
__ WATER
__ AIR

SECTION 8C

__ ORGANIC MATTER
__ BIOLOGY
__ LIFE AND DEATH

SECTION 8D

__ FLORA
__ AGRICULTURE

SECTION 9A
*ANIMALICS*

__ FAUNA

SECTION 9B

__ FOOD AND NUTRITION

SECTION 9C

__ SANITATION AND HEALTH

SECTION 9D

__ PARTS OF THE BODY

SECTION 10A
*SENSATIONS*

__ SENSATION
__ TACTILE
__ TASTE
__ SMELL

SECTION 10B

__ VISION
__ HEARING

SECTION 10C

__ CLOTHING
__ HOUSING
__ FURNISHINGS

SECTION 1OD CVC

Affixes, most of which are cores in their own right.

__ DOERS
__ QUALITY
__ MOST COMMON

SECTION 10D CVV

__ *QUANTITY. DEGREE*
__ *DIMENSIONS*
__ *DIRECTION*
__ *LOCATION*
__ *SHAPE*

These five items are in italics because they end in V rather than C. They also are in italics on the last line on p.23.

The section subheadings in slanted type, except for *CONTROL* and *ANIMALICS*, are taken from the "Synopsis of Categories" in Roget's Thesaurus.

# INDEX of CATEGORIES

| | K | sK | King | sKing | T | sT | Ting | sTing | P | sP | Ping | sPing | M | sM | Ming | sMing | L | sL | Ling | sLing |
|---|---|---|---|---|---|---|---|---|---|---|---|---|---|---|---|---|---|---|---|---|
| Ay | PERSONAL PRONOUNS | | | | AMENITIES 1 | | | | AGE AND STATUS | PERSONALITY | VOCATION | AVOCATION | RELATIONSHIPS | | | | PHRASES | | ABBREVIATIONS | |
| wAy | BEING | | | | NUMBER | | | | MATHEMATICS | | | | ARTICLES, CONNECTIVES | | RELATIVE ADJECTIVES | | AUXILIARIES | | ACTIONS | |
| Ah | TIME | | | | | | | | | | | | | | | | | | | |
| wAh | POWER | | | | | | | | | | | | | | | | | | | |
| Ee | INTELLECT | | | | | | | | | | | | | | | | | | | |
| wEe | ART | | | | | | | PUBLICATION | | | | | THEATER | | | | | DANCE | | |
| Eh | MUSIC | | | | MUSICAL INSTRUMENTS | | | | AMUSEMENT | | SPORTS | TEAM SPORTS | LANGUAGE | | GRAMMAR | | SPEECH | | | |
| wEh | COMMUNICATION | | | | | | | | | | | | EDUCATION | | | | | | | |
| I | VOLITION | | | | | | | | | | | | | | | | | | | |
| wYe | | | | | | | | | | | | | | | | | | | | |
| Ih | | | | | | | | | | | | | | | | | | | | |
| wIh | | | | | | | | | | | | | | | | | | | | |
| Aw | GOVERNMENT | | | | | | | | | | | | | | | | | | | |
| wAw | POLICE AND MILITARY | | | | | | | | | | | | | | | | | | | |
| ă | LAW AND ECONOMICS | | | | | | | | | | | | | | | | | | | |
| wă | BUSINESS AND FINANCE | | | | | | | | | | | | | | | | | | | |
| Ow | EMOTION | | | | | | | | | | | | | | | | | | | |
| wOw | SOCIABILITY | | | | | | | | | | | | | | | | | | | |
| Oh | MORALITY | | | | | | | | | | | | | | | | | | | |
| wOe | RELIGION | | | | | | | | | | | | | | | | | | | |

| | Ay | wAy | Ah | wAh | Ee | wEe | Eh | wEh | I | wYe | Ih | wIh | Aw | wAw | ă | wă | Ow | wOw | Oh | wOe |
|---|---|---|---|---|---|---|---|---|---|---|---|---|---|---|---|---|---|---|---|---|
| K | SPACE | | | | | | | | | | | | | | | | | | | |
| sK | DIMENSIONS | | | | | | | | | | | | | | | | | | | |
| King | STRUCTURE | | | | | | | | | | | | | | | | | | | |
| sKing | MOTION | | | | | | | | | | | | | | | | | | | |
| T | PHYSICAL SCIENCES | | | | | | | | | | | | | | | | | | | |
| sT | LIGHT | | | | | | | | ELECTRICITY | | | | TECHNOLOGY | | | | | | | |
| Ting | CHARACTER-ISTICS | | | | | | | | | | | | | | | | COLOR | | | |
| sTing | MATERIALS | | | | | | | | | | | | | | | | | | | |
| P | COSMOS | | | | | | | | | | | | | | | | | | | |
| sP | INORGANIC | | | | GEOLOGY | | | | WEATHER | | | WATER | | | | | AIR | | | |
| Ping | ORGANIC MATTER | | | | BIOLOGY | | | | LIFE AND DEATH | | | | | | | | | | | |
| sPing | FLORA | | | | | | | | | | | | | | | | AGRICULTURE | | | |
| M | FAUNA | | | | | | | | | | | | | | | | | | | |
| sM | FOOD AND NUTRITION | | | | | | | | | | | | | | | | | | | |
| Ming | SANITATION AND HEALTH | | | | | | | | | | | | | | | | | | | |
| sMing | PARTS OF THE BODY | | | | | | | | | | | | | | | | | | | |
| L | SENSATION | | | | TACTILE | | | | TASTE | | | | | | | | SMELL | | | |
| sL | VISION | | | | | | | | HEARING | | | | | | | | | | | |
| Ling | CLOTHING | | | | | | | | HOUSING | | | | | | | | FURNISHINGS | | | |
| sLing | DOERS *QUANTITY* *DEGREE* | | | | | | *DIMENSIONS* | | QUALITY *DIRECTION* | | | | MOST COMMON *LOCATION* | | *SHAPE* | | | | | |

The spreadsheets are the most useful item in our computer tool kit. What a tedious job it would have been without it. The spreadsheets are created directly from of the vocabulary listings on pages 67 to 103 inclusive. The computer is programmed to do it and the entire process including printing takes less than an hour. See page 148 about getting a copy of the program.

The program handles monads, diads and triads. It prints monads as a three column list not reproduced in this book. Diads are printed in a lattice format like the triads but there is no letter in the extreme upper left hand box. For diads the left vertical column has the first letter and the top row has the second letter. For triads the first letter appears in the box in the extreme upper left hand corner. The second letter in the left hand column and the third letter in the top row. The English equivalents are distributed into their proper boxes in the lattice. Of course if other languages were used in the vocabulary listing that language would appear on the spreadsheet in place of the English eqivalents. The program pays some attention to POTENTS by printing the English equivalents of the triads to which they are affixed but the program does not count the POTENT as a letter nor does it print it. When you see spouse husband wife all together in the same box you can assume that 'Spouse' is the neutral term and that it has been inflected by the gender POTENTS E and E to give husband and wife.

Except for page 65 which is CVV, all of the spreadsheets are either VCV or CVC. If the vocabulary contains VCC or CVV by intent or error a separate spreadsheet will be printed to accommodate those entries. This capability can be used to expand the vocabulary, modify categorization or to discover errors.

In some cases the entries in the spreadsheets are truncated because of programatic limitations. This is acceptable because the purpose of the spreadsheet is notational rather than to give the exact listing of the entire entry.

| | Ay | wAy | Ah | wAh | Ee | wEe | Eh | wEh | I | wYe | Ih | wIh | Aw | wAw | ǎ | wǎ | Ow | wOw | Oh | wOe |
|---|---|---|---|---|---|---|---|---|---|---|---|---|---|---|---|---|---|---|---|---|
| K | PLEASE | EXCUSE ME | THANKS | WELCOME | 1ST PERSON | | 2ND PERSON | | 3RD PERSON (DEFINITE FORM) | | 3RD PERSON (INDEFINITE FORM) | | IT (ANIMAL) | | IT (INANIMATE TANGIBLE) THING | | IT (INTANGIBLE) THING | | | |
| sK | FORMS OF ADDRESS 1 | | | | | | | | | | | | | | | | | | | |
| King | FORMS OF ADDRESS 2 | | | | | | | | | | | | | | | | | | | |
| sKing | FORMS OF ADDRESS 3 | | | | | | | | | | | | | | | | | | | |
| T | HELLO | GOOD BYE, ADIOS | BON CHANCE | ALL THE BEST TO YOU | NEICHEVO | | EH? | | OK | | | | GO, RECORDER IS ON | | HERE GOES | | HELLO, ARE YOU THERE? | SIGNING OFF, THANK YOU | OVER TO YOU | OVER AND OUT |
| sT | AMENITIES 2 | | | | | | | | | | | | | | | | | | | |
| Ting | AMENITIES 3 | | | | | | | | | | | | | | | | | | | |
| sTing | AMENITIES 4 | | | | | | | | | | | | | | | | | | | |
| P | PRENATAL | NEWBORN | BABY, INFANT | CHILD BOY GIRL | TEENS LAD LASS | MINOR | ADULT | MID-LIFE, PRIME | MATURE | ELDER | RETIRED | | PRESCHOOLER | GRADE-SCHOOLER | INTER-MEDIATE | HIGH-SCHOOLER | COLLEGIAN | | GRADUATE SCHOOLER | POST-GRADUATE |
| sP | CULTIVATED CRUDE | | | | PATRICIAN PLEBEIAN | | | | KIND MEAN | | | | SAINTLY EVIL | | | | TAME WILD | | | |
| Ping | VOCATION | | | | | | | | | | | | | | | | | | | |
| sPing | AVOCATION | | | | | | | | | | | | | | | | | | | |
| M | SPOUSE HUSBAND WIFE | PARENT FATHER MOTHER | OFFSPRING SON DAUGHTER | SIBLING BROTHER SISTER | UNCLE, AUNT UNCLE AUNT | NEPHEW/NIECE NEPHEW NIECE | COUSINS COUSIN COUSINE | CUZ M/F | GRAND-, GREAT- FOR UNCLES | GREATGRAND- | RELATIVE BY BLOOD | RELATIVE BY MARRIAGE | SURVIVING SPOUSE WIDOW WIDOWER | SINGLE PAR-ENT M/F | ORPHAN M/F | | DIVORCED M/F | SEPARATED, M/F | COURTESY, HONOR M/F | COMMON LAW M/F |
| sM | ACQUAINT-ANCE | FRIEND | -MATE, PLAY, TEAM ETC | CLUB, SOCIAL INTEREST | CO-ACTIVIST | ASSOCIATE | COLLEAGUE | PARTNER | LINGUISTIC GROUP | ETHNIC GROUP | NATIONAL GROUP | PROVINCIAL GROUP | NATIVE | ALIEN | TRIBE, CLAN | OFFICIAL OF | | | FOLLOWER, DISCIPLE | BELIEVER IN |
| Ming | DATING | LOVER | FIANCE | COHABITOR | RELATIONSHIP PATERNAL MATERNAL | | ANCESTOR | DESCENDENT | FAMILY | | FAMILY CHIEF PATRIARCH MATRIARCH | | CUSTODIAN | GUARDIAN | WARD | ADOPTED | IN-LAW COPARENT | | STEP- | |
| sMing | | | | | | | | | | | | | | | | | | | | |
| L | | | | | | | | | | | | | | | | | | | | |
| sL | | | | | | | | | | | | | | | | | | | | |
| Ling | PER SE | VIZ | Q V | I E | OP CIT | IBID | E G | C F | CUM | SEE ABOVE | SEE BELOW | ET SEQ | AS IN | VICE VERSA | A LA | ACCORDING TO | MOOT | SO TO SAY | AS IT WERE | IN A LIKE MANNER |
| sLing | SUPPOSEDLY | VIA | CIRCA | | RSVP | SO-SO | FIGURATIVELY | VS | AKA | TAKEN FROM | BY PERMISSION | | ETC | ET AL | AD INFINITUM | AD NAUSEAM | PAGE | PARAGRAPH | COLUMN | LINE |

| | Ay | wAy | Ah | wAh | Ee | wEe | Eh | wEh | I | wYe | Ih | wIh | Aw | wAw | ă | wă | Ow | wOw | Oh | wOe |
|---|---|---|---|---|---|---|---|---|---|---|---|---|---|---|---|---|---|---|---|---|
| K | EXIST | | BEING | | LIVING DEAD | | BECOME | | TANGIBLE INTANGIBLE | | | | NATURE | | KIND | | BASIC | | SYSTEM | CONDITION |
| sK | RELATIONSHIP | | DEPENDENCE INDEPEND-ENCE | | PERTAIN TO | | APART FROM | | RELEVANT IRRELEVANT | | WITH WITHOUT | | COMPARISON | | LIKE UNLIKE | | SUCH | | | |
| King | BLEND CONTRAST | | | | ENTITY NONENTITY | | SAME DIFFERENT | | OPPOSITE | | EQUIVALENT DIVERSE | | CONSISTENCY | | | | MIMIC MOCK | | | |
| sKing | | CREATE | | | SAMPLE | | | | AGREE DISAGREE | | PEACE CONFLICT | | UNDERSTAND | | | | EXAMPLE | | ADJUSTMENT | |
| T | NUMBER | NUMERAL | | | DECIMAL | | BINARY | | RATE | | FRACTION | | RATIO | | PERCENTAGE | | COUNTING | | | |
| sT | CALCULATING | ARITHMETIC | | | MATHEMATICS | | ADD SUBTRACT | | TOTAL | | DIFFERENCE | | MULTIPLY DIVIDE | | PRODUCT | | QUOTIENT | | REMAINDER | |
| Ting | PLUS MINUS | | | | | | | | ESTIMATING | | | | | | | | CORRELATE | | | |
| sTing | | | | | | | STATISTICS | | NORM | | AVERAGE | | MEDIAN | | RMS, ROOT MEAN SQUARE | | ANALOGY | | | |
| P | ALGEBRA | | | | | | | | | | | | | | | | | | DEMOBILIZE | |
| sP | GEOMETRY | | | | | | | | | | | | | | | | | | | |
| Ping | TRIGON-OMETRY | | SINE | COSINE | TANGENT | COTANGENT | SECANT | COSECANT | | | | | | | | | | | | |
| sPing | CALCULUS | | | | | | | | | | | | | | | | | | | |
| M | A | ANY | SOME | ALL NONE | EACH | EVERY | MANY FEW | | THE | THIS THESE | THAT THOSE | OF | AND | AND, FOR PAIRING | OR | AND/OR | EITHER NEITHER | BUT | YET | ERGO |
| sM | TIME TIMES | EVER NEVER | | | | THAN | AT | AS | SO SO' SO' | TO FROM | OTHER | IF, COND-ITIONAL IF' | YES | PERHAPS | | | | | | |
| Ming | WHERE | | WHEN | | WHAT | | WHY | | WAY | | HOW | | WHICH | | | | WHO | | WHOSE | |
| sMing | | | | | | | | | | | | | | | | | | | | |
| L | SHALL | SHOULD | WILL | WOULD | DO | DID | HAVE | HAD | BE | WAS | CAN | COULD | MAY | MIGHT | MUST | OUGHT | ALWAYS NEVER | OFTEN SELDOM | DEFINITELY MAYBE | |
| sL | | | | | | | | | | | | | | | | | | | | |
| Ling | COME GO | GET GIVE | PUT TAKE | MAKE LET | | REASON | SEE | LOOK | | | FEEL | GROPE | | | HEAR | LISTEN | | EAT | INTUIT | SEEM |
| sLing | | | | | | | | | | | | | | | | | | | | |

| | Ay | wAy | Ah | wAh | Ee | wEe | Eh | wEh | I | wYe | Ih | wIh | Aw | wAw | ă | wă | Ow | wOw | Oh | wOe |
|---|---|---|---|---|---|---|---|---|---|---|---|---|---|---|---|---|---|---|---|---|
| K | SECOND | MILLISECOND | MICROSECOND | NANOSECOND | MINUTE | HOUR | | DAY | WEEK | WEEKEND | FORTNIGHT | MONTH | YEAR | QUARTER | SEASON | | SPRING | SUMMER | AUTUMN | WINTER |
| sK | EQUINOX | SOLSTICE | ERA | AGE | DECADE | CENTURY | MILLENNIUM | ETERNITY | PREDAWN | DAWN | MORNING | FORENOON | NOON | MIDDAY | AFTERNOON | EVENING | DUSK | NIGHT | MIDNIGHT | OVERNIGHT |
| King | TODAY | TOMORROW | YESTERDAY | TONIGHT | ANNIVERSARY | BIRTHDAY | NEW YEAR'S DAY | NEW YEAR'S EVE | PERPETUAL | | | | HOLIDAY | VACATION | | | NATIONAL DAYS | | | |
| sKing | HOLY DAYS | EASTER | RAMADAN | | | | | | | | | | | | | | | | | |
| T | WHILE | | | | DURING | | | | SPELL | | | | TERM | | | | | | | |
| sT | MEANWHILE | | | | HIATUS | | | | WAIT | | | | | | | | | | | |
| Ting | | | | | | | | | PERSIST | | | | DELAY | | | | | | | |
| sTing | QUIT | | | | | | | | | | | | | | | | | | | |
| P | | NEW<br>OLD | | | RECENT | | MOD | | | | | | | | | | FLEETING<br>LASTING | | | |
| sP | NOW<br>THEN | | | | PAST | | | | PRESENT | | | | FUTURE | | | | SUDDENNESS | | | |
| Ping | EARLY<br>LATE | | | | EVENTUALLY | | | | SOONER<br>LATER | | | | YOUNG | | | | | | | |
| sPing | PREMATURE | | | | FREQUENT | | | | FOREVER | | | | PERSISTENT | | | | | | | |
| M | SEQUENCE | | | | PRECURSOR<br>SEQUEL | | | | SYNCHRO,<br>SIMULTANEITY | | | | INTERMIT-<br>TENT | | | | RHYTHM | | | |
| sM | REGULARITY<br>IRREGULARITY | | | | PERIODIC<br>ASYNCHRO-<br>NOUS | | | | RECURRENT | | | | ALTERNATELY | | | | | | | |
| Ming | STEADY | | | | CONSTANT<br>TRANSIENT | | | | PERMANENT<br>TEMPORARY | | | | BEFORE<br>AFTER | | | | | | | |
| sMing | AGAIN | | | | PHASE | | | | CONTINUE<br>CEASE | | | | BEGIN<br>END | | START<br>STOP | | USE | | | |
| L | ORIGIN | | | | HISTORY | | | | CONTEMP-<br>ORARY | | | | | | | | | | | |
| sL | PREHISTORIC | | | | STONE AGE | | | | | | | | | | | | EXTINCT | | | |
| Ling | GLACIAL ERA | | | | MILLION<br>YEARS AGO | | | | BILLION<br>YEARS AGO | | | | | | | | | | | |
| sLing | CLOCK | WATCH | | | TIMER | | | | CALENDAR | | | | | | | | | | | |

| | Ay | wAy | Ah | wAh | Ee | wEe | Eh | wEh | I | wYe | Ih | wIh | Aw | wAw | ă | wă | Ow | wOw | Oh | wOe |
|---|---|---|---|---|---|---|---|---|---|---|---|---|---|---|---|---|---|---|---|---|
| K | FORCE | | STRENGTH WEAKNESS | | HORSEPOWER | | MANPOWER | | | | | | ABLE UNABLE | | | | | | | |
| sK | POWER | | | | FUTILITY | | | | INFLUENCE | | | | ENABLE DISABLE | | | | WORK | | | |
| King | IMPREGNABLE VULNERABLE | | | | FRAILTY | | | | | | ENTERPRISE | | RIGOR | | | | ACTIVE | | | |
| sKing | VIOLENCE | | RAGE | | FRENZY | | EXPLOSION | | UNRULY | | RIOT | | ROWDY | | | | BRUTAL | | | |
| T | | | | | MODERATE | | | | | | | | RELAX | | | | GENTLE | | | |
| sT | OPERATION | PROCESS | | | | | | | PRODUCTIVE UNPRODUCT-IVE | | | | FERTILE BARREN | | | | FERTILIZER | | | |
| Ting | | | BUILD | | | | ARTIFACT | | | | | | | | | | | | MASTERPIECE | |
| sTing | | CROP | | | | | PRODUCT | | | | | | | | | | | | BY-PRODUCT | |
| P | | FAVOR | | | | | DOMINANCE SUBMISSION | | EFFECTIVE INEFFECTIVE | | | | | | | | | | TENDENCY | |
| sP | LIABILITY | RESPONSIBLE | | | PROBABILITY | | INVOLVE | | COOPERATION | | | | MAINTAIN | | | | FIX, REPAIR | | | |
| Ping | REST | | | | DEVELOP-MENT | | | | FOR, SUBSTITUTION | | | | OCCASION | | EVENT | | OCCUR | | | |
| sPing | TRADE | | | | EXCHANGE | | | | CAUSE | | | | | | | | | | | |
| M | LUCK | | | | SOURCE | | | | WELL | | | | EFFECT | | | | BECAUSE | | | |
| sM | | | | | ACCIDENT | | | | ODDS | | | | | | | | | | | |
| Ming | TOGETHER | | | | FRESH STALE | | | | PRISTINE | | | | PRIMITIVE | | | | | | | |
| sMing | ANALYSIS | | | | HEREDITY | | | | ADVANCE | | | | RETREAT | | | | | | | |
| L | | EVEN ODD | | | | | | | OCCASIONAL | | | | SYSTEMATIC HAPHAZARD | | | | | | | |
| sL | STOP | | | | TURN ON TURN OFF | | | | | | | | | | | | | | | |
| Ling | | | | | RANDOM | | | | PACE | | | | FAST | | | | | | | |
| sLing | CONSERVE | | | | REMAIN | | | | EVOLUTION | | | | | | | | | | | |

| ⊢ | Ay | wAy | Ah | wAh | Ee | wEe | Eh | wEh | I | wYe | Ih | wIh | Aw | wAw | ǎ | wǎ | Ow | wOw | Oh | wOe |
|---|---|---|---|---|---|---|---|---|---|---|---|---|---|---|---|---|---|---|---|---|
| K | INTELLECT | | MIND | | RATIONALITY | WITS | INTELLIGENCE | SENSE | | | | | KNOWLEDGE IGNORANCE | | SLY | | ASTUTE | | WISE | |
| sK | GENIUS | | SMART | TALENTED | STUPID | | SENILE | | FOOLISH | | SIMPLETON | | BOOR | | | | ODD | | | |
| King | LEARNING | LORE | LIBERAL ARTS | | THINK | | IDEA | | CONSIDER | | SPECULATE | | OPINION | | INTUITIVE | | | | | |
| sKing | PRO CON | ASSUMPTION | SINCERITY | | TOPIC | PROBLEM | QUESTION ANSWER | | TEST | | THEORY | | INSPECTION | | RESEARCH | | CHECKUP | | | |
| T | SPYING | | ENCODE DECODE | | SEARCH | | EXPLORE | | DISCOVER | | FIND LOSE | | EXPERIMENT | | LABORATORY | | PROVE DISPROVE | | | |
| sT | TACT | | APPROVAL CENSURE | | CRITICISM | | RATING | | CONCLUSION | | PRESUME | | CLUE | | | | | | | |
| Ting | GUESS | INFER | | | PHILOSOPHY | | METAPHYSICS | | MATERIALISM | | AESTHETICS | | IDEALISM | | BELIEF | | TRUST | | | |
| sTing | IMAGINE | | SUPERSTITION | | GULLIBLE | | NAIVE | | | | PROOF | | SKEPTICISM | | INCREDIBLE | | FACT | | DATA | |
| P | ENTIRE | POSSIBLE | PROBABLE | AVAILABLE | CHANCE | | | | RELIABLE | | VALID | INDEED | DOUBT | | EMBARRASS | | RISK | | BET | |
| sP | TRUTH | CORRECT | | GOOD BAD | NORMAL DEVIANT | | | | PROVERB | | FORMULA | SLOGAN | ERROR | | | | ILLUSION | | DELUSION | |
| Ping | | | ACCEPT REJECT | | PROTEST | | VOW | | ASSURE | | DECLARE | | | | DENIAL | | CONTRA-DICTION | | | |
| sPing | MOOD | MORALE DEMORAL(IZE) | | | TOLERANT INTOLERANT | | | | INTEREST | | ATTENTION | | OBSERVATION | | | | CARE | | IGNORE | |
| M | ASLEEP | DISTRACTION | | CONFUSE | NEGLECT | | LAZY | | SKIP | | SLIP | | IMAGINATION | | | | INVENTION | | INGENIOUS | |
| sM | | | PRACTICAL | | | | IDENTIFI-CATION | | TOKEN | | TROPHY | RELIC | KNOW | | | | CHERISH | | | |
| Ming | MEMORIZE | REMIND | | | REMEMBER FORGET | | SUSPENSE | ANTICIPATE | SURPRISE | | BLOW | | SHOCK | | STARTLE | | | | | |
| sMing | DISAPPOINT | | FRUSTRATE | | FORESIGHT | | PREDICTION | | OMINOUS | | OMEN | | PROMISE | WARNING | WHISTLE | SIREN | FORTUNATE | | IMPLY | |
| L | SILENCE | EVASIVE | SECRECY | | PRIVATE | | PUBLIC | | CONFIDENTIAL | | STIFLE | | DECEPTION | | MASK | ECLIPSE | LURK | | DISGUISED | |
| sL | HYPOCRISY | | LYING | | FORGERY | | CHEAT | TAMPERED | EXAGGER-ATION | | TRICK | BAIT | BLUFF | SNARE | NET | HOOK | FOOL | | LIAR | |
| Ling | MARK | BADGE | EMBLEM | NAME | PASSWORD | | LABEL | | STAMP | | STICKER | | BRAND | | LOGO | GESTURE | CROWN | | FLAG | |
| sLing | | | | | | | | | | | | | | | | | | | | |

| | Ay | wAy | Ah | wAh | Ee | wEe | Eh | wEh | I | wYe | Ih | wIh | Aw | wAw | ă | wă | Ow | wOw | Oh | wOe |
|---|---|---|---|---|---|---|---|---|---|---|---|---|---|---|---|---|---|---|---|---|
| K | ART | FINE ARTS | HANDICRAFTS | FOLK ARTS | ARCHITECTURE | CALLIGRAPHY | SCULPTURE | CERAMICS | | | | | OILS | WATER COLORS | ENGRAVING | | DECORATION | | PAINTING | |
| sK | PORTRAITURE | ILLUSTRATION | DRAWING | | TALENT | | | | TECHNIQUE | | | | DESIGN | | PERSPECTIVE | | PICTURE | SCENE | VIEW | |
| King | CARTOON | | COMIC STRIP | | STUDIO | | GALLERY | | | | | | STATUARY | | RELIEF | | EMBOSSMENT | | | |
| sKing | CAMEO | CARVE | | | MODEL | | MOLD | | POTTERY | | PORCELAIN | | CHINA | | CROCKERY | | KILN | | | |
| T | PHOTOGRAPHY | | SNAPSHOT | | PRINT | | SLIDE | | FILM | | NEGATIVE | | CAMERA PROJECTOR | | | | DEVELOP | | | |
| sT | ANIMATIONS | | | | GRAPHIC ARTS | | LITHOGRAPHY | | SILK SCREEN | | | | FONT | | TYPOGRAPHY | | PRESS | | PUBLISH | |
| Ting | LETTER | | NOTE | POSTCARD | MAIL | | PARCEL | | POSTAGE STAMP | MAILBOX | POST OFFICE | | ADDRESS | | ZIP CODE | | REPLY | | SEND | |
| sTing | BOOK | EDITION | VOLUME | | ANTHOLOGY | | HANDBOOK | ENCYCLOPEDIA | CATALOG | | DIRECTORY | | ATLAS | | DICTIONARY | | TEXTBOOK | | PRIMER | PAMPHLET |
| P | PERIODICAL | NEWSPAPER | | | NEWS | | BINDING | | COVER | | LIBRARY | | BOOKSTORE | | BIBLIOGRAPHY | | | | | |
| sP | INDEX | | | | EDITOR | | | | WRITING | | | | ESSAY | | | | EDITORIAL | | | |
| Ping | AUTHOR | | | | OUTLINE | | BIOGRAPHY | AUTOBIOGRAPHY | DIARY | | STORY | | FICTION | | MYTH | | | SCI-FI | NOVEL | |
| sPing | PLOT | | | | TELL | | | | POETRY | | VERSE | RHYME | METER | | PROSE | | | | | |
| M | THEATER | STAGE | | | SHOW | DRAMA | CIRCUS | MELODRAMA | STAGECRAFT | | PLAY | | SKIT | | TRAGEDY | | COMEDY | | MUSICAL | |
| sM | ACT | SCENE | INTERMISSION | FINALE | REPERTORY | | | | PART IN PLAY | HERO | VILLAIN | | LEAD | | | | STAR | | | |
| Ming | ENGAGEMENT | PERFORMANCE | | | PRODUCTION | | DIRECTION | REHEARSE | RODEO | CARNIVAL | FLOOR SHOW | SIDE SHOW | PUPPET | | MOVIE | FEATURE | DOCUMENTARY | | OPERA | |
| sMing | HALL | | ARENA | | BANDSTAND | | CABARET | | WINGS | PROP | SCENERY | FLATS | SCRIPT | LIBRETTO | SCENARIO | | | | | |
| L | PATRON | | | | OVERACT | | | | ENTERTAINER | | ACTOR | UNDERSTUDY | CLOWN | | | | CAST | | | |
| sL | DANCE | CHOREOGRAPHY | BALLET | BALLROOM | VARIOUS DANCES | | | | | | | | | | | | | | | |
| Ling | VARIOUS DANCES | | | | | | | | | | | | | | | | | | | |
| sLing | MUSIC | | | | MELODY | | HARMONY MUSICAL DISSONANCE | | COMPOSITION | | SCORE | ARRANGEMENT | SYMPHONY | | SYNCOPATION | | FOLK MUSIC | | MARCH | |

| | Ay | wAy | Ah | wAh | Ee | wEe | Eh | wEh | I | wYe | Ih | wIh | Aw | wAw | ă | wă | Ow | wOw | Oh | wOe |
|---|---|---|---|---|---|---|---|---|---|---|---|---|---|---|---|---|---|---|---|---|
| K | VOCAL | | SONG | BALLAD | ANTHEM | | SOLO | ARIA | LULLABY | | HYMN | | CHORUS | | ORCHESTRA | | POLYPHONY | COUNTER-POINT | CODA | |
| sK | OVERTURE | | STAFF | | MOTIF | | CHANT | | HUM | | WHISTLE | | INTONE | | CROON | | STRUM | | | |
| King | CONDUCT | | | | PITCH | KEY | MAJOR | MINOR | SCALE | | OCTAVE | | MUSICAL NOTE | | | | | | | |
| sKing | SHARP | FLAT | NATURAL | | HARMONIC | | CHORD | | TRILL | | TEMPO | | SOPRANO | ALTO | TENOR | BARITONE | BASS | | | |
| T | HARP | BANJO | GUITAR | MANDOLIN | VIOLIN | VIOLA | CELLO | BASS VIOLIN | HORN | BUGLE | TRUMPET | CORNET | TROMBONE | | | | | | | |
| sT | SAX | TUBA | FRENCH HORN | WOODWIND | FLUTE | FIFE | PICCOLO | REED | OBOE | BASSOON | CLARINET | | | | | | | | | |
| Ting | ENGLISH HORN | BAGPIPE | HARMONICA | KAZOO | ACCORDION | PIANO | HARPSICHORD | ORGAN | | | | | | | | | | | | |
| sTing | HURDY-GURDY | MUSIC BOX | CYMBALS | TRIANGLE | GONG | BELLS | CHIMES | CASTANETS | DRUM | TAMBOURINE | CARILLON | PLECTRUM | BOW | STICKS | BATON | METRONOME | ELECTRONIC KEYBOARD | TUNING FORK | PITCH PIPE | |
| P | AMUSEMENT | RECREATION | RELAXATION | PLEASURE | FUN | PLAY | SPORT | FAIR | FROLIC | ATHLETICS | GAME | SCORE | | PARK | PLAYGROUND | GYMNASIUM | FIELD | SWIMMING POOL | TOYS | DOLL |
| sP | CARD | VARIOUS GAMES | | | | | | | | | | | | | | | | | | |
| Ping | SPORTS | | | | | | | | | | | | | | | | | | | |
| sPing | TEAM SPORTS | | | | | | | | | | | | | | | | | | | |
| M | LANGUAGE | SPEECH | TALK | SAY | VOCABULARY | ROOT WORD | | WORD | AFFIX | PREFIX | SUFFIX | | POTENT | | PUNCTUATION | | IDIOM | | DIALECT | |
| sM | ALPHABET | LETTER | VOWEL | CONSONANT | | | | | SYMBOL | CHARACTER | GRAPHEME | | PHONEME | | SYLLABLE | | ETYMOLOGY | PHILOLOGY | LINGUISTICS | |
| Ming | GRAMMAR | SYNTAX | | | SUBJECT | PREDICATE | OBJECT | | NOUN | PRONOUN | ADJECTIVE | | VERB | ADVERB | INFINITIVE | | PARTICIPLE | PREPOSITION | CONJUNCTION | ARTICLE |
| sMing | GRAMMATICAL CASE | PERSON 1,2,3 | | | GENDER M/F | | MOOD OF VERB | | TENSE-PAST, PRESENT, FUTURE | TENSE-PERFECT | TENSE-ONGOING | | VOICE, ACTIVE-PASSIVE | | | | PRONUN-CIATION | | | |
| L | VULGARITY | | IMPROPER | UNCOUTH | CONCISE | | TERSE VERBOSE | | ACCENT | STRESS | VOICE | | STATEMENT | | | | PHRASE | | INFLECTION | |
| sL | TONE | | | | REMARK | | ORAL | | LISP | STUTTER | MUMBLE | | DISCUSSION | | CONVERS-ATION | | ORATE | | ARTICULATE | FLUENT |
| Ling | | | | | | | | | | | | | | | | | | | | |
| sLing | | | | | | | | | | | | | | | | | | | | |

| | Ay | wAy | Ah | wAh | Ee | wEe | Eh | wEh | I | wYe | Ih | wIh | Aw | wAw | ă | wă | Ow | wOw | Oh | wOe |
|---|---|---|---|---|---|---|---|---|---|---|---|---|---|---|---|---|---|---|---|---|
| K | MEANING | | INTENT | | SUGGESTION | | | | SYMBOLISM | | | | NONSENSE | | | | | | | |
| sK | INTELLIGIBLE | | | | | | | | COHERENCE | | | | LEGIBILITY ILLEGIBILITY | | | | | | | |
| King | PERCEPTION | | | | AMBIGUITY | | | | PUZZLE | | RIDDLE | | | | | | SCRAMBLE | | | |
| sKing | DESCRIBE | | ILLUSTRATE | | DEMON-STRATE | | | | INTER-PRETATION | | | | DEFINITION | | | | TEXT | | | |
| T | TRANSLATION | | | | PARAPHRASE | | COMMENT | | EDIT | | | | REPORT | | SIGNAL | | DISTORT | | MISUNDER-STANDING | |
| sT | COMMERCE | | CONTACT | | | | EXPRESSION | | DISCLOSURE | | | | DISPLAY | | DIVULGE | | CONFESSION | | | |
| Ting | PROMINENCE | | | | EXPLICIT | | | | ADMIT | | | | ADVICE | | | | INDICATE | | | |
| sTing | MEDIUM | | | | THE PRESS | | RADIO | | TELEVISION | | TELEGRAPH | | RUMOR | | GOSSIP | | SCANDAL | | | |
| P | | | | | ITEM | | NEWS ARTICLE | | | | | | PUBLICATION | | | | | | | |
| sP | PUBLICITY | | ADVERTISE-MENT | | POSTER | | SIGN | | NEWSLETTER | | | | MAGAZINE | | | | READING | | | |
| Ping | COMMUNI-CATIONS | | HAND SIGNALS | | TELEPHONE | | | TELETYPE | FAX | COMPUTER MODEM | INTERCOM | | MESSENGER | | POSTMAN | | PROPAGANDA | | MISLEAD | |
| sPing | | | | | | | | | | | | | | | | | | | | |
| M | TEACHING | | EDUCATION | | STUDY | PREPARATION | REARING | | DRILL | LESSON | LECTURE | | | | | | PROFESSOR | PRINCIPAL | DEAN | FACULTY |
| sM | STUDENT | | SCHOLAR | ALUMNUS | | | | | | | | | CLASS | | COURSE OF STUDY | | GRADE | | | |
| Ming | SCHOOL | | ACADEMY | | | KINDER-GARTEN | GRADE SCHOOL | | JUNIOR HIGH SCH | | HIGH SCHOOL | | COLLEGE | UNIVERSITY | GRADUATE SCHOOL | | TRADE SCHOOL | | | |
| sMing | | | | | | | | | | | | | | | | | | | | |
| L | RECORD | | ARCHIVES | | DOCUMENT | | CERTIFICATE | | TICKET | | VISA | | DIPLOMA | | ACCOUNT | | BULLETIN | | MONUMENT | |
| sL | | | | | | | | | | | | | | | | | | | | |
| Ling | ENROLLMENT | | SECRETARY | NOTARY | PEN | | PENCIL | | TYPEWRITER | | WORD-PROCESSOR | | PRESENT-ATION | | INK | | IMAGE | FIGURE | | |
| sLing | | | | | | | | | | | | | | | | | | | | |

| F | Ay | wAy | Ah | wAh | Ee | wEe | Eh | wEh | I | wYe | Ih | wIh | Aw | wAw | ă | wă | Ow | wOw | Oh | wOe |
|---|---|---|---|---|---|---|---|---|---|---|---|---|---|---|---|---|---|---|---|---|
| K |  | VOLITION | CHOICE |  | DISCRETION | PLEASURE |  |  | VOLUNTARI-NESS |  |  |  | SPONTANEITY |  | WILLINGNESS | EAGER | DEMUR |  | RELUCTANCE |  |
| sK |  |  | FIRMNESS |  | PERSEVER-ANCE |  |  | TENACITY | OBSTINACY | DILIGENCE | PERVERSITY | ADAMANT |  | CONTRARY |  |  | HESITATION |  |  |  |
| King | DEFECTION |  |  |  | BETRAY |  | TREASON |  |  | WHIM |  | FICKLENESS | IMPULSIVE |  |  | RECKLESS | IMPROVISE |  |  |  |
| sKing |  |  |  |  | ESCAPE |  |  |  | EVADE |  |  |  | FLEE |  |  |  | DERELICT |  |  |  |
| T | DESIRE |  |  |  |  |  | NEED |  |  |  |  |  | HOMESICK-NESS |  |  |  | APPETITE |  | HUNGER |  |
| sT | GREED |  |  |  | AMBITION |  |  |  |  | FERVOR | PASSION |  | DEVOTION |  | SERIOUSNESS |  |  |  |  |  |
| Ting |  | UNCONCERN | CARELESS-NESS |  |  | SELECTION |  |  | DILEMMA |  |  | PREFERENCE |  |  |  |  |  | ELIGIBILITY |  |  |
| sTing | NECESSITY |  |  |  | URGENCY |  | COMPULSORY |  |  | INSTINCTIVE |  |  | INEVITABLE | CERTAIN |  | FATE |  | DESTINY | DOOM |  |
| P | SCHEDULE |  |  |  | CUSTOM |  |  |  |  |  | FOLKWAY |  |  |  |  |  | CULTURE |  | CIVILIZATION |  |
| sP | HABIT |  | RULE | ROUTINE |  |  |  |  | ADDICTION |  |  |  | WEAN |  |  |  | FASHION |  | STYLE |  |
| Ping |  | FORMALITY |  | CONFORMITY |  |  |  |  | DIGNITY |  | POMP |  |  | MANNERS |  |  |  |  |  |  |
| sPing |  |  |  |  |  |  |  |  | CASUALNESS |  |  |  |  |  |  |  | CAUSE |  | IDEAL |  |
| M |  | PERSUASION |  | GOAD | INSPIRATION |  | PROVOKE |  | URGE |  |  | INVITE | NURTURE | REQUEST |  |  | TEMPTATION | FASCINATION | CHARM | GLAMOUR |
| sM | BRIBERY |  |  |  |  |  | DETERRENT |  | INTENTION |  | PURPOSE |  | TARGET | SCHEME | DIAGRAM |  | MAP | CHART |  |  |
| Ming | POLICY |  |  |  | CONSPIRE |  | ARTIFICE |  | SKETCH |  | QUEST |  | HUNT |  | FISH |  | PREY |  | PURSUE |  |
| sMing | ROUTE | PATH | ROAD |  | SEA LANE | AIR LANE | PASSAGE | CONDUIT | STREET |  | ALLEY |  | PAVEMENT |  | RAILROAD |  | BRIDGE |  |  |  |
| L | YET | MEANS | WHERE-WITHAL |  |  |  | AGENT |  | EQUIPMENT |  |  |  | SUPPLY |  | LODGINGS |  | HARNESS |  | SADDLE |  |
| sL |  | ENOUGH |  |  |  | SCARCE | WANT |  |  |  |  |  | EXCESS |  |  |  | OVERDO |  |  | SURFEIT |
| Ling | USE |  |  |  | TREATMENT |  | VALUE | WORTHY WORTHLESS |  |  |  |  |  |  |  |  |  |  |  |  |
| sLing |  |  |  |  | DISCARD |  |  |  | JUNK | OBSOLESCENT |  |  | WASTE | GARBAGE | RUBBISH | RUBBLE |  |  |  |  |

| F | Ay | wAy | Ah | wAh | Ee | wEe | Eh | wEh | I | wYe | Ih | wIh | Aw | wAw | ă | wă | Ow | wOw | Oh | wOe |
|---|---|---|---|---|---|---|---|---|---|---|---|---|---|---|---|---|---|---|---|---|
| K | | | ADVISABILITY | | FITNESS | APPROPRIATE | | ADVANTAGEOUS | | | | MAKESHIFT | DRAWBACK | | HANDICAP | | TROUBLE | | | |
| sK | IMPORTANT | | | | | | | | | | EMERGENCY | | | PERSON | SOMEBODY | CELEBRITY | | | CHIEF | |
| King | | | | | GREAT | | VITAL | | | | | SLIGHT | | | SILLY | PETTY | | | | |
| sKing | SORRY | | SAD | | DESPICABLE | | | | MISERABLE | | | | SHABBY | | CHEAP | | | | | |
| T | | EXCELLENCE | | | | | ADEQUATE | | WELFARE | | BENEFIT | | SUPERB | | | | WONDERFUL | | CHAMPION | PEERLESS |
| sT | | | | | | | | | | | | | | | | | | | | |
| Ting | | | | | | OUTRAGEOUS | LOATHSOME | | | | FOUL | | | HARM HARMLESS | | DAMAGE | | | DESTRUCTION | |
| sTing | JINX | VICIOUS | | | SHOCKING | | DISGUSTING | | DAMNABLE | | CURSE | | BLIGHT | | POISON | | PESTICIDE | | | |
| P | PERFECTION | FAULTLESS | SOUNDNESS | | DEFECT | | | | | | | | BLEMISH | | DEFACE | DEFORM | | | MAR | |
| sP | MEDIOCRITY | DULLNESS | | | COMMONPLACE | | | | | | | | | | | | | | | |
| Ping | | | | | | | | | | | | | | | | | | | | |
| sPing | | | | | | | | | | | | | | | | | | | | |
| M | | | PROGRESS | | REFORM | | | | | | | | | | | FALL | | | | ROT |
| sM | | | | | INJURY | | BRUISE | | WRECK | | | | | | | | | | | |
| Ming | COLLAPSE | | | SHATTER | FRAY | | RAMSHACKLE | | | | | | DOWNFALL | | DISASTER | | CRASH | | DISMANTLE | |
| sMing | | | ERASE | ANNIHILATION | VANDALISM | | | | | | | | | | | | | | | |
| L | RESTORE | | | | | | REHABILITATION | | | | RETRIEVAL | REVIVAL | RENEWAL | | | REPAIR | | | | REFRESH |
| sL | STIMULATE | | | | | | | | CHEER | | | | | | | | | | | |
| Ling | DANGER | | | | | | | | | | | | | | | | UNSAFE | | DELICATE | |
| sLing | | SAFE | SECURITY | | | COZY | | | HARBOR | SHELTER | | DOCK | PRESERVATION | | RESCUE | | | | | |

| F | Ay | wAy | Ah | wAh | Ee | wEe | Eh | wEh | I | wYe | Ih | wIh | Aw | wAw | ă | wă | Ow | wOw | Oh | wOe |
|---|---|---|---|---|---|---|---|---|---|---|---|---|---|---|---|---|---|---|---|---|
| K | | | | | | | BEHAVIOR MISBEHAVE | | | | | | DEED | | | | | | PRODUCE | |
| sK | INACTION | | | | ABSTAIN | | IDLE | | | | | | | | | | | | | |
| King | | | | | | | | | MOVEMENT | | | | QUICK | | AGILITY | | INITIATIVE | | | |
| sKing | BUSY | | | | | | | | SLOTH | | | | HASTE | | | | | | | |
| T | LEISURE | | EASE | | | | | | COMFORT DISCOMFORT | | RESPITE | | | | | | ABSENT | | | |
| sT | SLEEP | | | | COMA | | | | | | | | | | | | HIBERNATE | | | |
| Ting | | | AWAKE | | ENDEAVOR | | | | | | | | ATTEMPT | | | | | | ADVENTURE | |
| sTing | | | | | | | | | STRUGGLE | | STRIVE | | | | | | EXHAUSTION | | TIRED | |
| P | | | | | | | | | READY | | | | | | RIPE | | | | | |
| sP | RAWNESS | | | | | | | | UNCOOKED | | | | | | | | | | | |
| Ping | ACHIEVEMENT | | | | | | | | | | | | WINNER | | GAIN | | CAPTURE | | DEFEAT | |
| sPing | | | | | | | | | PROSPERITY | | | | LUXURY | | | | | | | |
| M | | | | | | | | | MISFORTUNE | | | | | | | | | | | |
| sM | HINDRANCE | | | | | | | | | | | | INTERRUP-TION | | | | | | | |
| Ming | | | | | | | | | | | | | | | | | PREVENT | | | |
| sMing | DIFFICULTY | | | | ANXIETY | | | | | | | | | | | | MESS | | | |
| L | | | | | FLEXIBILITY | | | | | | | | SKILL | | | | | | EXPERIENCE | |
| sL | CLUMSINESS | | | | INCOMPETENT | | | | | | | | BUNGLE | | | | CUNNING | | | |
| Ling | | | | | | | | | | | | | | | | | | | | |
| sLing | MISCHIEF | | | | | | | | IMP | | | | | | | | | | | |

| | Ay | wAy | Ah | wAh | Ee | wEe | Eh | wEh | I | wYe | Ih | wIh | Aw | wAw | ǎ | wǎ | Ow | wOw | Oh | wOe |
|---|---|---|---|---|---|---|---|---|---|---|---|---|---|---|---|---|---|---|---|---|
| K | | | | | DURESS | | PRESSURE | | | | REQUIRE | | STRICTNESS | | | | | | DISCIPLINE | AUSTERITY |
| sK | STERNNESS | | METICULOUSNESS | | | | | | | | | | | | RELENTLESS | | | | | |
| King | | | LENIENCY | | | | | | | | COMPASSION | | COMPLIANT | | | | | | HUMORING | |
| sKing | | | | | GENTLENESS | | | | FORBEARING | | | | | | LOCK | | KEY | | FREEDOM | |
| T | | | | | | | RIGHTS | | | | | | | | | FREE WILL | SELF-RELIANCE | | | |
| sT | | | | | | | | | FREE PERSON | | | | | | | | | | | |
| Ting | | | | | SERFDOM | | | BASENESS | | | | | | | MEEKNESS | | | | YIELD | |
| sTing | | | | | | | | | ALLEGIANCE | | | | | | REBEL | | | DEFY | HEED | |
| P | | | | | ENGAGEMENT | | | | SPONSORSHIP | | | | | | | | | | PERMISSION | |
| sP | REFUSE | | | | PROHIBITION | | FORBID | | LEGAL ILLEGAL | | | | | | | | DETECTIVE | | | |
| Ping | | | | | | | | | | HELP | | SYMPATHY | COMRADE | | | | | FRATERNITY | BELONG | |
| sPing | OPPOSITION | | | | HOSTILITY | | CONFRONT | | | | OPPONENT | | DEFIANCE | | | CHALLENGE | | | | |
| M | | | RAPPORT | | | | | | | | QUARREL | | | | | | | | | |
| sM | | | | | | | | | | | | | | | GIFT | | | | | |
| Ming | THRIFT | | | | | | | | | | STINGINESS | | | | | | | | | |
| sMing | GENEROUS | | | | | | | WASTEFULNESS | | | LAVISH | | SPEND | | | | | | | |
| L | | | | | NONVIOLENCE | | | | PACIFIST | | | | | | APPEASEMENT | | NEUTRALITY | | COMPROMISE | |
| sL | | | | | | | | | | GRIP | HOLD | HUG | KEEP | | RELEASE | | ABANDON | | | RENOUNCE |
| Ling | | | SHARING | CONTRIBUTE | | | | | GIVING | | CHARITY | | | | | | DOWRY | | | |
| sLing | GRAB | RAPACITY | RAPE | | RECOMPENSE | | | | PLAGIARISM | | BANDIT | | | | | | | | PAUPER | DESTITUTION |

| L | Ay | wAy | Ah | wAh | Ee | wEe | Eh | wEh | I | wYe | Ih | wIh | Aw | wAw | ǎ | wǎ | Ow | wOw | Oh | wOe |
|---|---|---|---|---|---|---|---|---|---|---|---|---|---|---|---|---|---|---|---|---|
| K | GOVERN | | | | SOCIAL SECURITY | | | | | AUTHORITY | | | RULE | | | | | | | |
| sK | | | | | | | | LORDSHIP | | | | | HIERARCHY | NOBILITY | ARISTOCRACY | | RULING CLASS | | | |
| King | CHAIRMAN | | | | PRESIDENT | | | | PREMIER | | | | PRINCE | | | | RECTOR | | REGENT | |
| sKing | MAYOR | | | | ALDERMAN | | | | AMBASSADOR | | | | CONSUL | | | | DICTATOR | | | |
| T | KING | | | | EMPEROR | | | | DUKE | | | | ROYALTY | | | | MAJESTY | | | |
| sT | SCEPTER | | THRONE | | ACCESSION | | | | | | | | | | APPOINTMENT | | OFFICIAL | | | |
| Ting | | | | | PLEBISCITE | | | | | | REGULATION | | ADMINISTRATION | | | | | | | |
| sTing | BUREAUCRACY | | RED TAPE | | | | CIVIL | | FEDERAL | | CONSTITUTIONAL | | EXECUTIVE | | | | JUDICIAL | | | |
| P | LEGISLATURE | | | | PARLIAMENT | | | | CONGRESS | | | | ASSEMBLY | | | | CHAMBER | | DIET | |
| sP | SENATE | | | | HOUSE | | REPRESENTATIVES | | DELEGATES | | | | COMMITTEES | | | | DEPARTMENTS | | | |
| Ping | COUNCIL | | CABINET | | CABINET SECRETARY | | MINISTER | | CAPITOL | | | | | | | | COURT HOUSE | | | |
| sPing | | | | DEBATE | VETO | | | | BILL | | FILIBUSTER | | POLITICS | | | | PARTY | | | |
| M | PLATFORM | | CONVENTION | CAUCUS | NOMINATE | | CANDIDATE | | ELECTIONEERING | | | | CAMPAIGN | | | | DISTRICT | | | |
| sM | PRECINCT | | WARD | | VOTE | | SUFFRAGE | | BALLOT | | POLLS | | ELECTORATE | | | | LOBBY | | | |
| Ming | GRAFT | | PATRONAGE | | | | | | PROCLAMATION | | | | TAX | | JUNTA | | FORUM | PANEL | SESSION | |
| sMing | TOWN MEETING | | REFERENDUM | NONPARTISAN | | | | | | | REVOLT | | | | REVOLUTION | | INSURRECTION | | INSURGENCY | |
| L | TREATY | | ALLIANCE | | | | | | PASSPORT | | | | EMBARGO | | | | REPEAL | | | RECALL |
| sL | | | | | | | | | DIPLOMAT | | | | ATTACHE | | | | SPY | | | |
| Ling | IMPEACHMENT | | OVERTHROW | | ABDICATION, ABANDON | | | | | | | | SOCIETY | | COMMUNITY | | | | | |
| sLing | | | | | CIVILIAN | | | | CITIZEN | | | | DEMOCRACY | | | | TARIFF | | | |

| L· | Ay | wAy | Ah | wAh | Ee | wEe | Eh | wEh | I | wYe | Ih | wIh | Aw | wAw | ă | wă | Ow | wOw | Oh | wOe |
|---|---|---|---|---|---|---|---|---|---|---|---|---|---|---|---|---|---|---|---|---|
| K | MIL POLICE | | PROTECT | | GUARD | | | | | | | | | | | | | | | |
| sK | WARDEN | NURSE MAID | | BABY SITTER | OUTPOST | | PICKET | VANGUARD | REARGUARD | | | | GARRISON | WATCH | WATCHMAN | LOOKOUT | SENTINEL | SCOUT | PATROL | |
| King | | | DOORKEEPER | | BODYGUARD | | ESCORT | | CONSTABLE | | OFFICER | | SHERIFF | | MARSHAL | | DEPUTY | | SERGEANT | |
| sKing | LIEUTENANT | | | | CAPTAIN | | | | INSPECTOR | | | | POLICE | | | | POSSE | | VIGILANTES | |
| T | | LOAD | SHOOT | | COMMISSIONED OFFICER | | | | GENERAL | | | | COLONEL | | | | MAJOR | | | |
| sT | COMMANDER | | | | NONCOM | | WARRANT OFFICER | CORPORAL | | | ADMIRAL | COMMODORE | ENSIGN | | | | PETTY OFFICER | | FORCE | |
| Ting | | | | | ARREST | | SHACKLE | | | | PRISON | | REFORMATORY | | CONFINE | | FETTER | | | |
| sTing | QUARANTINE | | ISOLATION | | | | | | CONCENTRATION CAMP | | | | PRISONER OF WAR | | SURRENDER | | MUTINOUS | | | |
| P | TRESPASS | | | | HOSTAGE | | | | ENLISTMENT | | CONSCRIPTION | MIL DRAFT | INDUCTION | | RECRUITMENT | | MUSTER | | MOBILIZE | |
| sP | ABET | ACCOMPLICE | | GANG | | | BATTLE | FIGHT | | | ENEMY | | SKIRMISH | | | | WARFARE | | ATTACK | |
| Ping | STRATEGY | | TACTICS | | SOLDIER | | | | DEPLOY | COUNTER-ATTACK | | | INVASION | | SIEGE | | BOMBARD | | STRAFE | GUNS |
| sPing | DEFENSE | | | | ARMOR | | FORTIFICATION | | | | | | BUNKER | | ENTRENCHMENT | | | | CASTLE | |
| M | KNIGHT | | CAVALRY | TANKS | INFANTRY | | | | ARTILLERY | | | | GUERRILLA | | | | MERCENARY | | | |
| sM | MILITARY | ARMY | DIVISION | | BRIGADE | | | | REGIMENT | | | | BATTALION | COMPANY | TROOP | SQUAD | PLATOON | | BATTERY | |
| Ming | UNIT | | | | MILITIA | | RESERVES | | NAVY | | FLEET | | MARINES | | | | AIR FORCE | | | |
| sMing | WEAPONS | | ARMORY | AMMUNITION | BALLISTICS | | | | SWORD | BLADE | RIFLE | SIDE ARM | CARTRIDGE | SHELL | MISSILE | BULLET | BOMB | | | |
| L | ARROW | | BOW | | SPEAR | | | | SHIELD | | | | SLINGSHOT | | | | BATTLEFIELD | | | |
| sL | | | CONSCIENTIOUS OBJECTOR | | TRUCE | | ARMISTICE | | DISARMAMENT | | | | | | | | | | | |
| Ling | | | | | | | | | | | | | | | | | | | | |
| sLing | | | | | | | | | | | | | | | | | | | | |

| L | Ay | wAy | Ah | wAh | Ee | wEe | Eh | wEh | I | wYe | Ih | wIh | Aw | wAw | ǎ | wǎ | Ow | wOw | Oh | wOe |
|---|---|---|---|---|---|---|---|---|---|---|---|---|---|---|---|---|---|---|---|---|
| K | LAW LAWLESS | | BAILIFF | JURISDICTION | | | | | ANARCHY | | | | | | NIHILISM | | CONSERVATISM | | REACTIONARY | |
| sK | LIBERALISM | RADICALISM | SOCIALISM | COMMUNISM | NATIONALIZATION | | CAPITALISM | | | | | | | | | | PRECEPT | | ORDER | |
| King | | | PRINCIPLE | | GUIDELINE | | STATUTE | | MANDATE | | DECREE | EDICT | RULING | | ORDINANCE | | | | | |
| sKing | NOTICE | | ENJOIN | | | | CHARGE | STIPULATION | PLEA | | INJUNCTION | | CUSTODY | | CATCH | | | | PAROLE | |
| T | VIOLATION | | INFRACTION | TRANSGRESSION | OATH | | SWORN | | PERJURY | | | | SETTLEMENT | | | | BAIL | | | |
| sT | MOVE | | PETITION | | APPEAL | | PRAYER | | SUIT | | WAIVER | | ANNUL | | OVERRULE | | | | SURROGATE | |
| Ting | ACCESSORY | | | | | | CARTEL | SYNDICATE | | | | | LEGITIMACY | | | | | | | |
| sTing | | | | | ACT | | | | | | | | | | | | | | | |
| P | ILLICIT | CRIME | FELONY | MISDEMEANOR | EXTORTION | BLACKMAIL | THEFT | FRAUD | SWINDLE | ROBBERY | BURGLARY | MUGGING | HIJACKING | LOOTING | RACKETEERING | SMUGGLING | CONTRABAND | | | |
| sP | | | | | | | | | | | | | | | | | | | | |
| Ping | | | JUDICIARY | | | | MAGISTRATE | | BUREAU | | | | TRIBUNAL | | | JUROR | ATTORNEY | ADVOCATE | PROSECUTOR | |
| sPing | | | COURT CASE | | SUMMONS | | | | WRIT | | WARRANT | | | | INDICTMENT | | | | | |
| M | COURT HEARING | INQUIRY | | DEPOSITIONS | PLEADINGS | | TESTIMONY | EVIDENCE | ARGUMENT | | DECISION | | | | VERDICT | | | | | |
| sM | | | | | TRY | | | | | | | ALLEGATION | CITATION | | | | ACCUSE | | VINDICATION | |
| Ming | ALIBI | | | | ACQUITTAL | | | DISMISSAL | | | | | AMNESTY | | REPRIEVE | | CONDEMNATION | | | CONVICTION |
| sMing | | | ATTAINDER | | PENALTY | | PUNISHMENT | FINE | | | | | | | IMPRISON | | | | | |
| L | SUE | | PLAINTIFF | | DEFENDANT | | | | COMPLAINT | | DISSENT | OBJECTION | MEDIATION | | REFEREE | | JUDGE | | | |
| sL | OCCUPANCY | | TENURE | | CONVEYANCE | | | | TRANSFER | | ASSIGNMENT | | BEQUEST | | LEGACY | | INHERITANCE | | | |
| Ling | | | | | REPOSSESSION | | FORECLOSURE | | GNP | DEPRESSION | RECESSION | | MARKET | | | | PANIC | | | |
| sLing | MONEY | | CURRENCY | LEGAL TENDER | | | | | | | | | CHECK | | INVESTMENT | | SOLVENCY | | FEE | PRICE INDEX |

| | Ay | wAy | Ah | wAh | Ee | wEe | Eh | wEh | I | wYe | Ih | wIh | Aw | wAw | ă | wă | Ow | wOw | Oh | wOe |
|---|---|---|---|---|---|---|---|---|---|---|---|---|---|---|---|---|---|---|---|---|
| K | BUSINESS | JOB | | | INSURANCE | | ANNUITY | INSURANCE POLICY | WORK | LABOR | WAGES | SALARY | SLAVE | | DRUDGE | | | | PROFESSIONAL | |
| sK | CRAFT | | JOURNEYMAN | MASTER | SMITHS | WRIGHTS | ENGINEERS | | | | | | SHOP | | BENCH | | DESK | | | |
| King | BUSINESS COMPANY | | CORPORATION | | SWEATSHOP | | INDUSTRIAL PLANT | FACTORY | POWER PLANT | MACHINE SHOP | MILL | YARD | | | FOUNDRY | | OFFICE | | | |
| sKing | SERVANT | EMPLOYEE | | | STEWARD | | WAITER | | STAFF | | AIDE | | | | | | | | | |
| T | FRANCHISE | | LICENSE | | FREE LANCE | | | | GUARANTEE | | CONTRACT | | BARGAIN | | DEAL | | DEED | | | |
| sT | SURETY | | PLEDGE | | | | DEPOSIT | | STAKE | | COLLATERAL | | MORTGAGE | | LIEN | | | | ENDORSE | |
| Ting | | | IN TRUST | | OFFER | | | | PROPOSITION | | SOLICITATION | | BEGGAR | | | | RENTAL | | LEASE | |
| sTing | | | INDENTURE | | MIDDLEMAN | | SPOKESMAN | | RAISE | | REDUCTION | | | DISMISS | RETIREMENT | PENSION | LIQUIDATE | VACATE | FINANCE | |
| P | | | PARTNERSHIP | | | | CO-WORKER | | ORGANIZATION | | | | FOUNDATION | | | | | | DIVISION | |
| sP | LABOR UNION | | MEMBERSHIP | | JOIN | | LOCAL | | STRIKE | WALKOUT | LOCKOUT | | | | | | COMPETITOR | | OWING | |
| Ping | | | MONOPOLY | | OWNER | LANDLORD | TENANT | ROOMER | PROPERTY | | | | | | GOODS | BELONGINGS | ESTATE | COMPETITION | | |
| sPing | INTEREST | | EQUITY | | REAL ESTATE | | ASSETS | | ACQUISITION | | | | EARNINGS | | PROFIT | RECEIPTS | DIVIDENDS | | | |
| M | | | | | LOSS | | DEPRECIATE | | | | | | BUDGETING | | DISTRIBUTION | | DELIVERY | | | |
| sM | SALE | | | | PREMIUM | BONUS | SUBSIDY | | ENDOWMENT | | SUBSCRIBER | | RECEIPT | | LENDING | | BORROWING | | NEGOTIATE | |
| Ming | | | | | CUSTOMER | | PROSPECT | BUYER SELLER | | | | | WHOLESALE | | RETAIL | | MERCHANDISING | | AUCTION | STORE |
| sMing | | | BROKER | | COMMODITY | | DRY GOODS | | APPLIANCES | | HARDWARE | | HOUSEWARES | | | | SUPERMARKET | | | |
| L | STOCKS | | BONDS | | SECURITIES | | DEBENTURES | | MARGIN | | | | TREASURER | CASHIER | TILL | BANK | PURSE | | WALLET | |
| sL | WEALTH | CREDIT | | | DEBT | | | | PAYMENT | REWARD | REIMBURSEMENT | | INCOME | | STIPEND | | PAID | NONPAYMENT | DEFAULT | BANKRUPTCY |
| Ling | EXPENDITURE | | | | | | | | FINAL STATEMENT | | INVOICE | | LEDGER | | | | | | | |
| sLing | ENTRY | | CREDIT | DEBIT | BOOKKEEPING | | AUDITING | | CLERK | | BALANCE | | PRICE | | | | ASSESSMENT | | DISCOUNT | |

| | Ay | wAy | Ah | wAh | Ee | wEe | Eh | wEh | I | wYe | Ih | wIh | Aw | wAw | ă | wă | Ow | wOw | Oh | wOe |
|---|---|---|---|---|---|---|---|---|---|---|---|---|---|---|---|---|---|---|---|---|
| K | EMOTIONS | | SENTIMENT | | CALLOUS | | | | THRILL | | AGITATION | | EXCITEMENT | | | | | | | |
| sK | IMPASSIVE | | | | PATIENT | | | | CALM | | | | NONCHAL-<br>ANCE | | | | NERVOUS | | TENSE | |
| King | | INDULGENCE | DOMINANT<br>SUBMISSIVE | ENDURE<br>CONDONE | IMPATIENT<br>HOPE<br>DESPAIR | LIVELY<br>FUNEREAL | ENTHUSIASTIC<br>INDIFFERENT | ENERGETIC<br>LETHARGIC | HAPPY<br>SAD | POSITIVE<br>NEGATIVE | FOR<br>AGAINST | PRAISE<br>DEPRECATE | EXALT<br>DEBASE | LOVE<br>HATE | ADORE<br>DETEST | FAMILIAR<br>STRANGE | ENCOURAGE<br>DISCOURAGE | | | |
| sKing | PLEASANT | DELIGHTFUL | CHEERFUL | | | | BLISSFUL | | UGLY | | OFFENSIVE | | | | | | MORTIFI-<br>CATION | | ANNOY | |
| T | | | JOYFUL | | ECSTACY | | SATISFY | | LAUGH | | | | ENJOY | | | | CONTENT-<br>MENT | | COMFORT-<br>ABLE | |
| sT | | | | | REJOICING | | SMILE | | EXULT | | CELEBRATE | | | | | | JOKE | | | |
| Ting | | | MISERY | | | | | | GRIEF | | SUFFER | | | | DISLIKE | | | | | |
| sTing | SOLEMNITY | | MELANCHOLY | | | GLUM | FORLORN | | REGRET | PENITENCE | DEPLORE | | SHAME | | | | LAMENT | WEEPING | MOURN | SOB |
| P | TEDIOUS | | | | | | | | BORE | | | | RELIEF | | | | | | | |
| sP | | | | | | | | | OPTIMISM | | | | EXPECTATION | | | | | | | |
| Ping | DESPERATION | | | | PESSIMISM | | | | | | | | IMPOSSIBILITY | | | | INCURABLE | | | |
| sPing | WORRY | FEAR | ALARM | | DREAD | TERROR | SCARINESS | | | INTIMIDATION | | | | | | | BOLD | | RASH | |
| M | CAUTIOUS | | | | FASTIDIOUS | | | | TASTEFUL-<br>NESS | | ELEGANCE | | REFINEMENT | | | | CONNOISSEUR | | GOURMET | |
| sM | INDECENCY | | | | GROSS | | | | OBSCENE | | | | HOMELY | | | | HIDEOUS | | MONSTROSITY | |
| Ming | BEAUTIFUL | | | | ORNAMENT | | JEWEL | | SIMPLICITY | | NATURALNESS | | | | | | OSTENTATION | PRIDE | CONCEITED | |
| sMing | DIGNIFIED | | HUMILITY | | | | | | SERVILITY | | SYCOPHANT | | MODESTY | | SHYNESS | TIMIDITY | COYNESS | | DEMURENESS | |
| L | VANITY | | SMUGNESS | | EGOTIST | | | BOASTFUL | BLUSTER | | BULLY | | ARROGANCE | | SNOBBERY | | PRESUMP-<br>TUOUS | | | |
| sL | IMPERIOUS | | INSOLENCE | | BRAZENNESS | | | | | | | | IMPUDENCE | | | | DISREPUTE | DISGRACE | STIGMA | |
| Ling | REPUTATION | | ESTEEM | DEAR | HONOR | | PRESTIGE | | DISTINCTION | HONORS | AWARDS | LAURELS | BRAVERY<br>COWARDICE | VALOR | MEDAL | | TITLE | HONORIFIC | ACADEMIC<br>DEGREE | |
| sLing | THE PEOPLE | | RABBLE | | THE MASSES | | PEASANT | | WONDER | | AMAZEMENT | | | | AWE | | PRODIGY | | | PHENOMENON |

| | Ay | wAy | Ah | wAh | Ee | wEe | Eh | wEh | I | wYe | Ih | wIh | Aw | wAw | ă | wă | Ow | wOw | Oh | wOe |
|---|---|---|---|---|---|---|---|---|---|---|---|---|---|---|---|---|---|---|---|---|
| K | SOCIABILITY | GREGARIOUS-NESS | CONVIVIALITY | | FELLOWSHIP | | PARTY | | SECLUSION | | | | HOSPITALITY | | WELCOME | | GREETINGS | | | |
| sK | HOST | | | | GUEST | | VISITOR | | BANISHMENT | | | | EXILE | | BLACKLIST | | | | | |
| King | | | | | INTIMATE | | CORDIAL | | DEVOTE | | DEDICATE | | BEFRIEND | | | | INTRODUCE | | | |
| sKing | ENMITY | | | | | | | | GRUDGE | | SPITE | | | | | | | | | |
| T | ROMANCE | | | | INFATUATION | | SWEETHEART | | ADMIRER | | | | LOVEMAKING | | | | KISS | | | |
| sT | WOOING | | | | FLIRTATION | | | | PHILANDER | | | | COPULATE | | | | PROPOSAL | | | |
| Ting | MARRIED | | WEDDING | | HONEYMOON | | | | BRIDE | | BRIDEGROOM | | | | | | | | | |
| sTing | HAREM | | BIGAMIST | | | | | | CELIBACY | | | | | | | | | | | |
| P | COURTESY | | GRACIOUS-NESS | | GALLANTRY | | | | SUAVITY | | | | POLITE | | | | | | | |
| sP | | | | | | | | | | | | | BROTHER-HOOD | | | | | | | |
| Ping | | | | | MALICE | | | | RANCOR | | VIRULENCE | | | | | | CRUELTY | | | |
| sPing | | | | | | | | | | | | | | | | | | | | |
| M | BENEFACTOR | | | | | | | | SAVIOR | | | | | | | | | | | |
| sM | | | BARBARIAN | | WITCH | | | | PITY | | | | MERCY | | | | RUTHLESS | | | |
| Ming | CONSOLE | | | | FORGIVE | | | | | | | | CONGRATUL-ATE | | | | | | | |
| sMing | GRATITUDE | | | | | | | | | | | | | | | | | | | |
| L | ILL HUMORED | | | | SCOWL | | | | FROWN | | | | SULK | | | | | | | |
| sL | ANGRY | | | | | | | | RESENTMENT | | | | | | | | | | | |
| Ling | | | | | JEALOUS | | | | SUSPICIOUS | | | | | | | | ENVY | | | |
| sLing | RETALIATE | | | | | | | | | | | | REVENGE | | | | | | | |

| | Ay | wAy | Ah | wAh | Ee | wEe | Eh | wEh | I | wYe | Ih | wIh | Aw | wAw | ă | wă | Ow | wOw | Oh | wOe |
|---|---|---|---|---|---|---|---|---|---|---|---|---|---|---|---|---|---|---|---|---|
| K | ETHICS | | | | | | MORALITY IMMORALITY | | CONSCIENCE | | | | | | | | RIGHT WRONG | PROPER | DECENT | |
| sK | PRIVILEGE | | | | HUMAN RIGHTS | | CIVIL RIGHTS | | | | | | | | | | | | | |
| King | | | MERIT | EARN | IMPOSITION | | | | USURP | | | | DUTY | | | | | | | |
| sKing | NECESSARY UNNECESSARY | | | | DEMAND | | | | | | | | | | | | | | INFLICT | |
| T | RESPECT DISRESPECT | | | | | | | | REVERENCE | | | | | | | | | | | |
| sT | | | | | OFFEND | | | | | | INSULT | | CONTEMPT | | | | SCORN | | SNUB | |
| Ting | RIDICULE | DERISION | SARCASM | IRONY | CYNICISM | SATIRE | BURLESQUE | LAMPOON | PARODY | CARICATURE | SNEER | INVECTIVE | | JEST | FARCE | HUMOR | LEVITY | FANTASY | INCREDULITY | |
| sTing | | | APPLAUSE | | | | | | POPULARITY | | | | | | | | | | COMPLIMENT | FLATTER |
| P | | | | | BLAME | | | | REBUKE | | | | SCOLD | | | | | NAG | | |
| sP | | | | | | | SLANDER | LIBEL | | | | | ABUSE | | | | | | PROFANITY | |
| Ping | THREAT | | | | DECEIT | | INFIDELITY | TREACHERY | CORRUPTION | | | | | | | | SELFISH | | | |
| sPing | JUSTICE INJUSTICE | | | | FAIRNESS | | IMPARTIAL | | | HONESTY | TRUST-WORTHY | | | VIRTUE | | LOYAL | | | | |
| M | VICE | | | | | | EVIL | | | MISCONDUCT | SIN | | | | | | ATROCITY | | | |
| sM | WRETCH | | RASCAL | | | | | | CHASTITY | | VIRGINITY | | DISSOLUTE | | WANTON | | LEWD | | | |
| Ming | SEDUCTION | | | | ADULTERY | | | | PROSTI-TUTION | PIMP | BROTHEL | | DEBAUCHERY | | | | PARAMOUR | | | |
| sMing | SEXY | | LUSTFUL | | SMUT | | | | FORNICATION | | | | IMMODEST | | | | RISQUE | PORNO-GRAPHIC | RIBALD | SCATOLOG-ICAL |
| L | ASCETIC | | | | | | | | INTEMPER-ANCE | | GLUTTONY | | FASTING | | | | INTOXICATION | | | |
| sL | | | | | | | | | | | | | CHAMPAIGN | | | | TOAST | | COCKTAILS | |
| Ling | | | | | TAVERN | | | | PUB | | | | BREWERY | | | | DISTILLERY | | | |
| sLing | SOBRIETY | | | | ATONEMENT | | WHIP | | | | REDRESS | | APOLOGY | | EXCUSE | | PENANCE | | | |

| | Ay | wAy | Ah | wAh | Ee | wEe | Eh | wEh | I | wYe | Ih | wIh | Aw | wAw | ă | wă | Ow | wOw | Oh | wOe |
|---|---|---|---|---|---|---|---|---|---|---|---|---|---|---|---|---|---|---|---|---|
| K | RELIGION | | | | CULT | | | | SECT | | | | DENOMINATION | | | | | | | |
| sK | THEISM | POLYTHEISM | MONOTHEISM | PANTHEISM | AGNOSTICISM | ATHEISM | CHRISTIANITY | JUDAISM | ISLAM | BUDDHISM | CONFUCIANISM | SHINTOISM | TAOISM | | | | | | | |
| King | SCRIPTURE | | | | BIBLE | | | | KORAN | | | | VEDAS | | | | TORAH | | | |
| sKing | REVELATION | | | | PROPHECY | MIRACLE | PROPHETS | | EVANGELISTS | | | | APOSTLES | | DISCIPLES | | THEOLOGY | | DIVINITY | |
| T | DOCTRINE | | | | DOGMA | | | | ORTHODOXY | | | | FAITH | | | | FUNDAMENTALISM | HETERODOXY | | |
| sT | HERESY | | FALLACY | | INFIDEL | | PAGAN | | | | | | NONBELIEVER | | BIGOT | | DEITY | GOD | SPIRIT | SOUL |
| Ting | MOTHER NATURE | | GHOST | | CREATOR | | DEMIGODS | | FAIRY | | LIKE | | | | FOLKLORE | | ANGELS | SAINTS | | |
| sTing | | DEMONS | DEVIL | GOBLIN | WEREWOLF | | | | HEAVEN | PARADISE | HELL | PURGATORY | | | RESURRECTION | REINCARNATION | HOLINESS | CONSECRATION | PROFANENESS | |
| P | SECULAR | | | | TEMPORAL | | | | PIETY IMPIETY | | | | ZEAL | | | | FANATICISM | | | |
| sP | BELIEVER | | | | DEVOTEE | | | | | | | | | | | | | | | |
| Ping | | | SACRILEGE | | BLASPHEMY | | DESECRATION | | IRRELIGIOUS | | | | SKEPTIC | | HUMANISM | | ICONOCLASM | | | |
| sPing | WORSHIP | | | PAEAN | PSALM | PRAY | SUPPLICATION | | INVOCATION | GRACE | BENEDICTION | BLESSING | PROPITIATION | OFFERING | SACRIFICE | IMMOLATION | SERVICES | | LITURGY | |
| M | IDOLATRY | | | | FETISHISM | | | | | | | | OCCULTISM | | | | MYSTICISM | | | |
| sM | THEOSOPHY | | SUPERNATURALISM | | TRANSCENDENTALISM | | | PSYCHICS | PARAPSYCHOLOGY | | SPIRITUALISM | ECTOPLASM | CLAIRVOYANCE | TELEPATHY | | EXTRASENSORY | DIVINATION | | | |
| Ming | SORCERY | MAGIC | | | WITCHCRAFT | | VOODOOISM | | EXORCISM | | TRANCE | | | | INCANTATION | | TALISMAN | | | |
| sMing | RELIGIONS, VARIOUS | | | | | | | | | | | | | | | | | | | |
| L | PRIESTHOOD | | MINISTRY | CLERIC | MONASTICISM | | | ORDINATION | CLERGY | | CHAPLAIN | PREACHER | IMAM | MULLAH | RABBI | | MONK | | NUN | |
| sL | | HIGH PRIEST | POPE | | CARDINAL | ARCHBISHOP | BISHOP | | | | | | | | | | | GURU | BONZE | LAMA |
| Ling | LAITY | | CONGREGATION | PARISH | | | | | RITUAL | BAPTISM | ANOINTING | | EUCHARIST | | MASS | | VESTMENTS | | | |
| sLing | TEMPLE | CHURCH | MOSQUE | PAGODA | SHRINE | | | | CATHEDRAL | | ABBEY | CONVENT | ALTAR | | PULPIT | LECTERN | PEW | | | |

| | K | sK | King | sKing | T | sT | Ting | sTing | P | sP | Ping | sPing | M | sM | Ming | sMing | L | sL | Ling | sLing |
|---|---|---|---|---|---|---|---|---|---|---|---|---|---|---|---|---|---|---|---|---|
| Ay | SPACE | | | | | | MEASURE | | | | VOID | | RANGE | | | | | | | |
| wAy | | | | | ROOMINESS | | | | REGION | | | | TERRITORY | | | | PLACE | | | |
| Ah | | | | | | | QUARTER | | | | NEIGHBOR-HOOD | | | | | | | | PROVINCE | |
| wAh | | | | | STATE | | | | | | TOWNSHIP | | | PATCH CITY | TOWN | VILLAGE | DIOCESE | | | |
| Ee | COUNTRY | | REPUBLIC | | COMMON-WEALTH | | | | KINGDOM | | EMPIRE | | PRINCIPALITY | | | | COLONY | | | |
| wEe | THE COUNTRY | | | | | | | | | | | | WASTELAND | | | | FRONTIER | | | |
| Eh | | | | | | | | | PASTORAL | | | | AGRARIAN | | | | | | | |
| wEh | METROPOLIS | | MUNICIPALITY | | SUBURB | | | | CAPITAL | | COUNTY SEAT | | BLOCK | | | | SQUARE | | | |
| I | LOCATION | | | | | | POSITION | | ORIENTATION | | | | | | | | ESTABLISH-MENT | | | |
| wYe | | | | | | | | | | | | | | | | | | | ELSEWHERE | |
| Ih | | | | | | | | | | | | | | | | | | | | |
| wIh | | | | | | | | | | | | | | | | | | | | |
| Aw | PRESENCE | | | | | | | | | | | | | | | | | UBIQUITY | | |
| wAw | ATTENDANCE | | | | | | | | PERVADE | | APPEAR DISAPPEAR | | | | | | | | | |
| ă | | | | | | | RESIDENT NONRESIDENT | | UNINHABITED | | | | HABITATION | | | | TENANCY | | | |
| wă | | | POPULATION | | | | | | DWELL | | | | | | | | | | | |
| Ow | | | | | SETTLER | | | | | | | | PIONEER | | | | | | | |
| wOw | CONTAINER | BOTTLES | | | CASKS | | CASES | BOX | BASINS | BASKETS | BAGS | LUGGAGE | | | PANS | | | | LADLES | BUCKET |
| Oh | CUPBOARDS | | | | CONTENTS | | | | COMPONENTS | | | | INGREDIENTS | | | | PARTS | | INVENTORY | |
| wOe | LOAD | | | | | | | | FILLING | | | | | | | | SUBSTANCE | | MATERIAL | |

| | K | sK | King | sKing | T | sT | Ting | sTing | P | sP | Ping | sPing | M | sM | Ming | sMing | L | sL | Ling | sLing |
|---|---|---|---|---|---|---|---|---|---|---|---|---|---|---|---|---|---|---|---|---|
| Ay | | | | | | | BIGNESS | | | | | | DIMENSIONS | | PROPORTIONS | | | | | |
| wAy | HUGE | PLUMPNESS | GIANT | | | | | | | | | | | | | | | | | |
| Ah | | | | LITTLENESS | SHORTNESS | SCANTINESS | RUNT | MINIATURE | | | DEVELOPMENT | | EXPANSION | | EXTENSION | ENLARGEMENT | | SPREAD | | DISTENTION |
| wAh | | COMPRESSION | | SHRINKING | SQUEEZING | | SHRIVELING | WITHERING | | | | | | | PUCKER | | | | PINCH | |
| Ee | LINEAR MEASURES | AREA MEASURES | VOLUME MEASURES | | SURVEY | | INSTRUMENTATION | GAUGE | | | | CRITERION | PATTERN | | | | GEODESY | ASSAY | WEIGH | METRICAL |
| wEe | | REMOTENESS | | | | | | BEYOND | | | VICINITY | | CONVENIENT | NEIGHBORING | INTERVAL | | ENCOUNTER | | TANGENCY | GRAZE |
| Eh | | | CLEARANCE | | CRACK | GULF | BREACH | | | | | | | | | | STRETCH | | | |
| wEh | | | SUCCINCTNESS | | | | LOWNESS | | ABBREVIATION | | CONDENSATION | | CURTAILMENT | | | | | | ABRIDGE | |
| I | | | | | | RADIUS | | | WIDE NARROW | | | | TAPERING | BOTTLENECK | | | LEANNESS | | | |
| wYe | | TALLNESS | | | STATURE | | | | TOWER | | | STEEPLE | | | | | BASE | | | |
| Ih | | | DEEPNESS | | HOLE | | CAVITY | | CHASM | | | | UNDERGROUND | | UNDERWATER | | SHALLOWNESS | | SUPERFICIALITY | |
| wIh | | | | | | | CLIMAX | | | UNDERSIDE | UNDERNEATH | | NADIR | | | | GROUND | | FLOOR | FOUNDATION |
| Aw | VERTICALNESS | ERECTNESS | | PERPENDICULARITY | STEEP | | | | HORIZONTALNESS | | LEVELNESS | FLATNESS | RECUMBENCY | | | | HORIZON | | SKYLINE | |
| wAw | | | | | | | | | RAZE | | | | PENDENCY | | | | SAG | DANGLE | DROOPING | |
| ǎ | SUPPORT | AID | SUSTAINING | BRACKET | BRACE | BUTTRESS | BEAM | TRUSS | FOOTING | PILLAR | SCAFFOLD | PLATFORM | | TRESTLE | SAWHORSE | | ROSTRUM | | | |
| wǎ | SHAFT | | POLE | | BAR | | ROD | | | | | | STAFF | | CANE | | RAFTER | | | |
| Ow | ZIGZAG | BENT | STAGGER | CROOKED | LEANING | SLOPE | | | BIAS | BEND | | TWIST | TURN | SKEW | SWERVE | | | | | |
| wOw | INVERSION | | | | | TRANSPOSITION | | | OVERTURN | UPSET | | SOMERSAULT | | | | | | | | |
| Oh | INTERSECTION | CROSSROAD | CROSSWALK | NETWORK | | WEBBING | NETTING | MESH | WICKERWORK | | CRISSCROSS | | ROOD | CROSS | SALTIRE | ANKH | MALTESE CROSS | SWASTIKA | CROSSWISE | TRAVERSE |
| wOe | WEAVING | | LACING | | TWINING | BRAIDING | INTERWEAVING | | WREATH | | | | WARP | WOOF | WEFT | | LOOM | SHUTTLE | TREADLE | |

| | K | sK | King | sKing | T | sT | Ting | sTing | P | sP | Ping | sPing | M | sM | Ming | sMing | L | sL | Ling | sLing |
|---|---|---|---|---|---|---|---|---|---|---|---|---|---|---|---|---|---|---|---|---|
| Ay | | | | | | | FRINGE | | OUTDOORS | | | | | | | | | | | |
| wAy | INLAND | | MIDLAND | | | | | | | | | | | | | | HEAD-QUARTERS | | CONCENTRIC | |
| Ah | LAYER | | | | | | | | | | | VENEER | | COATING | PATINA | SLICE | SLAB | | PLY | |
| wAh | COVERING | | | VEILING | | LID | | ROOF | UMBRELLA | CRUST | SHELL | HULL | WRAPPER | | BANDAGE | ENVELOPE | CRATE | PACKAGE | PLASTER | ELECTRO-PLATE |
| Ee | ENVIRONMENT | | | | | ENVIRONS | CIRCUM-STANCES | | | | CONTEXT | SITUATION | SETTING | | BACKGROUND | | ELEMENTS | ENVELOP-MENT | | |
| wEe | | | | | PATENT | COPYRIGHT | TRADEMARK | | | RESTRICT | RESTRAIN | | | | | | REGISTER | | TERMINAL | |
| Eh | | | | | | | | PROFILE | | | BORDER | | | | | | | BRINK | | |
| wEh | | | | | YARD | | | | PEN | | | | FENCE | RAIL | | | | | | |
| I | | | | | INJECTION | | INSERTION | | INTERMED-IARY | | PARTITION | | BUFFER | | BUMPER | | | | | |
| wYe | INTRUSION | INTERFER-ENCE | | | | | | | | | | | | | CONFRONT-ATION | | | | ANTIPODAL | |
| Ih | | | | | | | | PROW | | | ONWARDS | | | | | | | | | |
| wIh | | | ASKANCE | | PORT | STARBOARD | LEEWARD | WINDWARD | BESIDE | | | | SIDE BY SIDE | | | | | | | |
| Aw | STRUCTURE | ARCH | CONSTRUCT-ION | FRAME | FORM | | SYMMETRY | ASYMMETRY | | | GRIMACE | GARBLE | DIRECTNESS | LINE, LINEAR | ANGLE, ANGULARITY | TRIANGLE | CURVE | FLEXURE | BOW, HAIR | PARABOLIC |
| wAw | CIRCLE | RING | CIRCUMFER-ENCE | | ROUND | | | LOOP | OVAL | ELLIPSE | CURLY | WAVY | CONVOLUTION | WINDING | MEANDER | | COIL | | SPIRAL | HELIX |
| ă | SPHERE | | BALL | GLOBE | | | BEAD | | CYLINDER | | CONE | | CONVEXITY | RIDGE | SWELLING | PROTUBER-ANCE | EXTRUSION | | BULGE | HUMP |
| wă | PIT | | DIGGER | | HOLLOWNESS | | CRATER | DENT | | | | | CONCAVITY TUNNEL | | BURROW | | DIMPLE | RECESS | NICHE | |
| Ow | SHARPNESS DULLNESS | | POINT | | HONE | KEEN | BARBED | | SMOOTH ROUGH | | | | SLEEKNESS | | | | SHINE | | SLIPPERY | |
| wOw | | | | | | | | | NOTCH | | | GASH | GROOVE | | TRENCH | | TROUGH | | DITCH | RUT |
| Oh | FOLD | | | | TUCK | | WRINKLE | CREASE | OPEN | | | | GAP | | PUNCTURE | | | | | |
| wOe | | | | | | | | | SHUT | | | | | | | | BLOCKAGE | | PLUG | |

| | K | sK | King | sKing | T | sT | Ting | sTing | P | sP | Ping | sPing | M | sM | Ming | sMing | L | sL | Ling | sLing |
|---|---|---|---|---|---|---|---|---|---|---|---|---|---|---|---|---|---|---|---|---|
| Ay | MOTION INERTNESS | VELOCITY | ACCELERATION DECELERATION | RAPIDITY SLOWNESS | WALK | RUN | DASH | GALLOP | CRAWL | | PLOD | | STEP | | | | JUMP | SPRING | SKIP | |
| wAy | IMPEL | KICK | IMPACT | | THRUST | MOMENTUM | | PUSH | | CRUSH | | POKE | JOSTLE | COLLISION | BUMP | BOUNCE | HIT MISS | TAP | REACTION | REFLEX |
| Ah | THROWING | | | | | | TOSS | | SALVO | | PROJECTILE | SHOT | PULLING | | TRACTION | | TUG | | JERK | |
| wAh | LEVERAGE | | PRY | | FULCRUM | | AXIS | PIVOT | CROWBAR | | | | TACKLE | WINDLASS | CAPSTAN | WINCH | ATTRACTION REPULSION | | MAGNET | |
| Ee | | | WAY | | AIM | | HEADING | COURSE (ROUTE) | NORTH | SOUTH | EAST | WEST | | | | | | | THROUGH | |
| wEe | DEVIATION | | | VARIATION | | WANDERING | DEFLECTION | | REFRACTION | | DIFFRACTION | | SCATTER | SHIFT | DIVERT | | | PRECEDING TRAILING | | LAG |
| Eh | | | PROMOTION DEMOTION | | ONGOING | | | | | | | SETBACK | | | REVERSE | | | | | |
| wEh | | RETRACT | | | CONVERGENCE DIVERGENCE | | FOCAL | | | | | | | | | | ARRIVAL DEPARTURE | DESTINATION | REACH | |
| I | | | | | ENTRY EXIT | | | INTAKE OUTLET | PENETRATION | | INFLUX | | IMMIGRATION EMIGRATION | EMERGENCE | EMISSION | | | | LEAK | EXUDE |
| wYe | | | | | OVERPASS | | | | INFESTATION | | | | INFRINGEMENT | | | | OVERSHOOT | | | |
| Ih | SUCCESS FAILURE | | | | RAISE LOWER | | SOARING DIVING | | CLIMB DESCEND | STAIRS | LADDER | ELEVATOR | ESCALATOR | | RAMP | | DROP LIFT | | | |
| wIh | STAND | | | | KNEEL | | SQUAT | | SIT | | LIE | | | | | | | | | |
| Aw | EXCURSION | | DETOUR | REVOLUTION | | WHEELS | ROLL | | VIBRATION | FLUCTUATION | | PULSE | | SWING | SHAKE | | DISTURBANCE | | | |
| wAw | TRANSPORT | CART | TRUCKING | FREIGHT | SHIPMENT | BEARER | PORTER | IMPORT EXPORT | | DRAY | WHEELBARROW | PIPE | FUNNEL | EXPRESS | POST | | BRING REMOVE | | IN TRANSIT | |
| ă | VEHICLE | | | STATION | WAGON | CARRIAGE | WHEELCHAIR | | UNICYCLE | BICYCLE | TRICYCLE | MOTORCYCLE | PRAM | AUTOMOBILE | BUS | TAXICAB | STAGECOACH | TRAIN | COACH | BOX CAR |
| wă | WAGON-LITS | DINING CAR | STREETCAR | TRACTOR | TRAILER | SEMITRAILER | SLED | SNOWMOBILE | ICE SKATES | ROLLER SKATES | SKIS | SNOWSHOES | HOVERCRAFT | SCOOTER | FORKLIFT | | | | | |
| Ow | TRAVEL | | | | TOURISM | ITINERARY | JOURNEY | TRIP | | | | | RIDE | | DRIVE | | PASSENGER | | COMMUTER | MIGRANT |
| wOw | SAILING | RADAR | SONAR | LORAN | SWIMMING | PILOT | BOAT | SEXTANT | LATITUDE | LONGITUDE | WAKE | SUBMARINE | | ANCHOR | BALLAST | OAR | PADDLE | KNOT | FATHOM | |
| Oh | SAILOR | SHIP | VESSEL | RAFT | RIGGING | MAST | SAIL | | AVIATE | TAKE OFF | FLIGHT | LANDING | AIRPORT | | RUNWAY | | | | | |
| wOe | JET PROPULSION | MACH NUMBER | PARACHUTE | AIRCRAFT | HELICOPTER | HYDROPLANE | BLIMP | DIRIGIBLE | BALLOON | GLIDER | KITE | ROCKETRY | SPACE TRAVEL | ASTRONAUTICS | | SPACE PROBE | | | | |

| | K | sK | King | sKing | T | sT | Ting | sTing | P | sP | Ping | sPing | M | sM | Ming | sMing | L | sL | Ling | sLing |
|---|---|---|---|---|---|---|---|---|---|---|---|---|---|---|---|---|---|---|---|---|
| Ay | PHYSICS | | | | NUCLEONICS | | | | SCIENCE | | | | THERMO-DYNAMICS | | | | | | | |
| wAy | ELEMENT | MOLECULE | ATOM | NUCLEUS | NEUTRON | POSITRON | PROTON | | ELECTRON | ION | ANION | MUON | ISOTOPE | | | | FISSION | FUSION | CRITICAL MASS | REACTOR |
| Ah | | | | | | | | | | | | | QUARK | | | | RADIATION | | | COSMIC RAY |
| wAh | HALF-LIFE | URANIUM | PLUTONIUM | RADIUM | GEIGER COUNTER | CURIE | ROENTGEN | | CHEMICALS | REAGENT | ACID | ALKALI | MOLECULAR WEIGHT | VALENCE | ATOMIC NUMBER | | | | | |
| Ee | TEMPER-ATURE | DEGREE FARENHEIT | DEGREE CELSIUS | DEGREE KELVIN | HEAT | | | | | | | | | | | | | | | |
| wEe | FIRE | FLAME | | | IGNITION | | | | | | | | | | | | | | | |
| Eh | SPARK | | | | SCINTILL-ATION | | | | COAL | | | | EMBER | | | | | CINDER | ASH | |
| wEh | FIREWORKS | | | | CALORIE | | BTU | | | | ENGINE | | SMOKE | | | | | | FIERY | |
| I | STOVE | FURNACE | OVEN | | HEATING | | BOILING | | | | | | | | | | | | | |
| wYe | MELTING | | | | KINDLING | | | | | MOTOR | | | CAUTERIZING | | | | INCINERATION | | | |
| Ih | | | | | BURN | | | | SCALD | | | | ARSON | | | | | | | |
| wIh | FIREPLACE | | ANDIRON | | BLOWTORCH | | | | SLAG | | | | COKE | | | | CHARCOAL | | SOOT | |
| Aw | | | | | REHEATED | | | | SEARED | | | | | | | | GALLEY | | BAKERY | |
| wAw | FUEL | | PEAT | | GASOLINE | | ALCOHOL | | KEROSENE | | GAS | | PROPANE | | FIREWOOD | | BAGASSE | | | |
| ă | MATCH | | | | TINDER | | | | | | FUSE | | | | | | | | | |
| wă | | | | | | EXTINGUISH-ING | | | FIREFIGHTER | | | | FIREPROOFING | | | | | | | |
| Ow | | | CHILL | | | | | | SHIVERS | | | | | | | | | | | |
| wOw | FREEZE THAW | | FROST | | ICICLE | | FLOE | | ICEBERG | | GLACIER | | SLEET | | HAIL | | | | | |
| Oh | HOARFROST | | | | ICE | | SNOW | | | | SLUSH | | REFRIGERATE | | | | ARCTIC | | | |
| wOe | CRYOGENICS | | | | AIR CONDITIONING | | COLD STORAGE | | COOLANT | | DRY ICE | | FREON | | LIQUID AIR | | | | | |

| | K | sK | King | sKing | T | sT | Ting | sTing | P | sP | Ping | sPing | M | sM | Ming | sMing | L | sL | Ling | sLing |
|---|---|---|---|---|---|---|---|---|---|---|---|---|---|---|---|---|---|---|---|---|
| Ay | LIGHT | | GLOW | | INCAND-ESCENCE | BRILLIANCE | SPLENDOR | | | | RAY | | GLITTER | | | | SPARKLE | | | |
| wAy | DAYLIGHT | SUNLIGHT | | | MOONLIGHT | | | | STARLIGHT | | | | | | FLUOR-ESCENCE | | PHOSPHOR-ESCENCE | | | |
| Ah | HALO | | | | RAINBOW | | AURORA | | LIGHTNING | | THUNDER | | IRIDESCENCE | | | | | | | |
| wAh | PHOTON | | QUANTUM | | CANDLE | | | | | | | | PRISMS | | LENSES | | LASERS | | | |
| Ee | | | | | | | | | TWINKLING | | | | FLICKERING | | | | LIT | | | |
| wEe | | LAMP | TORCH | FLARE | TRAFFIC LIGHT | | FIREFLY | | CHANDELIER | | WICK | LANTERN | FLASHLIGHT | | FLASHBULB | | BEACON | LIGHTHOUSE | STROBOSCOPE | FLUORESCENT TUBE |
| Eh | SUN GLASSES | EYESHADE | FILTER | BLINDS | | SHADOW | SHADE | | BLACKOUT | | | | | | SCREEN | CURTAIN | AWNING | | | |
| wEh | TRANSPAR-ENCY OPACITY | | CLEARNESS | | | | | | | | | | TRANSLUC-ENCE | | | | | | | |
| I | | ELECTRIC CURRENT | AMPERES | VOLTAGE | ELECTRIC RESISTANCE | OHMS | CONDUCTION | REACTANCE | IMPEDANCE | CAPACITANCE | CONDUCTOR | | CONDENSER | ELECTRIC CHARGE | BATTERY | | CIRCUIT | ELECTRIC SHOCK | | |
| wYe | MAGNETISM | | POLARITY | | WATTAGE | | ELECTROLYSIS | | GENERATOR | | | | INSULATE | GROUND | METERS | WIRE | ELECTRONICS | VACUUM TUBE | TRANSISTOR | COMPUTER CHIP |
| Ih | | FREQUENCY | BAND WIDTH | MODULATION | AMPLIFI-CATION | BROADCAST-ING | MICROPHONE | SPEAKER | TRANSMITTER | RECEIVER | ANTENNAS | AUDIO | VIDEO | STEREO | DIGITAL | | ANALOG | | | |
| wIh | | | | | | | | | OSCILLOSCOPE | | | | | | | | | | | |
| Aw | MECHANICS | | STATICS | | DYNAMICS | | | | HYDRAULICS | | | | PNEUMATICS | | | | | | | |
| wAw | TOOLS | | INSTRUMENT | | | | APPARATUS | | DEVICE | SCISSORS | HAND TOOL | MACHINE TOOL | | | | | | | | |
| ă | MACHINERY | | MACHINE | | MECHANISM | | | | GEAR | | | | TRANS-MISSION | | CLUTCH | BRAKE | MECHANIC | | MACHINIST | |
| wă | HAMMER | | SAW | | SHOVEL | SPADE | TROWEL | | PLANE | | DRILL | | WRENCH | | | | | | | |
| Ow | MILLS | | WELDERS | | DIES | | PRESSES | | LATHES | | SHAPERS | | PUMPS | | | | | | | |
| wOw | AUTOMATIC | CONTROL | FEEDBACK | | REMOTE CONTROL | | SERVO-MECHANISM | CONTROL PANEL | COMPUTER | COMPUTER MEMORY | STORAGE | | INPUT OUTPUT | | | | PROGRAM | PRINTOUT | | |
| Oh | FRICTION | RUBBING | ABRASION | | ATTRITION | EROSION | SCRAPING | SCUFF | | BUFF | BURNISH | POLISH | SANDING | | GRINDING | | RASPING | | GRATING | |
| wOe | FASTENING | PIN | NAIL | RIVET | SCREW | BUTTON | ZIPPER | VELCRO | CHAIN | LINK | CLAMP | LATCH | | ADHERE | | GLUE | RUBBER CEMENT | PASTE | | |

| | K | sK | King | sKing | T | sT | Ting | sTing | P | sP | Ping | sPing | M | sM | Ming | sMing | L | sL | Ling | sLing |
|---|---|---|---|---|---|---|---|---|---|---|---|---|---|---|---|---|---|---|---|---|
| Ay | TEXTURE | | SURFACE | | GRAIN | | NAP | | | | | | WEIGHT | | BURDEN | | OPPRESSIVE | | | |
| wAy | GRAVITY | | MASS | | | | | | GRAM | POUND | OUNCE | TON | CARAT | | | | | | | |
| Ah | LIGHTNESS | | BUOYANCY | LEVITATE | VOLATILITY | | | | | | | | | | | | | | | |
| wAh | | | | | LEAVEN | | FERMENT | | | | YEAST | | | | | | | | | |
| Ee | | | | | INDIVISIBILITY | | | | COAGULATION | | | | | | | | | | | |
| wEe | CURDLING | | | | PRECIPIT-ATION | | | | | | | | CLOT | | | | GEL | | | |
| Eh | | | | | | | | | TENUOUS | | | | | | | | | | | |
| wEh | | | | | | | | | | | | | | | | | | | | |
| I | HARD SOFT | | | | | | | | | | | | | | | | | | | |
| wYe | | | | | STUBBORN | | | | TEMPER | | | | TOUGH | | | | | | | |
| Ih | | | | | PETRIFY | | | | STIFF | | | | | | | | | | | |
| wIh | | | | | | | | | | | | | YIELDING | | | | | | | |
| Aw | ELASTIC | | | | | | | | RUBBER | | | | SPRINGS | | | | | | | |
| wAw | | | | | UNBREAKABLE | | | | STRONG FEEBLE | | | | | | | | FRAGILITY | | | |
| ă | POWDER | | | | | | | | | | | | DUST | | | | CRUMB | | | |
| wă | MEAL | | | | | | | | GRATE | | | | SHRED | | | | MASH | | | |
| Ow | COLOR | | STAIN | | DYE | | PAINT | | BLOND | | | | BRUNETTE | | | | REDHEAD | | | |
| wOw | | | | | FADING | | | | PALENESS | | | | GRAY | | | | BLEACHED | | | |
| Oh | WHITE | | | | | | ALBINO | | BLACK | | | | | | | | | | | |
| wOe | BROWN | | | | RED | PURPLE | | | ORANGE | | | | YELLOW | GREEN | BLUE | | VARIEGATION | SPECKLE | | |

| | K | sK | King | sKing | T | sT | Ting | sTing | P | sP | Ping | sPing | M | sM | Ming | sMing | L | sL | Ling | sLing |
|---|---|---|---|---|---|---|---|---|---|---|---|---|---|---|---|---|---|---|---|---|
| Ay | METALS | ORE | ALLOY | AMALGAM | CASTING | | INGOT | | MINE | | | | | | | | | | | |
| wAy | ALUMINUM | BRASS | COPPER | IRON | STEEL | GOLD | SILVER | PLATINUM | MERCURY | LEAD | NICKEL | TIN | ZINC | BRONZE | CHROMIUM | PEWTER | SOLDER | | | |
| Ah | PHOSPHORUS | POTASSIUM | SODIUM | | | | | | | | | | | | | | | | | |
| wAh | | | | | | | | | | | | | | | | | | | | |
| Ee | | | | | WOOD | FIBER | PAPER | CLOTH | PLASTIC | | | | GLASS | | | | CERAMIC | | | |
| wEe | | | | | | | | | | | | | | | | | | | | |
| Eh | | | | | | | | | | | | | | | | | | | | |
| wEh | | | | | | | | | | | | | | | | | | | | |
| I | FLUID | | SAP | VISCOSITY | EMULSION | MUD | SOLUBILITY | SOLUTION | SOLVENT | | NAPHTHA | TURPENTINE | | | | | | | | |
| wYe | | | | | | | | | | | | | | | | | | | | |
| Ih | | | | | | | | | | | | | | | | | | | | |
| wIh | | | | | | | | | | | | | | | | | | | | |
| Aw | HELIUM | HYDROGEN | OXYGEN | NITROGEN | CARBON DIOXIDE | CARBON MONOXIDE | NEON | POISON GAS | LAUGHING GAS | | | | | | | | | | | |
| wAw | | | | | | | | | | | | | | | | | | | | |
| ă | | | | | | | | | | | | | | | | | | | | |
| wă | | | | | | | | | | | | | | | | | | | | |
| Ow | LUBRICANTS | GREASE | GRAPHITE | | MINERAL OILS | FUEL OILS | VEGETABLE OILS | | ANIMAL FATS | GLYCEROL ESTERS | | | WAXES | | | | RESINS | | GUMS | |
| wOw | | | | | | | | | | | | | | | | | | | | |
| Oh | | | | | | | | | | | | | | | | | | | | |
| wOe | | | | | | | | | | | | | | | | | | | | |

| | K | sK | King | sKing | T | sT | Ting | sTing | P | sP | Ping | sPing | M | sM | Ming | sMing | L | sL | Ling | sLing |
|---|---|---|---|---|---|---|---|---|---|---|---|---|---|---|---|---|---|---|---|---|
| Ay | MATTER | | | | COSMOS | | UNIVERSE | | WORLD | | | | NATURE | | | | HEAVENS | | SKY | |
| wAy | | | ETHER | OUTER SPACE | STARS | | COMETS | | POLE STAR | | CONSTELL-ATION | | GALAXY | | NEBULA | | MILKY WAY | | | |
| Ah | PLANET | | | | EARTH | | MOON | SATELLITE | SUN | | | | METEOR | | | | ASTEROID | | | |
| wAh | MERCURY | | VENUS | | MARS | | JUPITER | | URANUS | | NEPTUNE | | SATURN | | PLUTO | | | | | |
| Ee | | | | | ORBIT | | | | | | | | ZODIAC | | | | | | | |
| wEe | ECLIPTIC | | | | OBSERVATORY | | | | PLANETARIUM | | | | TELESCOPE | | | | | | | |
| Eh | SPECTRUM | | | | ASTRONOMY | | | | STARGAZING | | | | | | | | | | | |
| wEh | ASTROLOGY | | | | | | | | EXTRATER-RESTRIAL | | | | | | | | | | | |
| I | | | | | | | | | | | | | | | | | | | | |
| wYe | | | | | | | | | | | | | | | | | | | | |
| Ih | | | | | | | | | | | | | | | | | | | | |
| wIh | | | | | | | | | | | | | | | | | | | | |
| Aw | RAW MATERIALS | | | | BRICKS | | | | MORTAR | | | | | | | | | | | |
| wAw | TIMBER | BOARD | LUMBER | | FABRIC | | | | | | | | PAPER | | | | SYNTHETICS | | | |
| ă | WOOD | | | | | | | | PLASTICS | | | | | | | | | | | |
| wă | | | | | | | | | | | | | | | | | | | | |
| Ow | | | | | | | | | | | | | | | | | | | | |
| wOw | | | | | | | | | | | | | | | | | | | | |
| Oh | | | | | | | | | | | | | | | | | | | | |
| wOe | | | | | | | | | | | | | | | | | | | | |

| | K | sK | King | sKing | T | sT | Ting | sTing | P | sP | Ping | sPing | M | sM | Ming | sMing | L | sL | Ling | sLing |
|---|---|---|---|---|---|---|---|---|---|---|---|---|---|---|---|---|---|---|---|---|
| Ay | INORGANIC MATTER | | QUARRY | MINERALS | | | | | | | | | | | | | | | | |
| wAy | | | | | | | | | | | | | | | | | | | | |
| Ah | ROCK | STONE | SAND | GRAVEL | PEBBLE | BOULDER | BASALT | CHALK | FLINT | GNEISS | GRANITE | LAVA | MARBLE | QUARTZ | SLATE | SANDSTONE | LIMESTONE | | | |
| wAh | GEM | DIAMOND | RUBY | EMERALD | AMETHYST | OPAL | CORAL | GARNET | JADE | LAPIS LAZULI | ONYX | CHRYSOLITE | SAPPHIRE | TOPAZ | TURQUOISE | ZIRCON | | | | |
| Ee | LAND | | | | | SOIL | | | SHORE | | | | GEOLOGY | | | | GEOGRAPHY | | | |
| wEe | ALLUVIAL | | | | LITTORAL | | | | CLAY | | | | SILT | | | | LOESS | | MARL | |
| Eh | | CONTINENT | MAINLAND | | AFRICA | | ASIA | | EUROPE | | ANTARCTICA | | SOUTH AMERICA | | NORTH AMERICA | | AUSTRALIA | | PENINSULA | ISLAND |
| wEh | PLAIN | | PRAIRIE | | STEPPE | | TUNDRA | | PAMPAS | | PLATEAU | | VELD | | MOOR | | HEATH | MOUNTAIN | MESA | |
| I | | | | | | | | | | | | | | | | | | | | |
| wYe | | | | | | | | | MOIST | | HUMIDITY | | | | DEW | | SPRAY | SPRINKLE | SPLASH | |
| Ih | FLOODING | IRRIGATION | SOAKING | | | | | SATURATE | SUBMERGE | | | | RAIN | | MIST | | RAINSTORM | THUNDER-STORM | WET DRY | THIRST |
| wIh | STREAM | BROOK | TRIBUTARY | RIVER | CURRENT | TORRENT | DELUGE | TRICKLE | DRIP | | SEEP | RAPIDS | WATERFALL | WHIRLPOOL | TIDE | | WAVE | SWELL | SURF | |
| Aw | CHANNEL | AQUEDUCT | CANAL | | GUTTER | | DRAIN | | HOSE | | NOZZLE | | VALVE | | FAUCET | | | | | |
| wAw | FLOODGATE | | SLUICE | | WEIR | | DAM | LOCK | HYDRANT | | | | VENT | | VENTILATOR | | CHIMNEY | FLUE | | |
| ă | OCEAN | SEA | WATER | MARITIME | LAKE | | POOL | | POND | | PUDDLE | | LAGOON | | RESERVOIR | | WELL | CISTERN | OASIS | |
| wă | INLET | GULF | BAY | FJORD | ESTUARY | STRAIGHT | SOUND | BIGHT | SHALLOWS | REEFS | TIDAL FLATS | | MARSH | | | | MORASS | BOG | MIRE | QUAGMIRE |
| Ow | VAPOR | | FUME | | REEK | | | | | | STEAM | | GASES | | | | | | | |
| wOw | | | EVAPORATION | | | | VENTILATE | | | | | | | | | | | | | |
| Oh | AIR | ATMOSPHERE | WEATHER | CLIMATE | METEOR-OLOGY | | FORECAST | BAROMETER | WIND | DRAFT | BREEZE | STORM | GALE | HURRICANE | BLIZZARD | | CYCLONE | TORNADO | VANE | FAN |
| wOe | CLOUD | FOG | CUMULUS | NIMBUS | HAZE | DRIZZLE | CIRRUS | OVERCAST | BUBBLE | | | FOAM | | | | | LATHER | | | |

| | K | sK | King | sKing | T | sT | Ting | sTing | P | sP | Ping | sPing | M | sM | Ming | sMing | L | sL | Ling | sLing |
|---|---|---|---|---|---|---|---|---|---|---|---|---|---|---|---|---|---|---|---|---|
| Ay | ORGANIC MATTER | | BIO-DEGRADABLE | | FLORA | | FAUNA | | ORGANISM | | CELL | | PROTOPLASM | | | | | | | |
| wAy | CHROMOSOME | | GENE | | DNA | | RNA | | GAMETE | | GERM | | SPERM | | | | | | | |
| Ah | | | | | | | | | SPORE | | | | | | | | | | | |
| wAh | | | | | YOLK | | | | ALBUMEN | | | | | | | | | | | |
| Ee | BIOLOGY | | | | | | | | | | | | BACTERI-OLOGY | | | | | | | |
| wEe | BIOCHEM-ISTRY | | | | | | | | | | | | | | | | | | | |
| Eh | PHYSIOLOGY | | | | | | | | | | | | ANATOMY | | | | | | | |
| wEh | BOTANY | | | | LIFE<br>LIFELESS | | | | | | | | LIVE, TO LIVE<br>DIE, TO DIE | | | | | | | |
| I | BIRTH<br>DEATH | | | | | | | | | | | | | | | | BEREAVEMENT | | OBITUARY | |
| wYe | | | | | CORPSE | CADAVER | | CARRION | | | | | | | | | | | | |
| Ih | | | | | | | | | AUTOPSY | POSTMORTEM | INQUEST | | | | | | | | EXPIRE | |
| wIh | DROWN | | | | MORTAL | | | | PERISHABLE | | | | | | | | | | | |
| Aw | | | | | KILLING | | | | | | | | | | | | | | | |
| wAw | | | | | MURDER | | | | ASSASSIN-ATION | | | | | | | | | | | |
| ă | | | | | | | | | SUICIDE | | | | | | | | | | | |
| wă | ASPHYXIATION | | STRANGUL-ATION | | | | | | FATALITY | | | | | | | | HOMICIDE | | | |
| Ow | | | | | BURIAL | | | | CREMATION | | | | EMBALMMENT | | | | | | | |
| wOw | LAST RITES | | | | WAKE | | | | FUNERAL | | | | | | | | | | | |
| Oh | MORTICIAN | | | | MORGUE | | | | COFFIN | | | | HEARSE | | | | URN | | | |
| wOe | CEMETERY | | | | TOMB | | | | EPITAPH | | | | | | | | | | | |

| | K | sK | King | sKing | T | sT | Ting | sTing | P | sP | Ping | sPing | M | sM | Ming | sMing | L | sL | Ling | sLing |
|---|---|---|---|---|---|---|---|---|---|---|---|---|---|---|---|---|---|---|---|---|
| Ay | PLANTS | | | | WEED | | LEGUME | | HERB | | | | | | | | MOSS | | WORT | |
| wAy | ALGAE | | | | SEAWEED | | | | FUNGUS | | | | MOLD | | | | LICHEN | | | |
| Ah | | | | | | | | | MEADOW | | LAWN | | | | | | PASTURE | | | |
| wAh | SHRUBBERY | | | | TREE | | FOREST | | JUNGLE | | GROVE | | | | | | | | UNDER-GROWTH | |
| Ee | FOLIAGE | | | | LEAF | | | | FROND | | | | BLADE | | | | | | | |
| wEe | NEEDLE | | | | PETAL | | | | THORN | | | | | | | | | | | |
| Eh | BRANCH | | | | TWIG | | | | SPROUT | | | | | | | | | | | |
| wEh | STEM | | | | | | | | TRUNK | | | | | | | | | | | |
| I | ROOT | | | | RHIZOME | | | | TUBER | | | | BULB | | | | | | | |
| wYe | SEED | | | | BUD | | | | FLOWER | | | | | | | | | | | |
| Ih | NUT | | | | BERRY | | | | KERNEL | | | | VERDANT | | | | | | | |
| wIh | PERENNIAL | | | | ANNUAL | | | | FERNS | | | | | | | | | | | |
| Aw | | | | | | | | | | | | | | | | | | | | |
| wAw | GRASS | | | | GRAIN | | | | | | | | | | | | | | | |
| ă | | | | | SHRUBS | | | | | | | | | | | | | | | |
| wă | VINES | | | | | | | | | | | | | | | | | | | |
| Ow | | | | | AGRICULTURE | | | | FARMING | | | | | | | | | | | |
| wOw | HORTI-CULTURE | | | | GARDEN | | | | CULTIVATION | | | | SOWING | | | | | | | |
| Oh | HOEING | | | | | | | | | | | | PLOW | | | | HARROW | | | |
| wOe | HARVEST | | | | REAP | | | | PICK | | | | GLEANING | | | | | | | |

| | K | sK | King | sKing | T | sT | Ting | sTing | P | sP | Ping | sPing | M | sM | Ming | sMing | L | sL | Ling | sLing |
|---|---|---|---|---|---|---|---|---|---|---|---|---|---|---|---|---|---|---|---|---|
| Ay | MICROFAUNA | ZOOLOGY | PROTOZOA | PARAZOA | METAZOA | CHORDATA | VERTEBRATE | INVERTE-BRATE | MAMMAL | MARSUPIAL | PRIMATE | HUMANS | BIPED | QUADRUPED | UNGULATE | RUMINANT | CREATURE | VERMIN | LEECH | WORM |
| wAy | INSECT | BEETLE | SPIDER | SCORPION | TICK | FLY | BEE | HORNET | MOSQUITO | MOTH | BUTTERFLY | ANT | TERMITE | LOCUST | GRASSHOPPER | CRICKET | LOUSE | FLEA | ROACH | |
| Ah | REPTILE | | | | LIZARD | ALLIGATOR | | | TURTLE | | SNAKE | | AMPHIBIAN | FROG | TOAD | | | | | |
| wAh | BIRD | | | | | | | | | | | | | | | | | | | |
| Ee | FOWL | | POULTRY | | CHICKEN | | GOOSE | | DUCK | | TURKEY | | | | | | | | | |
| wEe | SEA-LIFE | | | | CORAL | | | | PLANKTON | | | | SHRIMP | | | | | | | |
| Eh | FISHES | SALMON | MINNOW | | | | | | | | | | | | | | | | | |
| wEh | WHALE | | | | PORPOISE | | DOLPHIN | | OTTER | | | | | | | | | | | |
| I | DEER | ELK | MOOSE | REINDEER | ANTELOPE | BUFFALO | CAMEL | GIRAFFE | | | | | | | | | | | | |
| wYe | BEAR | | | | | | | | | | | | | | | | | | | |
| Ih | ELEPHANT | | | | | | | | | | | | | | | | | | | |
| wIh | | | | | | | | | | | | | | | | | | | | |
| Aw | | | | | | | | | | | | | | | | | | | | |
| wAw | CANINES | FOX | WOLF | COYOTE | HYENA | DOG | | | | | | | | | | | | | | |
| ă | FELINES | CAT | LION | TIGER | LEOPARD | | | | | | | | | | | | | | | |
| wă | RODENT | RAT | MOUSE | | RACCOON | | OPOSSUM | SKUNK | HARE | | RABBIT | | | | | | | | | |
| Ow | HORSE | STEED | COLT | PONY | ASS | | DONKEY | | BURRO | | MULE | | | | | | | | | |
| wOw | MONKEY | APE | GIBBON | CHIMP | ORANG | GORILLA | BABOON | LEMUR | TARSIER | | | | | | | | | | | |
| Oh | ANIMAL HUSBANDRY | BREEDING | STOCK | PEDIGREE | | BROOD | RANCHER | | | HERD | CATTLE | BOVINE | STEER | OX | HEIFER | SHEEP | GOAT | | SWINE | |
| wOe | RACE | | ETHNICITY | | CAUCASIAN | | MONGOLOID | | INDIAN | ARABIAN | SEMITIC | NILOTIC | SLAVIC | NORDIC | MELANESIAN | ABORIGINE | BUSHMAN | PYGMY | | |

| | K | sK | King | sKing | T | sT | Ting | sTing | P | sP | Ping | sPing | M | sM | Ming | sMing | L | sL | Ling | sLing |
|---|---|---|---|---|---|---|---|---|---|---|---|---|---|---|---|---|---|---|---|---|
| Ay | COOK | FRY | DEEP-FRY | SAUTE | BROIL | BAKE | ROAST | CAUTERIZE | BARBECUE | SMOKE | MICROWAVE | STIR | BLEND | WHIP | FOLD | | | | GRIND | CHOP |
| wAy | EATING | FEEDING | CHEWING | BITE | SUCKLE | SWALLOW | CONSUME | DRINK | MEAL | BREAKFAST | LUNCH | TEA TIME HARMFUL | DINNER | SUPPER | | | SICK | | | |
| Ah | | | | | | | | | | | | | | | PICNIC | FEAST | BANQUET | PORTION | MENU | |
| wAh | CHOP-STICKS | KNIFE | FORK | SPOON | PLATE | BOWL | CUP | PLATTER | NAPKIN | | | | GLASS | POT | PAN | SKILLET | WOK | KETTLE | | |
| Ee | | | | | CARNIVORE | CANNIBAL | VEGETARIAN | | | | | | NOURISH | | | | | | | |
| wEe | | | | | | | | | | | | | | | | | | | | |
| Eh | | | | | | | | | | | | | | | | | | | | |
| wEh | | | | | | | | | | | | | | | | | | | | |
| I | | | | | | | | | | | | | | | | | | | | |
| wYe | RESTAURANT | COURSE (FOOD) | ENTRE | DESERT | | RESERVATION | TIP | AMBIENCE | CAFETERIA | TRAY | CAFE | FOOD | EDIBLE | DRINKABLE | GROCERIES | SOUP | BROTH | SALAD | SLAW | STEW |
| Ih | MEAT | | | | BEEF | | VEAL | | MUTTON | | LAMB | | PORK | HAM | BACON | | STEAK | | | |
| wIh | SEAFOOD | SAUSAGES | EGGS | | FISH | | | | SHELLFISH | | | | EEL | | | | ROE | | | |
| Aw | STUFFING | CEREAL | PANCAKES | DOUGHNUTS | BREAD | TOAST | BISCUIT | ROLLS | PASTA | DUMPLINGS | PASTRY | RICE | WHEAT | RYE | CORN | OATS | BARLEY | MILLET | | POTATO |
| wAw | VEGETABLES | CABBAGE | CELERY | LETTUCE | CARROT | BEET | | PEANUTS | AVOCADO | BOK CHOY | SOYBEANS | YAMS | ONION | GARLIC | LEEK | PEPPERS | SQUASHES | CUCUMBERS | RADISHES | SPINACH |
| ă | FRUIT | DATES | FIGS | COCONUTS | ORANGES | LEMONS | TOMATO | BANANAS | APPLES | PEARS | PEACHES | APRICOTS | MELONS | BERRIES | GRAPES | CHERRIES | NUTS | OLIVES | PIMENTO | POMEGRAN-ATE |
| wă | SUGAR | CANDY | JELLY | PUDDING | ICE CREAM | SHERBET | CAKE | COOKIES | CHOCOLATE | | | | BUTTER | OLEO | CHEESE | GHEE | YOGURT | SOUR CREAM | TOFU | LARD |
| Ow | WATER | | JUICE | | MILK | | | | COFFEE | | TEA | | BEVERAGES | | | | WINE | BEER | LIQUOR | |
| wOw | | | | | | | | | | | | | | | | | | | | |
| Oh | DIGESTIBILITY | | NUTRIENT | | VITAMIN | | | | CARBO-HYDRATE | STARCH | PROTEIN | FATS | ENZYME | | | | METABOLISM | | | |
| wOe | | | | | | | | | | | | | | | | | | | | |

| | K | sK | King | sKing | T | sT | Ting | sTing | P | sP | Ping | sPing | M | sM | Ming | sMing | L | sL | Ling | sLing |
|---|---|---|---|---|---|---|---|---|---|---|---|---|---|---|---|---|---|---|---|---|
| Ay | CLEAN DIRTY | SANITATION | HYGIENE | STERILIZATION | PROPHYLACTIC | ASEPTIC | PASTEURIZATION | | FUMIGATION | DELOUSING | WASHING | LAUNDERING | SCRUB | BATH | SHOWER | | BATHTUB | SINK | CLEANSER | SOAP |
| wAy | DETERGENT | SHAMPOO | MOUTHWASH | TOOTHPASTE | PURGE | DIURETIC | SWAB | MOP | SCOUR | COMB | WHOLESOMENESS | BENEFICIAL | HEALTH | IMMUNITY | RESISTANCE | ANTIGEN | WELL | HEARTY | | |
| Ah | SQUALOR | | POLLUTION | | SLIME | | TOXICITY | | NOXIOUS | | MALIGNANT | | | | | | | | | |
| wAh | | | | | | | | | | | | | | | | | | | | |
| Ee | DISEASE | | | | | | DISABILITY | | | SYMPTOMS | PATHOLOGY | SYNDROME | INFECTION | CONTAGION | VIRUS | | EPIDEMIC | PLAGUE | PESTILENCE | |
| wEe | SEIZURE | | STROKE | | CONVULSION | EPILEPSY | FEVER | PROSTRATION | INFLAMMATION | | ARTHRITIS | GOUT | RHEUMATISM | | COLITIS | HEPATITIS | LARYNGITIS | CHOLERA | CHICKEN POX | SMALL POX |
| Eh | LEPROSY | INFLUENZA | MALARIA | ASTHMA | MONONUCLEOSIS | MEASLES | TONSILLITIS | RABIES | TETANUS | CONJUNCTIVITIS | ANEMIA | COMMON COLD | PNEUMONIA | EMPHYSEMA | TUBERCULOSIS | VENEREAL DISEASE | SYPHILIS | GONORRHEA | ANGINA | HEART ATTACK |
| wEh | JAUNDICE | CIRRHOSIS | | HEADACHE | | SHOCK | | ULCER | INDIGESTION | CONSTIPATION | DIARRHEA | NAUSEA | ALLERGY | ECZEMA | ACNE | RASH | | | | |
| I | LESION | TUMOR | CANCER | | | GANGPENE | | PATHOGEN | MICROBE | BACTERIA | | | INVALID | PATIENT | | CRIPPLE | | | AFFLICT | |
| wYe | | | | | | | | | | | | | | | | | | | | |
| Ih | | CURE | MEDICINE | DRUG | DOSE | POTION | PILL | | CAPSULE | TONIC | STIMULANT | BALM | LOTION | SALVE | OINTMENT | UNGUENT | LINIMENT | | MEDICATE | |
| wIh | SEDATIVE | TRANQUILIZER | ANALGESIC | SLEEPING PILL | NARCOTIC | OPIATE | HALLUCINOGEN | ANESTHETIC | LAXATIVE | | DISINFECTANT | CONTRACEPTIVE | ANTACID | ANTIDOTE | ANTITOXIN | ANTIBODY | VACCINE | WOUND DRESSING | | |
| Aw | SURGERY | DENTISTRY | THERAPY | | MIDWIFE | OSTEOPATH | CHIROPRACTOR | DOCTOR | PHYSICIAN | INTERN | | VETERINARY | NURSE | HOSPITAL | AMBULANCE | | RADIOLOGY | X-RAY | | |
| wAw | DIAGNOSIS | | TRANSFUSION | OPERATION | | | AMPUTATION | TRANSPLANT | CLINIC | | PHARMACY | NURSING HOME | | WARD | SPA | | MEDICAL | | | |
| ă | | | | | | | | | | | | | | | | | | | | |
| wă | PSYCHOLOGY | PSYCHOTHERAPY | PSYCHIATRY | PSYCHOSOMATIC | PSYCHOANALYSIS | INTROVERT | EXTROVERT | NEUROTIC | PSYCHOPATH | PSYCHOTIC | NEUROSIS | | INHIBITION | | PSYCHE | | | EGO | | |
| Ow | CYST | | | RIND | PELT | | | | BARK | HYMEN | MANE | BRAID | PIGTAIL | WHISKERS | WIG | HAIRSTYLE | HAIRCUT | | FLUFF | HAIRY |
| wOw | EVACUATION | | VOMITING | | RETCHING | HICCUP | FLATULENCE | | DEFECATION | | DYSENTERY | | | DUNG | FESTERING | MENSTRUATION | SPIT | | DROOL | |
| Oh | | | | | | | | | | | | | | | | | | | | |
| wOe | INNARDS | GUTS | | | BOWEL | SPHINCTER | BUTTOCKS | PHYSIQUE | GASP | SNIFF | SMELL | COUGH | BREATH | SPASM | INHALATION | EXHALATION | PUFF | SNEEZE | RESUSCITATION | |

| | K | sK | King | sKing | T | sT | Ting | sTing | P | sP | Ping | sPing | M | sM | Ming | sMing | L | sL | Ling | sLing |
|---|---|---|---|---|---|---|---|---|---|---|---|---|---|---|---|---|---|---|---|---|
| Ay | BODY | TORSO | BACK | CHEST | ABDOMEN | SKELETON | MUSCULATURE | CIRCULATORY SYSTEM | NERVOUS SYSTEM | LYMPH SYSTEM | SKIN | HEAD | FACE | NECK | WAIST | HIPS | RUMP | ARMS | LEGS | LAP |
| wAy | SKULL | MANDIBLE | SPINE | VERTEBRA | RIB | STERNUM | CLAVICLE | SCAPULA | HUMERUS | ULNA | RADIUS | WRIST BONES | HAND BONES | PELVIS | FEMUR | KNEE CAP | TIBIA | FIBULA | ANKLE BONES | FOOT BONES |
| Ah | SHOULDER | ARM PIT | UPPER ARM | BICEPS | ELBOW | CRAZY BONE | FORE ARM | WRIST | HAND | FIST | PALM | HEEL OF THE HAND | KNUCKLE | FINGER | THUMB | INDEX FINGER | MIDDLE FINGER | FOREFINGER | LITTLE FINGER | FINGER NAIL |
| wAh | | CROTCH | THIGH | KNEE | LOWER LEG | CALF | SHIN | ANKLE | FOOT | HEEL | BALL | ARCH | ACHILLES TENDON | SOLE | | | TOE | BIG TOE | LITTLE TOE | |
| Ee | PATE | BROW | HAIR | HAIR LINE | TEMPLE | EYE BROW | EYE | NOSE | EAR | CHEEK | MOUTH | LIP | MUSTACHE | CHIN | | | | | BEARD | |
| wEe | EYE LID | EYE LASH | TEAR DUCT | | EYEBALL | PUPIL | IRIS | LENS | CORNEA | | UVEA | | RETINA | | | | OPTIC NERVE | | | |
| Eh | EAR LOBE | OUTER EAR | MIDDLE EAR | INNER EAR | EAR DRUM | HAMMER | ANVIL | | OSSICLES | LABYRINTH | COCHLEA | AUDITORY NERVE | EUSTACHIAN TUBE | EAR WAX | NOSTRIL | OLFACTORY BULB | CILIA | SINUS | | |
| wEh | TONGUE | GUMS | HARD PALATE | SOFT PALATE | TOOTH | INCISOR | CANINE | BICUSPID | MOLAR | TASTE BUD | SALIVARY GLAND | THROAT | TONSIL | PHARYNX | LARYNX | ESOPHAGUS | EPIGLOTTIS | TRACHEA | VOCAL CHORD | THYROID GLAND |
| I | THORAX | LUNG | BRONCHI | DIAPHRAGM | HEART | VENTRICLE | VALVE | AORTA | VENA CAVA | ARTERY | VEIN | CAPILLARY | BLOOD | LYMPH | | | PLATELET | PLASMA | BREAST | NIPPLE |
| wYe | ALIMENTARY CANAL | CARDIA | DUODENUM | STOMACH | SMALL INTESTINE | LARGE INTESTINE | COLON | APPENDIX | RECTUM | ANUS | KIDNEY | BLADDER | URETHRA | LIVER | GALL BLADDER | PANCREAS | SPLEEN | VISCERA | NAVEL | |
| Ih | BRAIN | FRONTAL LOBE | TEMPORAL LOBE | CEREBELLUM | BRAIN STEM | PITUITARY | HYPOTHAL-AMUS | CORTEX | MEDULLA OBLONGATA | SPINAL CHORD | AUTONOMOUS NERVOUS SYSTEM | NERVE | NEURON | SYNAPSE | | | | | | |
| wIh | EPIDERMIS | DERMIS | SUBCUTANE-OUS TISSUE | PORE | SWEAT GLAND | FOLLICLE | FRECKLE | BIRTH MARK | MOLE | WART | BLISTER | CALLUS | PIMPLE | BLACKHEAD | BURN | BOIL | SCAR | TATTOO | WOUND | SCAB |
| Aw | PENIS | GLANS | FORESKIN | TESTICLE | SCROTUM | SEMINAL VESICLE | PROSTATE | VAS DEFERENS | ERECTION | EJACULATION | SEMEN | | | | | | | | PUBIC HAIR | INTERCOURSE |
| wAw | MOUND OF VENUS | ORGASM | LABIA | CLITORIS | VULVA | VAGINA | CERVIX | UTERUS | FALLOPIAN TUBE | OVARY | OVUM | | UMBILICAL CORD | PLACENTA | EMBRYO | FETUS | MITOSIS | MEIOSIS | MISCARRIAGE | ABORTION |
| ă | SECRETION | EXCRETION | HORMONE | ENDOCRINE | | BILE | SALIVA | MUCOUS | URINE | FECES | | | SWEAT | | TEAR | | SPUTUM | | PHLEGM | |
| wă | MARROW | | BONES | | CARTILAGE | LIGAMENT | TENDON | MUSCLE | FAT | FLESH | TISSUE | NAILS | RIGHT | LEFT | RIGHT HANDED | LEFT HANDED | PHYSICAL | | | |
| Ow | | CRAW | GULLET | TUSK | SNOUT | MUZZLE | ANTLER | HORN | TRUNK | TAIL | WING | FIN | FLUKE | FLIPPER | TALON | PAW | CLAW | PAD | HOOF | |
| wOw | HIDE | FUR | FLEECE | FEATHER | QUILL | DOWN | FUZZ | PLUME | SCALE | UDDER | POUCH | GILL | BLOW HOLE | CARCASS | | | | | | |
| Oh | | | | | | | | | | | | | | | | | | | | |
| wOe | | | | | | | | | | | | | | | | | | | | |

| | K | sK | King | sKing | T | sT | Ting | sTing | P | sP | Ping | sPing | M | sM | Ming | sMing | L | sL | Ling | sLing |
|---|---|---|---|---|---|---|---|---|---|---|---|---|---|---|---|---|---|---|---|---|
| Ay | SENSATION | | | | SENSE | | SENSIBILITY | | SENSITIVITY INSENSITIVITY | | | | SUSCEPTIBLE | | | | RECEPTIVE | | | |
| wAy | AWARE | | CONSCIOUS UNCONSCIOUS | | NUMB | | FAINT | | STUPOR | | STUNNED | | PAIN | | | | DISTRESS | | | |
| Ah | HURT | | PANG | | TWINGE | | | | STING | | | | ACHE | | | | | | | |
| wAh | AGONY | | ANGUISH | | TORMENT | | TORTURE | | INFLAMED | | TENDER | | SORE | | RAW | | THROBBING | | | |
| Ee | RUB | TOUCH | | | | | CARESS | | MANIPULATE | | STROKE | | PET | | | | LICK | | | |
| wEe | TACTILE | | | | BRUSH | | MASSAGE | | TINGLE | | PRICKLE | | | | | | ITCH | | | |
| Eh | GOOSEFLESH | | | | | | | | SEX | | | | SEXUALITY | | | | | | | |
| wEh | SEXUAL PREFERENCE | HETERO-SEXUALITY | BISEXUALITY | | HOMO-SEXUALITY | LESBIANISM | | | SADISM | | MASOCHISM | | INCEST | | SODOMY | | MASTURBATE | | APHRODISIAC | |
| I | TASTE | | | | SAVOR UNSAVORINESS | | | | FLAVOR | | | | TANG | | ZEST | | GUSTO | | | |
| wYe | SEASONING | | | | CONDIMENT | SPICE | SALT | | | | | | | | | | PEPPER | | | |
| Ih | SWEET SOUR | | | | | | | | HONEY | | | | NECTAR | | | | CLOYING | | | |
| wIh | | | | | INEDIBLE | | TASTELESS | | | | | | | | | | | | | |
| Aw | BITTER | | | | | | | | TARTNESS | | | | | | | | DRYNESS | | | |
| wAw | VINEGAR | | | | PICKLE | | | | PUNGENCY | | | | PIQUANCY | | | | SALTINESS | | | |
| ă | | | | | | | | | RANK | | | | GAMEY | | | | ACRID | | | |
| wă | | | | | | | | | | | | | | | | | | | | |
| Ow | TOBACCO | | | | CIGAR | | CIGARETTE | | PIPE | | CHEWING TOBACCO | | SNUFF | | NICOTINE | | SMOKING | | | |
| wOw | STINK | | | | FETIDNESS | | MUSTINESS | | ODOROUS ODORLESS | | | | | | SCENT | | SNIFF | | | |
| Oh | FRAGRANCE | | | | PERFUME | | AROMA | | BOUQUET | | INCENSE | | | | | | SACHET | | | |
| wOe | | | | | | | | | | | | | | | | | | | | |

| | K | sK | King | sKing | T | sT | Ting | sTing | P | sP | Ping | sPing | M | sM | Ming | sMing | L | sL | Ling | sLing |
|---|---|---|---|---|---|---|---|---|---|---|---|---|---|---|---|---|---|---|---|---|
| Ay | VISION | SIGHT | | | EYESIGHT | | | | | | | | WATCHING | | VIEWING | | | | | |
| wAy | NOTICE | | | | GLANCE | | GAZE | | STARE | | WINK | | BEHOLD | | WITNESS | | | | | |
| Ah | GLARE | | | | DEFECTIVE VISION | | ASTIGMATISM | | NEARSIGHTED | | FARSIGHTED | | SQUINT | | CROSS-EYED | | TUNNEL VISION | | | |
| wAh | BLINDNESS | | BLIND SPOT | | DAY BLINDNESS | | NIGHT BLINDNESS | COLOR BLINDNESS | BRAILLE | | | | BLINDFOLDED | | | | | | | |
| Ee | SPECTATOR | | | | SIGHT-SEEING | | | | OPTICAL INSTRUMENTS | | | | SPECTACLES | | | | CONTACT LENSES | | | |
| wEe | FIELD GLASSES | | OPERA GLASSES | | BINOCULARS | | MIRROR | | OPTICS | | OPTOMETRY | | OCULIST | | OPHTHALMOL-OGIST | | MICROSCOPE | | SPECTRO-SCOPES | |
| Eh | VISIBILITY INVISIBILITY | | | | DISTINCT INDISTINCT | | | | CONSPICUOUS INCONSPIC-UOUS | | | | APPARENT HIDDEN | | | | | | | |
| wEh | | | | | BLURRED | | | | | | | | | | | | PHANTOM | | | |
| I | HEARING | | | | AUDIENCE | | INTERVIEW | | CONFERENCE | | | | EAVESDROP | | EARSHOT | | | | | |
| wYe | SOUND | | | | HEARING AID | | | | MEGAPHONE | | | | OTOLOGY | | | | DEAFNESS | | | |
| Ih | SOUND | | | | ACOUSTICS | | | | SONICS | | | | DECIBEL | | | | | | | |
| wIh | HEADSET | | | | PHONOGRAPH | | | | PUBLIC ADDRESS SYSTEM | | BULL HORN | | | | TAPE REC | | DIGITAL RECORDING | | | |
| Aw | QUIET | | MUTE | | DUMB | | MUFFLE | | GAG | | SOUND-PROOFING | | INAUDIBLE | | TACIT | | IMPLICIT | | | |
| wAw | THUD | | | | PATTER | | | | WHISPER | | MURMUR | | UNDERTONE | | HUMMING | | RUSTLE | | | |
| ă | SIGH | | | | MUTTER | | | | MOAN | | | | WHINE | | | | | | | |
| wă | LOUD | | NOISE | | BLAST | | RACKET | | | | NOISEMAKER | | RESONANCE | | SONORITY | | RUMBLE | | ECHO | |
| Ow | RING | | | | TINKLE | | REPEATED SOUNDS | | STACCATO | | | | BEAT | | CLICKING | | TICKING | | RATTLE | |
| wOw | DETONATION | BOOM | | | POP | | BURST | | HISSING | | SHRILLNESS | | HOARSENESS | | | | SCREAM | SQUEAL | SQUAWK | |
| Oh | CALLING | | | | CRYING | | | | YELLING | | | | CHEERING | | | | SHOUTING | | | |
| wOe | ANIMAL SOUNDS | | | | | | | | | | | | | | | | | | | |

| | K | sK | King | sKing | T | sT | Ting | sTing | P | sP | Ping | sPing | M | sM | Ming | sMing | L | sL | Ling | sLing |
|---|---|---|---|---|---|---|---|---|---|---|---|---|---|---|---|---|---|---|---|---|
| Ay | CLOTHING | POCKET | | | SEWING | NEEDLE | | SEWING MACHINE | STITCH | SEAM | BASTE | | BUTTONHOLE | COLLAR | LAPEL | PLEAT | CROCHET | EMBROIDER | HEMSTITCH | NEEDLEPOINT |
| wAy | DRESS | FROCK | COSTUME | WARDROBE | SUIT | UNIFORM | MUFTI | | CLOAK | | COAT | | JACKET | | | | OVERCOAT | | TOPCOAT | |
| Ah | WAISTCOAT | VEST | SHIRT | SKIRT | APRON | BELT | TROUSERS | DIAPER | NEGLIGEE | NIGHTWEAR | UNDERWEAR | LINGERIE | CORSET | GIRDLE | BRASSIERE | LOINCLOTH | MILLINERY | CAP | HAT | |
| wAh | KERCHIEF | VEIL | FOOTWEAR | SHOES | BOOTS | SANDALS | SOCKS | STOCKING | BATHING SUIT | CHILDREN'S WEAR | TAILORING | SWEATERS | PANTS | BATHROBE | KIMONO | GLOVES | LEGGINGS | | | |
| Ee | | | | | | | | | THREAD | | | | STRAND | | | | CORD | | STRING | |
| wEe | TWINE | | KNOT | | ROPE | HAWSER | CABLE | | RIBBON | | | | TAPE | | | | | | | |
| Eh | | | COTTON | CANVAS | SILK | | WOOL | LINEN | RAYON | NYLON | DACRON | POLYESTER | LEATHER | | FELT | | YARN | | | |
| wEh | | | UNDRESS | | MOLT | SHEDDING | BALDNESS | | PEEL | STRIP | HUSK | FLAKE | NUDITY | | | | BAREFOOT | | | |
| I | | | | | HOUSE | | HOME | HOUSEHOLD | HEARTH | | BUILDING | | | | | | | | HOMESTEAD | |
| wYe | MANSION | VILLA | CHATEAU | PALACE | BUNGALOW | | CABIN | | SHACK | | SHED | | TENT | | | | APARTMENT | | | |
| Ih | INN | HOTEL | MOTEL | | DORMITORY | | | | MOBILE HOME | | MOTOR HOME | | | | | | GREENHOUSE | | BARN | STABLE |
| wIh | DOGHOUSE | | | | COOP | AVIARY | NEST | | | | DEN | | RESORT | | CAVE | | CAMP | | BARRACKS | HOUSE BOAT |
| Aw | ROOM | | | | | | CELL | | | | HALLWAY | | LIVING ROOM | | | | BEDROOM | | | |
| wAw | DINING ROOM | | | | | | | | PLAYROOM | | | NATATORIUM | KITCHEN | | PANTRY | | | | | |
| ă | STOREROOM | | CLOSET | | ATTIC | | BASEMENT | | CORRIDOR | | VESTIBULE | | THRESHOLD | | | | PORCH | | BALCONY | |
| wă | FLOOR | | CEILING | | WALL | | | | DOOR | | WINDOW | TRANSOM | BATHROOM | | | | GARAGE | | CARPORT | |
| Ow | FURNITURE | CHEST | DRAWER | SEAT | TABLE | | CHAIR | | COUNTER | | SHELF | | REFRIGERATOR | | | | FREEZER | | | |
| wOw | COUCH | BED | BUNK | | | | | | | | | | | | | | | | | |
| Oh | | | | | BEDDING | BLANKET | BEDSPREAD | QUILT | MATTRESS | | PILLOWS | | SHEET | | PILLOWCASE | | | | | |
| wOe | RUG | CARPET | MAT | UPHOLSTERY | CUSHIONS | ARMCHAIR | SOFAS | DAYBED | BASSINET | CRIB | COT | CRADLE | HAMMOCK | PALLET | WATER BED | | | | | |

| | K | sK | King | sKing | T | sT | Ting | sTing | P | sP | Ping | sPing | M | sM | Ming | sMing | L | sL | Ling | sLing |
|---|---|---|---|---|---|---|---|---|---|---|---|---|---|---|---|---|---|---|---|---|
| Ay | DOER, ONE WHO DOES THE ACTION | | RECIPIENT, OBJECT OF THE ACTION | | INITIATOR OF | | CREATOR OF SOMETHING DESTROYER OF | | DEVICE FOR | MAKER OF THE DEVICE THAT DOES THE ACTION | CARETAKER OF THE DEVICE | OPERATOR OF A DEVICE THAT DOES THE ACTION | PRACTITIONER OF | ARTIST IN | ARTISAN IN OR OF, -SMITH | ARTISTE, PROFESSIONAL PERFORMER | MANAGER, EXECUTIVE | ONE CONNECTED WITH OR BELONGING TO | INTERN, APPRENTICE | AMATEUR, DILETTANTE |
| wAy | STUDY OF SOMETHING | FACTS REGARDING SOMETHING | PURPOSE, USE, APPLICATION | USER OF, CONSUMER | MAKER OF | INDUSTRY, TRADE IN SOMETHING | VENDOR OF | FANCIER, LOVER OF FEAR, DREAD OF | PLACE WHERE THE ACTION OCCURS | PLACE WHERE SOMETHING IS MADE | PLACE WHERE SOMETHING IS STORED | PLACE WHERE SOMETHING IS USED | TEACHER OF | STUDENT OF | PROMOTER OF | POSSESSOR OF | PLAYER, PARTICIPANT | | ENTHUSIAST, FAN OF | |
| Ah | | | | | | | | | | | | | | | | | | | | |
| wAh | | | | | | | | | | | | | | | | | | | | |
| Ee | | | | | | | | | | | | | | | | | | | | |
| wEe | | | | | | | | | | | | | | | | | | | | |
| Eh | | | | | | | | | | | | | | | | | | | | |
| wEh | | | | | | | | | | | | | | | | | | | | |
| I | HEAVY LIGHT | DENSE THIN | RICH IN POOR IN | OPEN CLOSED | ORIGINAL COPY OF | GENUINE FAKE | SUBTLE OBVIOUS | OVERT SECRET | TRUE FALSE | ACTUAL VIRTUAL | REAL UNREAL | NATURAL ARTIFICIAL | TORRID FRIGID | HOT COLD | WARM COOL | | LIQUID | VISCOUS THIN | MOLTEN SOLID | VAPOROUS, EPHEMERAL |
| wYe | LOGICAL ILLOGICAL | ORDERLY CHAOTIC | | STATIONARY, FIXED PORTABLE | RICH POOR | LIGHT DARK | BRIGHT DIM | INTENSE MILD | | | | | | | | | | | | |
| Ih | | | | | | | | | | | | | | | | | | | | |
| wIh | | | | | | | | | | | | | | | | | | | | |
| Aw | | | RE-; SEE AGAIN | | EX-, FORMER | | DE-, OUT OF | | VICE-, SUBSTITUTE | | -IC,-AL, PERTAINING TO | | -ISH, LIKE | | -ERN,-ESE, OF OR RELATING | | -ED, OF THAT NATURE | | -LY, SIMILAR IN MANNER | |
| wAw | -FUL, TENDING, ABLE TO | | -TUDE; STATE, QUALITY | | -ANT, -ENT, AGENCY | | -PAROUS, BEARING | | -MONY, RESULT | | -FY, -IFY, TO MAKE, FORM INTO | | -FACIENT, MAKING, CAUSING | | -ADE, DENOTES ACTION | | -ESCENT, BEGINNING TO BE | | -ICE, STATE, CHARACTERISTIC | |
| ă | -AR, -ARY, IN THE NATURE OF | | -NESS; QUALITY | | -HOOD, STATE, CONDITION | | -ESQUE, STYLE | | -ATE, RESULT OF ACTION | | -ANCE, -ENCE | | -ITY, CONDITION | | -OSITY, EXCESSIVE CONDITION | | -EN, APPEARANCE, MADE OF | | -ORY, HAVING THE EFFECT OF | |
| wă | -WORTHY | | -ABLE, CAPABLE OF | | UNI-, MONO-, SINGLE | | BI-, DUAL | | TRI-, TRIPLE | | MULTI-, MANY | | AMBI-, BOTH | | -ILITY | | | | | |
| Ow | FUNCTION | | MENTOR | PROTEGE | RELATIVE TO | | -CRACY | -CRAT PEACE | WAR | PATRIOTIC | | | SPEAKER, AUDITOR, READER | | | | | | | |
| wOw | | | | | | | | | | | | | | | | | | | | |
| Oh | | | | | | | | | | | | | | | | | | | | |
| wOe | | | | | | | | | | | | | | | | | | | | |

| | Ay | wAy | Ah | wAh | Ee | wEe | Eh | wEh | I | wYe | Ih | wIh | Aw | wAw | ă | wă | Ow | wOw | Oh | wOe |
|---|---|---|---|---|---|---|---|---|---|---|---|---|---|---|---|---|---|---|---|---|
| Ay | AMOUNT | ABOUNDING<br>RARE | SUFFICIENT<br>LACKING | MUCH<br>LITTLE | SUPERFLUOUS,<br>BEYOND<br>NEED<br>DEVOID OF | MORE<br>LESS | MOST<br>LEAST | SEMI, HEMI,<br>DEMI | USUAL<br>UNUSUAL | LIMITED<br>INFINITE | EXCEEDING<br>SHORT OF | EXACTLY<br>APPROXIM-<br>ATELY | MAXIMUM<br>MINIMUM | HYPER<br>HYPO | | SUPERIOR<br>INFERIOR | SURPASSING,<br>OUT-<br>FALLING<br>SHORT | SUCCEEDING<br>FAILING | VARIETY,<br>MISC-<br>UNIFORMITY | THROUGHOUT |
| wAy | ABOUT<br>ALMOST | MACRO<br>MICRO | ULTRA<br>INFRA | | SORTED<br>MIXED | HOMOGEN-<br>EOUS<br>HETEROGEN-<br>EOUS | EQUAL<br>UNEQUAL | | COMPLETELY<br>PARTIALLY | | BOTH<br>EXCLUDING | INCLUDING | CAPACITY | VOLUME | FULL, -OUS<br>EMPTY | | DEGREE | SCALE | | |
| Ah | STILL | THOUGH | MATCH | GRAND | VERY | GLORY | HEROIC<br>CRAVEN | REMARKABLE | NICE<br>AWFUL | EXTREME | MAJOR<br>MINOR | | BETTER<br>WORSE | BEST<br>WORST | INCREASE<br>DECREASE | EXPAND<br>CONTRACT | GROW<br>DIMINISH | | INTENSIFY<br>WEAKEN | |
| wAh | SIMPLE<br>COMPLEX | PURE<br>IMPURE | EASY<br>DIFFICULT | PLAIN<br>ORNATE | UNITE | SPLINTER | CONNECT<br>DISCONNECT | REPETITION | FREE<br>FIXED | | TIGHT<br>LOOSE | | INTACT<br>BROKEN | CUT | SEPARATE | | BIT | IN<br>OUT | QUITE | |
| Ee | FACTOR | ELEMENT | DETAIL | WHOLE<br>PART | | HARMONY<br>DISCORD | | FORM | | ARRANGE-<br>MENT<br>DISARRANGE-<br>MENT | SORT<br>SHUFFLE | GRADE | FIRST<br>LAST | FINISHED<br>UNFINISHED | CONTINUITY<br>DISCONTIN-<br>UITY | CHANGE | | | | |
| wEe | CONTAIN | COMMON<br>UNCOMMON | GENERAL<br>SPECIFIC | SPECIAL | QUALITY | EXPERT | | LIST | UNIT | INDIVIDUAL | ONLY | GUIDE | PAIR | COPY | HALF | SPLIT | | MEETING | GROUP | BAND |
| Eh | LENGTH | | | | WIDTH | SIDEWAYS | | AREA | HEIGHT<br>DEPTH | | THICK<br>THIN | | | | CUBIC | | | | | |
| wEh | DIAMETER | | RADIANS | | | PERIMETER | | ARC | | DEGREE | MINUTE | SECOND | DISTANCE | | | | AU, ASTRO-<br>NOMICAL<br>UNIT | LY,<br>LIGHTYEAR | MLY, MILLION<br>LIGHTYEARS | BLY, BILLION<br>LIGHTYEARS |
| I | NEAR<br>FAR | | | | ABUTTING<br>APART | | CONTIGUOUS<br>NONCONTIG-<br>UOUS | | DIRECTION | | | | TOWARD<br>AWAY FROM | | | | FORWARD<br>BACKWARD | | | |
| wYe | GO OVER<br>GO UNDER | | GO THROUGH<br>GO AROUND | | | | | | | | -WAYS | -WISE | INTO<br>OUT OF | | UPWARD<br>DOWNWARD | | ROTATION | | SPIN | |
| Ih | PARALLEL TO<br>DIVERGING<br>FROM | | ACROSS | CROSSING | LEAVING<br>RETURNING | | APPROACHING<br>RECEDING | | LEADING<br>FOLLOWING | | | | INWARD<br>OUTWARD | | | | | | | |
| wIh | RISING<br>FALLING | | | | CLOCKWISE<br>COUNTER-<br>CLOCKWISE | | DIAGONALLY | ATHWART | | | | | THIS SIDE OF<br>THAT SIDE<br>OF | | AHEAD<br>BEHIND | | ATOP<br>BENEATH | OVER<br>UNDER | UP<br>DOWN | |
| Aw | INSIDE OF<br>OUTSIDE OF | | HERE<br>THERE | IN SITU | ON<br>OFF | | ENCLOSE | | SOURCE,<br>-HEAD<br>TERMINUS | | FOREMOST<br>HINDMOST | | FRONT<br>BACK | | TOP<br>BOTTOM | | SIDE | CORNER | EDGE | |
| wAw | | | INTERIOR<br>EXTERIOR | | | | ABOVE<br>BELOW | | HIGH<br>LOW | | INNER<br>OUTER | | BETWEEN | AMONG | ALONGSIDE | | MIDDLE,<br>CENTERED<br>SURROUNDING | | AROUND,<br>PERIPHERAL | |
| ă | LARGE<br>SMALL | | STRAIGHT<br>BOWED | | | RECTANGLE | SQUARE | | | | | | | | | | | | | |
| wă | | | | MULTI-<br>FACETED | PYRAMID | | CUBE | | | | OVATE, SOLID | | CRUCIFORM | | CRESCENT | | STELLATE | | -FORM | PLANE |
| Ow | | | | | | | | | | | | | | | | | | | | |
| wOw | | | | | | | | | | | | | | | | | | | | |
| Oh | | | | | | | | | | | | | | | | | | | | |
| wOe | | | | | | | | | | | | | | | | | | | | |

VN.1 ⊧ᒧΓ2ₓ is intended to be a polite language so it is appropriate that its first words be please, excuse (or pardon) me, thanks, and welcome. These four words and the pronouns appear in both one and three letter forms. During the development of ⊧ᒧΓ2ₓ all 40 of the letters were used as single letter words and also a long list of affixes was generated in two letter format. In the end however, it was thought best that all of the words of the general vocabulary be standardized at triads (POTENTS and punctuation are not counted as letters), because if one could be sure that the core words always had three letters, it would reduce the need to use linkages in many compound words of six or even nine letters. The twelve monads we retained pose no problems because they are not compounded with other cores and are often inflected by punctuation and POTENTS.

VN.2 There need be no objective case since sentence format takes care of the direction of the action, but there is the possibility of using a punctuational grapheme with the single letter forms to indicate the objective case. In the first person three letter form the objective could be Γ˥⊧ for instance.

VN.3 The gender POTENTS may be appended to the above if for some reason the writer wants his speaker to add gender emphasis as in "I, a woman,...", but for the most part there is little need for this in the first or second person. In the third person however modern American practice often requires non-differentiation by gender so the absence of these POTENTS gives us an undifferentiated or 'neutral' pronoun while their presence gives positive gender designation when needed.

The triad forms are inflected by punctuation in the same way as the monad forms.

VN.4 As a universal second language ⊧ᒧΓ2ₓ is not apt to develop much in these categories (Forms of Address and Amenities) aside from what is needed for telephone or radio communication. Local situations and customs dictate current usage and most of that will be in the local idiom. What does enter into ⊧ᒧΓ2ₓ may be different from place to place, but so long as they are confined to words beginning with Γ, Γ, Γ or Γ they will always be recognized as considerate expressions of goodwill. The same considerations apply to forms of address.

These categories are left open to be filled in as the need develops.

VN.5 American usage requires a gender neutral form. The use of the gender POTENTS E and E takes care of this awkward problem very well. Thus if Γ˥Γ is the undifferentiated term for Mr. or Ms., EΓ˥Γ is Mr. and EΓ˥Γ is Ms. In situations where marital status is a factor Γ˥Γ is the root word. Many forms are possible, delineating age and/or status. These forms may develop differently in different communities, but an initial Γ followed by a letter of the ˥ or ⊣ families assures universal recognition of the intent even when the exact definition is not known. One can always safely assume that the intention is flattering and respectful. Please note that only these two very limited categories have this degree of freedom since universality requires that all definitions be well established and recorded.

## VOCABULARY

### 1A

See note VN.1

__ please

__ please

__ excuse me

__ excuse me

__ thanks

__ thanks

__ welcome

__ welcome

### PRONOUNS

### FIRST PERSON

__ 1st person

__ I, me

__ me, I

See note VN.2

__ we, us

__ us, we

__ my, mine

__ mine, my

__ myself

__ our

__ ourselves

__ mine

__ ours

See note VN.3

### SECOND PERSON

__ 2nd person

__ you

youse? (slang) English has no distinctive plural form for

__ you

__ your

__ yourself

__ yours

__ yourselves

__ your own

__ your (pl.) own

### THIRD PERSON
definite forms

__ 3rd person (definite forms)

__ he, she, one (undifferentiated)

__ one

__ person

__ he, him

__ him, he

__ she, her

__ her, she

__ they, them

__ them, they

__ one's

__ his

__ her

__ oneself

__ himself

__ herself

__ their

__ themselves

__ one's own

__ their own

### THIRD PERSON
indefinite forms

__ 3rd person indefinite

__ one (a person)

__ man

__ woman

__ people

__ men

__ women

__ one's

__ man's

__ woman's

__ oneself (ego?)

__ male ego

__ female ego

__ peoples'

__ men's

__ women's

__ themselves

__ one's own

__ their own

__ it (animal)

__ it (animal)

__ male animal, e.g. cock.

__ female animal, e.g. hen.

__ they or them, animals

__ males, rams, etc.

__ females, ewes, etc.

__ its, animal

__ his, animal

__ her, animal

__ itself, animal

__ himself, animal

__ herself, animal

__ their, animal

__ animals', bulls', etc.

__ animals', cows', etc.

__ themselves, animal

__ one's own, animal

__ their own, animal

__ it (inanimate tangible)

__ thing

__ it (inanimate tangible)

__ thing

__ things

__ thing's

__ itself

__ things'

__ it, thing (intangible)

__ it (intangible)

__ thing

See note VN.5

__ FORMS OF ADDRESS 1

__ FORMS OF ADDRESS 2

__ FORMS OF ADDRESS 3

### AMENITIES 1

__ hello

__ good bye, adios

__ bon chance

__ all the best to you

__ neichevo

__ eh?

__ OK

__ go, recorder is on

__ here goes

__ hello, are you there?

__ signing off, thank you

__ over to you

__ over and out

__ AMENITIES 2

Include expressions, interjections, inanities etc. such as oh? well! zatso? yuhno, doansay, gosh, go to.

__ AMENITIES 3

__ AMENITIES 4

See note VN.4

### AGE and STATUS

__ prenatal

__ newborn

__ baby, infant

__ child

__ boy

__ girl

__ teens

__ lad

__ lass

__ minor

__ adult

__ mid-life; prime

__ mature

__ elder

__ retired

__ preschooler

__ grade-schooler

__ intermediate
__ high-schooler
__ collegian
__ graduate schooler
__ post-graduate

__ cultivated
__ crude
__ patrician
__ plebeian
__ kind
__ mean
__ saintly
__ evil
__ tame
__ wild

__ VOCATION

__ AVOCATION

## PERSONAL RELATIONSHIPS

__ spouse
__ husband
__ wife
__ parent
__ father
__ mother
__ offspring
__ son
__ daughter
__ sibling
__ brother
__ sister
__ uncle, aunt
__ uncle
__ aunt
__ nephew/niece
__ nephew
__ niece
__ cousins
__ cousin
__ cousine

__ cuz m/f
__ grand-, great- for uncles
__ greatgrand-
__ relative by blood
__ relative by marriage
__ surviving spouse
__ widow
__ widower
__ single parent m/f
__ orphan m/f
__ divorced m/f
__ separated, m/f
__ courtesy, honor m/f
__ common law m/f

__ acquaintance
__ friend
__ -mate; play, team etc.
__ club, social interest
__ co-activist
__ associate
__ colleague
__ partner
__ linguistic group
__ ethnic group
__ national group
__ provincial group
__ native
__ alien
__ tribe, clan
__ official of
__ follower, disciple
__ believer in

__ dating
__ lover
__ fiance
__ cohabitor
__ relationship
__ paternal
__ maternal
__ ancestor
__ descendent

__ family
__ family chief
__ patriarch
__ matriarch
__ custodian
__ guardian
__ ward
__ adopted
__ in-law coparent
__ step-

## MANUSCRIPT ABBREVIATIONS

__ per se
__ viz.
__ q.v.
__ i.e.
__ op.cit.
__ ibid
__ e.g.
__ c.f.
__ cum
__ see above
__ see below
__ et seq.
__ as in
__ vice versa
__ a la
__ according to
__ moot
__ so to say
__ as it were
__ in a like manner

__ supposedly
__ via
__ circa
__ rsvp
__ so-so
__ figuratively
__ vs.
__ aka
__ taken from
__ by permission

__ etc.
__ et al
__ ad infinitum
__ ad nauseam
__ page
__ paragraph
__ column
__ line

1B

__ exist
__ being
__ living
__ dead
__ become
__ tangible
__ intangible
__ nature
__ kind
__ basic
__ system
__ condition
__ relationship
__ dependence
__ independence
__ pertain to
__ apart from
__ relevant
__ irrelevant
__ with
__ without
__ comparison
__ like
__ unlike
__ such
__ blend
__ contrast
__ entity
__ nonentity
__ same
__ different
__ opposite
__ equivalent

— diverse
— consistency
— mimic
— mock
— create
— sample
— agree
— disagree
— peace
— conflict
— understand
— example
— adjustment

— number
— numeral
— decimal
— binary
— rate
— fraction
— ratio
— percentage
— counting
— calculating
— arithmetic
— mathematics
— add
— subtract
— total
— difference
— multiply
— divide
— product
— quotient
— remainder
— plus
— minus
— estimating
— correlate
— statistics
— norm
— average
— median

— RMS, root mean square
— analogy
— algebra
— geometry
— trigonometry
— sine
— cosine
— tangent
— cotangent
— secant
— cosecant
— calculus

## ARTICLES, CONNECTIVES

— a
— any
— some
— all
— none
— each
— every
— many
— few
— the
— this
— these
— that
— those
— of
— and
— and, for pairing
— or
— and/or
— either
— neither
— but
— yet
— ergo
— time
— times
— ever
— never
— than

— at
— as
— so
— so?
— so!
— to
— from
— other
— if, conditional
— if?
— yes
— perhaps

The following are relative adjectives or adverbs that become interrogatory pronouns with the addition of a question mark ; exclamatories or interjections by the addition of the exclamation point .

— where
— when
— what
— why
— way
— how
— which
— who
— whose

## AUXILIARIES

— shall
— should
— will
— would
— do
— did
— have
— had
— be
— was
— can
— could
— may
— might

— must
— ought
— always
— never
— often
— seldom
— definitely
— maybe

## ACTIONS

— come
— go
— get
— give
— put
— take
— make
— let
— reason
— see
— look
— feel
— grope
— hear
— listen
— eat
— intuit
— seem

## 1C

— second
— millisecond
— microsecond
— nanosecond
— minute
— hour
— day
— week
— weekend
— fortnight
— month
— year

__ quarter
__ season
__ spring
__ summer
__ autumn
__ winter

__ equinox
__ solstice
__ era
__ age
__ decade
__ century
__ millennium
__ eternity
__ predawn
__ dawn
__ morning
__ forenoon
__ noon
__ midday
__ afternoon
__ evening
__ dusk
__ night
__ midnight
__ overnight
__ today
__ tomorrow
__ yesterday
__ tonight
__ anniversary
__ birthday
__ new year's day
__ new year's eve
__ perpetual
__ holiday
__ vacation
__ national days

__ holy days
__ easter
__ ramadan

__ while
__ during
__ spell
__ term
__ meanwhile
__ hiatus
__ wait
__ delay
__ persist
__ quit

__ new
__ old
__ recent
__ mod
__ fleeting
__ lasting
__ now
__ then
__ past
__ present
__ future
__ suddenness
__ early
__ late
__ eventually
__ sooner
__ later
__ young
__ premature
__ frequent
__ forever
__ persistent

__ sequence
__ precursor
__ sequel
__ synchro, simultaneity
__ intermittent
__ rhythm
__ regularity
__ irregularity
__ periodic

__ asynchronous
__ recurrent
__ alternately
__ steady
__ constant
__ transient
__ permanent
__ temporary
__ before
__ after
__ again
__ phase
__ continue
__ cease
__ begin
__ end
__ start
__ stop
__ use

__ origin
__ history
__ contemporary
__ prehistoric
__ stone age
__ extinct
__ glacial era
__ million years ago
__ billion years ago
__ clock
__ watch
__ timer
__ calendar

1D

__ force
__ strength
__ weakness
__ horsepower
__ manpower
__ able
__ unable
__ power

__ futility
__ influence
__ enable
__ disable
__ work
__ impregnable
__ vulnerable
__ frailty
__ enterprise
__ rigor
__ active
__ violence
__ rage
__ frenzy
__ explosion
__ unruly
__ riot
__ rowdy
__ brutal

__ moderate
__ relax
__ gentle
__ operation
__ process
__ productive
__ unproductive
__ fertile
__ barren
__ fertilizer
__ build
__ artifact
__ masterpiece
__ crop
__ product
__ by-product

__ favor
__ dominance
__ submission
__ effective
__ ineffective
__ tendency

__ liability
__ responsible
__ probability
__ involve
__ cooperation
__ maintain
__ fix, repair
__ rest
__ development
__ for, substitution
__ occasion
__ event
__ occur
__ trade
__ exchange
__ cause

__ source
__ well
__ effect
__ because
__ luck
__ accident
__ odds
__ together
__ fresh
__ stale
__ pristine
__ primitive
__ analysis
__ heredity
__ advance
__ retreat

__ even
__ odd
__ occasional
__ systematic
__ haphazard
__ stop
__ turn on
__ turn off
__ random
__ pace

__ fast
__ conserve
__ remain
__ evolution

2A

__ intellect
__ mind
__ rationality
__ wits
__ intelligence
__ sense
__ knowledge
__ ignorance
__ sly
__ astute
__ wise
__ genius
__ smart
__ talented
__ stupid
__ senile
__ foolish
__ simpleton
__ boor
__ odd
__ learning
__ lore
__ liberal arts
__ think
__ idea
__ consider
__ speculate
__ opinion
__ intuitive
__ pro
__ con
__ assumption
__ sincerity
__ topic
__ problem
__ question
__ answer

__ test
__ theory
__ inspection
__ research
__ checkup

__ spying
__ encode
__ decode
__ search
__ explore
__ discover
__ find
__ lose
__ experiment
__ laboratory
__ prove
__ disprove
__ tact
__ approval
__ censure
__ criticism
__ rating
__ conclusion
__ presume
__ clue
__ guess
__ infer
__ philosophy
__ metaphysics
__ materialism
__ aesthetics
__ idealism
__ belief
__ trust
__ imagine
__ superstition
__ gullible
__ naive
__ proof
__ skepticism
__ incredible
__ fact

__ data

__ entire
__ possible
__ probable
__ available
__ chance
__ reliable
__ valid
__ indeed
__ doubt
__ embarrass
__ risk
__ bet
__ truth
__ correct
__ good
__ bad
__ normal
__ deviant
__ proverb
__ formula
__ slogan
__ error
__ illusion
__ delusion
__ accept
__ reject
__ protest
__ vow
__ assure
__ declare
__ denial
__ contradiction
__ mood
__ morale
__ demoral(ize)
__ tolerant
__ intolerant
__ interest
__ attention
__ observation
__ care

— ignore

— asleep
— distraction
— confuse
— neglect
— lazy
— skip
— slip
— imagination
— invention
— ingenious
— practical
— identification
— token
— trophy
— relic
— know
— cherish
— memorize
— remind
— remember
— forget
— suspense
— anticipate
— surprise
— blow
— shock
— startle
— disappoint
— frustrate
— foresight
— prediction
— ominous
— omen
— promise
— warning
— whistle
— siren
— fortunate
— imply

— silence
— evasive
— secrecy
— private
— public
— confidential
— stifle
— deception
— mask
— eclipse
— lurk
— disguised
— hypocrisy
— lying
— forgery
— cheat
— tampered
— exaggeration
— trick
— bait
— bluff
— snare
— net
— hook
— fool
— liar
— mark
— badge
— emblem
— name
— password
— label
— stamp
— sticker
— brand
— logo
— gesture
— crown
— flag

2B

— art
— fine arts
— handicrafts
— folk arts
— architecture
— calligraphy
— sculpture
— ceramics
— oils
— water colors
— engraving
— decoration
— painting
— portraiture
— illustration
— drawing
— talent
— technique
— design
— perspective
— picture
— scene
— view
— cartoon
— comic strip
— studio
— gallery
— statuary
— relief
— embossment
— cameo
— carve
— model
— mc'd
— pottery
— porcelain
— china
— crockery
— kiln

— photography
— snapshot
— print
— slide
— film
— negative
— camera
— projector
— develop
— animations
— graphic arts
— lithography
— silk screen
— font
— typography
— press
— publish
— letter
— note
— postcard
— mail
— parcel
— postage stamp
— mailbox
— post office
— address
— zip code
— reply
— send
— book
— edition
— volume
— anthology
— handbook
— encyclopedia
— catalog
— directory
— atlas
— dictionary
— textbook
— primer
— pamphlet

— periodical
— newspaper
— news
— binding
— cover
— library

__ bookstore
__ bibliography
__ index
__ editor
__ writing
__ essay
__ editorial
__ author
__ outline
__ biography
__ autobiography
__ diary
__ story
__ fiction
__ myth
__ sci-fi
__ novel
__ plot
__ tell
__ poetry
__ verse
__ rhyme
__ meter
__ prose

__ theater
__ stage
__ show
__ drama
__ circus
__ melodrama
__ stagecraft
__ play
__ skit
__ tragedy
__ comedy
__ musical
__ act
__ scene
__ intermission
__ finale
__ repertory
__ part in play

__ hero
__ villain
__ lead
__ star
__ engagement
__ performance
__ production
__ direction
__ rehearse
__ rodeo
__ carnival
__ floor show
__ side show
__ puppet
__ movie
__ feature
__ documentary
__ opera
__ hall
__ arena
__ bandstand
__ cabaret
__ wings
__ prop
__ scenery
__ flats
__ script
__ libretto
__ scenario

__ patron
__ overact
__ entertainer
__ actor
__ understudy
__ clown
__ cast
__ dance
__ choreography
__ ballet
__ ballroom
__ various dances
__ various dances

__ music
__ melody
__ harmony
__ musical dissonance
__ composition
__ score
__ arrangement
__ symphony
__ syncopation
__ folk music
__ march

2C

__ vocal
__ song
__ ballad
__ anthem
__ solo
__ aria
__ lullaby
__ hymn
__ chorus
__ orchestra
__ polyphony
__ counterpoint
__ coda
__ overture
__ staff
__ motif
__ chant
__ hum
__ whistle
__ intone
__ croon
__ strum
__ conduct
__ pitch
__ key
__ major
__ minor
__ scale
__ octave
__ musical note

__ sharp
__ flat
__ natural
__ harmonic
__ chord
__ trill
__ tempo
__ soprano
__ alto
__ tenor
__ baritone
__ bass

__ harp
__ banjo
__ guitar
__ mandolin
__ violin
__ viola
__ cello
__ bass violin
__ horn
__ bugle
__ trumpet
__ cornet
__ trombone
__ sax
__ tuba
__ french horn
__ woodwind
__ flute
__ fife
__ piccolo
__ reed
__ oboe
__ bassoon
__ clarinet
__ english horn
__ bagpipe
__ harmonica
__ kazoo
__ accordion
__ piano

_ harpsichord
_ organ
_ hurdy-gurdy
_ music box
_ cymbals
_ triangle
_ gong
_ bells
_ chimes
_ castanets
_ drum
_ tambourine
_ carillon
_ plectrum
_ bow
_ sticks
_ baton
_ metronome
_ electronic keyboard
_ tuning fork
_ pitch pipe

_ amusement
_ recreation
_ relaxation
_ pleasure
_ fun
_ play
_ sport
_ fair
_ frolic
_ athletics
_ game
_ score
_ park
_ playground
_ gymnasium
_ field
_ swimming pool
_ toys
_ doll

_ card
_ various games

_ sports

_ team sports

_ language
_ speech
_ talk
_ say
_ vocabulary
_ root word
_ word
_ affix
_ prefix
_ suffix
_ potent
_ punctuation
_ idiom
_ dialect
_ alphabet
_ letter
_ vowel
_ consonant
_ symbol
_ character
_ grapheme
_ phoneme
_ syllable
_ etymology
_ philology
_ linguistics
_ grammar
_ syntax
_ subject
_ predicate
_ object
_ noun
_ pronoun
_ adjective
_ verb
_ adverb
_ infinitive
_ participle
_ preposition
_ conjunction
_ article
_ grammatical case
_ person 1,2,3
_ gender M/F
_ mood of verb
_ tense-past, present, future
_ tense-perfect
_ tense-ongoing
_ voice, active-passive
_ pronunciation

_ vulgarity
_ improper
_ uncouth
_ concise
_ terse
_ verbose
_ accent
_ stress
_ voice
_ statement
_ phrase
_ inflection
_ tone
_ remark
_ oral
_ lisp
_ stutter
_ mumble
_ discussion
_ conversation
_ orate
_ articulate
_ fluent

2D

_ meaning
_ intent
_ suggestion
_ symbolism
_ nonsense
_ intelligible
_ coherence
_ legibility
_ illegibility
_ perception
_ ambiguity
_ puzzle
_ riddle
_ scramble
_ describe
_ illustrate
_ demonstrate
_ interpretation
_ definition
_ text

_ translation
_ paraphrase
_ comment
_ edit
_ report
_ signal
_ distort
_ misunderstanding
_ commerce
_ contact
_ expression
_ disclosure
_ display
_ divulge
_ confession
_ prominence
_ explicit
_ admit
_ advice
_ indicate
_ medium
_ the press
_ radio
_ television
_ telegraph
_ rumor

__ gossip
__ scandal

__ item
__ news article
__ publication
__ publicity
__ Advertisement
__ poster
__ sign
__ newsletter
__ magazine
__ reading
__ communications
__ hand signals
__ telephone
__ teletype
__ fax
__ computer modem
__ intercom
__ messenger
__ postman
__ propaganda
__ mislead

__ teaching
__ education
__ study
__ preparation
__ rearing
__ drill
__ lesson
__ lecture
__ professor
__ principal
__ dean
__ faculty
__ student
__ scholar
__ alumnus
__ class
__ course of study
__ grade

__ school
__ academy
__ kindergarten
__ grade school
__ junior high sch.
__ high school
__ college
__ university
__ graduate school
__ trade school

__ record
__ archives
__ document
__ certificate
__ ticket
__ visa
__ diploma
__ account
__ bulletin
__ monument
__ enrollment
__ secretary
__ notary
__ pen
__ pencil
__ typewriter
__ word-processor
__ presentation
__ ink
__ image
__ figure

3A

__ volition
__ choice
__ discretion
__ pleasure
__ voluntariness
__ spontaneity
__ willingness
__ eager
__ demur

__ reluctance
__ firmness
__ perseverance
__ tenacity
__ obstinacy
__ diligence
__ perversity
__ adamant
__ contrary
__ hesitation
__ defection
__ betray
__ treason
__ whim
__ fickleness
__ impulsive
__ reckless
__ improvise
__ escape
__ evade
__ flee
__ derelict

__ desire
__ need
__ homesickness
__ appetite
__ hunger
__ greed
__ ambition
__ fervor
__ passion
__ devotion
__ seriousness
__ unconcern
__ carelessness
__ selection
__ dilemma
__ preference
__ eligibility
__ necessity
__ urgency
__ compulsory

__ instinctive
__ inevitable
__ certain
__ fate
__ destiny
__ doom

__ schedule
__ custom
__ folkway
__ culture
__ civilization
__ habit
__ rule
__ routine
__ addiction
__ wean
__ fashion
__ style
__ formality
__ conformity
__ dignity
__ pomp
__ manners
__ casualness
__ cause
__ ideal

__ persuasion
__ goad
__ inspiration
__ provoke
__ urge
__ invite
__ nurture
__ request
__ temptation
__ fascination
__ charm
__ glamour
__ bribery
__ deterrent
__ intention
__ purpose

__ target
__ scheme
__ diagram
__ map
__ chart
__ policy
__ conspire
__ artifice
__ sketch
__ quest
__ hunt
__ fish
__ prey
__ pursue
__ route
__ path
__ road
__ sea lane
__ air lane
__ passage
__ conduit
__ street
__ alley
__ pavement
__ railroad
__ bridge

__ yet
__ means
__ wherewithal
__ agent
__ equipment
__ supply
__ lodgings
__ harness
__ saddle
__ enough
__ scarce
__ want
__ excess
__ overdo
__ surfeit
__ use

__ treatment
__ value
__ worthy
__ worthless
__ discard
__ junk
__ obsolescent
__ waste
__ garbage
__ rubbish
__ rubble

3B

__ advisability
__ fitness
__ appropriate
__ advantageous
__ makeshift
__ drawback
__ handicap
__ trouble
__ important
__ emergency
__ person
__ somebody
__ celebrity
__ chief
__ great
__ vital
__ slight
__ silly
__ petty
__ sorry
__ sad
__ despicable
__ miserable
__ shabby
__ cheap
__ excellence
__ adequate
__ welfare
__ benefit
__ superb

__ wonderful
__ champion
__ peerless
__ outrageous
__ loathsome
__ foul
__ baseness
__ harm
__ harmless
__ damage
__ destruction
__ jinx
__ vicious
__ shocking
__ disgusting
__ damnable
__ curse
__ blight
__ poison
__ pesticide

__ perfection
__ faultless
__ soundness
__ defect
__ blemish
__ deface
__ deform
__ mar
__ mediocrity
__ dullness
__ commonplace

__ progress
__ reform
__ fall
__ rot
__ injury
__ bruise
__ wreck
__ collapse
__ shatter
__ fray
__ ramshackle

__ downfall
__ disaster
__ crash
__ dismantle
__ erase
__ annihilation
__ vandalism

__ restore
__ rehabilitation
__ retrieval
__ revival
__ renewal
__ repair
__ refresh
__ stimulate
__ cheer
__ danger
__ unsafe
__ delicate
__ safe
__ security
__ cozy
__ harbor
__ shelter
__ dock
__ preservation
__ rescue

3C

__ behavior
__ misbehave
__ deed
__ produce
__ inaction
__ abstain
__ idle
__ movement
__ quick
__ agility
__ initiative
__ busy
__ sloth

__ haste

__ leisure
__ ease
__ comfort
__ discomfort
__ respite
__ absent
__ sleep
__ coma
__ hibernate
__ awake
__ endeavor
__ attempt
__ adventure
__ struggle
__ strive
__ exhaustion
__ tired

__ ready
__ ripe
__ rawness
__ uncooked
__ achievement
__ winner
__ gain
__ capture
__ defeat
__ prosperity
__ luxury

__ misfortune
__ hindrance
__ interruption
__ prevent
__ difficulty
__ anxiety
__ mess
__ flexibility
__ skill
__ experience
__ clumsiness
__ incompetent

__ bungle
__ cunning
__ mischief
__ imp

3D

__ duress
__ pressure
__ require
__ strictness
__ discipline
__ austerity
__ sternness
__ meticulousness
__ relentless
__ leniency
__ compassion
__ compliant
__ humoring
__ gentleness
__ forbearing
__ lock
__ key
__ freedom

__ rights
__ free will
__ self-reliance
__ free person
__ serfdom
__ meekness
__ yield
__ allegiance
__ rebel
__ heed
__ defy

__ engagement
__ sponsorship
__ permission
__ refuse
__ prohibition
__ forbid

__ legal
__ illegal
__ detective
__ help
__ sympathy
__ comrade
__ fraternity
__ belong
__ opposition
__ hostility
__ confront
__ opponent
__ defiance
__ challenge

__ rapport
__ quarrel
__ gift
__ thrift
__ stinginess
__ generous
__ wastefulness
__ lavish
__ spend
__ nonviolence
__ pacifist
__ appeasement
__ neutrality
__ compromise
__ grip
__ hold
__ hug
__ keep
__ release
__ abandon
__ renounce
__ sharing
__ contribute
__ giving
__ charity
__ dowry
__ grab
__ rapacity

__ rape
__ recompense
__ plagiarism
__ bandit
__ pauper
__ destitution

4A

__ govern
__ social security
__ authority
__ rule
__ lordship
__ hierarchy
__ nobility
__ aristocracy
__ ruling class
__ chairman
__ president
__ premier
__ prince
__ rector
__ regent
__ mayor
__ alderman
__ ambassador
__ consul
__ dictator

__ king
__ emperor
__ duke
__ royalty
__ majesty
__ scepter
__ throne
__ accession
__ appointment
__ official
__ plebiscite
__ regulation
__ administration
__ bureaucracy

— red tape
— civil
— federal
— constitutional
— executive
— judicial

— legislature
— parliament
— congress
— assembly
— chamber
— diet
— senate
— house
— representatives
— delegates
— committees
— departments
— council
— cabinet
— cabinet secretary
— minister
— capitol
— court house
— debate
— veto
— bill
— filibuster
— politics
— party

— platform
— convention
— caucus
— nominate
— candidate
— electioneering
— campaign
— district
— precinct
— ward
— vote
— suffrage
— ballot
— polls
— electorate
— lobby
— graft
— patronage
— proclamation
— tax
— junta
— forum
— panel
— session
— town meeting
— referendum
— nonpartisan
— revolt
— revolution
— insurrection
— insurgency

— treaty
— alliance
— passport
— embargo
— repeal
— recall
— diplomat
— attache
— spy
— impeachment
— overthrow
— abdication, abandon
— society
— community
— civilian
— citizen
— democracy
— tariff

4B

— Mil. police
— protect
— guard
— warden
— nurse maid
— baby sitter
— outpost
— picket
— vanguard
— rearguard
— garrison
— watch
— watchman
— lookout
— sentinel
— scout
— patrol
— doorkeeper
— bodyguard
— escort
— constable
— officer
— sheriff
— marshal
— deputy
— sergeant
— lieutenant
— captain
— inspector
— police
— posse
— vigilantes
— load
— shoot
— commissioned officer
— general
— colonel
— major
— commander
— noncom
— warrant officer
— corporal
— admiral
— commodore
— ensign
— petty officer
— force
— arrest
— shackle
— prison
— reformatory
— confine
— fetter
— quarantine
— isolation
— concentration camp
— prisoner of war
— surrender
— mutinous

— trespass
— hostage
— enlistment
— conscription
— mil draft
— induction
— recruitment
— muster
— mobilize
— demobilize
— abet
— accomplice
— gang
— battle
— fight
— enemy
— skirmish
— warfare
— attack
— strategy
— tactics
— soldier
— deploy
— counterattack
— invasion
— siege
— bombard
— strafe

__ guns
__ defense
__ armor
__ fortification
__ bunker
__ entrenchment
__ castle

__ knight
__ cavalry
__ tanks
__ infantry
__ artillery
__ guerrilla
__ mercenary
__ military
__ army
__ division
__ brigade
__ regiment
__ battalion
__ company
__ troop
__ squad
__ platoon
__ battery
__ unit
__ militia
__ reserves
__ navy
__ fleet
__ marines
__ air force
__ weapons
__ armory
__ ammunition
__ ballistics
__ sword
__ blade
__ rifle
__ side arm
__ cartridge
__ shell
__ missile
__ bullet
__ bomb

__ arrow
__ bow
__ spear
__ shield
__ slingshot
__ battlefield
__ conscientious objector
__ truce
__ armistice
__ disarmament

4C

__ law
__ lawless
__ bailiff
__ jurisdiction
__ anarchy
__ nihilism
__ conservatism
__ reactionary
__ liberalism
__ radicalism
__ socialism
__ communism
__ nationalization
__ capitalism
__ precept
__ order
__ principle
__ guideline
__ statute
__ mandate
__ decree
__ edict
__ ruling
__ ordinance
__ notice
__ enjoin
__ charge
__ stipulation
__ plea
__ injunction
__ custody
__ catch
__ parole

__ violation
__ infraction
__ transgression
__ oath
__ sworn
__ perjury
__ settlement
__ bail
__ move
__ petition
__ appeal
__ prayer
__ suit
__ waiver
__ annul
__ overrule
__ surrogate
__ accessory
__ cartel
__ syndicate
__ legitimacy
__ act

__ illicit
__ crime
__ felony
__ misdemeanor
__ extortion
__ blackmail
__ theft
__ fraud
__ swindle
__ robbery
__ burglary
__ mugging
__ hijacking
__ looting
__ racketeering
__ smuggling
__ contraband
__ judiciary
__ magistrate
__ bureau
__ tribunal
__ juror
__ attorney
__ advocate
__ prosecutor
__ court case
__ summons
__ writ
__ warrant
__ indictment

__ court hearing
__ inquiry
__ depositions
__ pleadings
__ testimony
__ evidence
__ argument
__ decision
__ verdict
__ try
__ allegation
__ citation
__ accuse
__ vindication
__ alibi
__ acquittal
__ dismissal
__ amnesty
__ reprieve
__ condemnation
__ conviction
__ attainder
__ penalty
__ punishment
__ fine

__ imprison

__ sue
__ plaintiff
__ defendant
__ complaint
__ dissent
__ objection
__ mediation
__ referee
__ judge
__ occupancy
__ tenure
__ conveyance
__ transfer
__ assignment
__ bequest
__ legacy
__ inheritance
__ repossession
__ foreclosure
__ GNP
__ depression
__ recession
__ market
__ panic
__ money
__ currency
__ legal tender
__ check
__ investment
__ solvency
__ fee
__ price index

4D

__ business
__ job
__ insurance
__ annuity
__ insurance policy
__ work
__ labor
__ wages
__ salary
__ slave
__ drudge
__ professional
__ craft
__ journeyman
__ master
__ smiths
__ wrights
__ engineers
__ shop
__ bench
__ desk
__ business company
__ corporation
__ sweatshop
__ industrial plant
__ factory
__ power plant
__ machine shop
__ mill
__ yard
__ foundry
__ office
__ servant
__ employee
__ steward
__ waiter
__ staff
__ aide

__ franchise
__ license
__ free lance
__ guarantee
__ contract
__ bargain
__ deal
__ deed
__ surety
__ pledge
__ deposit
__ stake
__ collateral
__ mortgage
__ lien
__ endorse
__ in trust
__ offer
__ proposition
__ solicitation
__ beggar
__ rental
__ lease

__ indenture
__ middleman
__ spokesman
__ raise
__ reduction
__ dismiss
__ retirement
__ pension
__ liquidate
__ vacate
__ finance

__ partnership
__ co-worker
__ organization
__ foundation
__ division
__ labor union
__ membership
__ join
__ local
__ strike
__ walkout
__ lockout
__ competitor
__ competition
__ owing
__ monopoly
__ owner
__ landlord
__ tenant
__ roomer
__ property
__ goods
__ belongings
__ estate
__ interest
__ equity
__ real estate
__ assets
__ acquisition
__ earnings
__ profit
__ receipts
__ dividends

__ loss
__ depreciate
__ budgeting
__ distribution
__ delivery
__ sale
__ premium
__ bonus
__ subsidy
__ endowment
__ subscriber
__ receipt
__ lending
__ borrowing
__ negotiate
__ customer
__ prospect
__ buyer
__ seller
__ wholesale
__ retail
__ merchandising
__ auction
__ store
__ broker
__ commodity
__ dry goods
__ appliances

__ hardware
__ housewares
__ supermarket

__ stocks
__ bonds
__ securities
__ debentures
__ margin
__ treasurer
__ cashier
__ till
__ bank
__ purse
__ wallet
__ wealth
__ credit
__ debt
__ payment
__ reward
__ reimbursement
__ income
__ stipend
__ paid
__ nonpayment
__ default
__ bankruptcy
__ expenditure
__ final statement
__ invoice
__ ledger
__ entry
__ credit
__ debit
__ bookkeeping
__ auditing
__ clerk
__ balance
__ price
__ assessment
__ discount

5A

__ emotions
__ sentiment
__ callous
__ thrill
__ agitation
__ excitement
__ impassive
__ patient
__ impatient
__ calm
__ nonchalance
__ nervous
__ tense
__ indulgence
__ dominant
__ submissive
__ endure
__ condone
__ hope
__ despair
__ lively
__ funereal
__ enthusiastic
__ indifferent
__ energetic
__ lethargic
__ happy
__ sad
__ positive
__ negative
__ for
__ against
__ praise
__ deprecate
__ exalt
__ debase
__ love
__ hate
__ adore
__ detest
__ familiar
__ strange

__ encourage
__ discourage
__ pleasant
__ delightful
__ cheerful
__ blissful
__ ugly
__ offensive
__ mortification
__ annoy

__ joyful
__ ecstacy
__ satisfy
__ laugh
__ enjoy
__ contentment
__ comfortable
__ rejoicing
__ smile
__ exult
__ celebrate
__ joke
__ misery
__ grief
__ suffer
__ like
__ dislike
__ solemnity
__ melancholy
__ glum
__ forlorn
__ regret
__ penitence
__ deplore
__ shame
__ lament
__ weeping
__ mourn
__ sob

__ tedious
__ bore

__ relief
__ optimism
__ expectation
__ desperation
__ pessimism
__ impossibility
__ incurable
__ worry
__ fear
__ alarm
__ dread
__ terror
__ scariness
__ intimidation
__ cowardice
__ bold
__ rash

__ cautious
__ fastidious
__ tastefulness
__ elegance
__ refinement
__ connoisseur
__ gourmet
__ indecency
__ gross
__ obscene
__ homely
__ hideous
__ monstrosity
__ beautiful
__ ornament
__ jewel
__ simplicity
__ naturalness
__ ostentation
__ pride
__ conceited
__ dignified
__ humility
__ servility
__ sycophant

__ modesty
__ shyness
__ timidity
__ coyness
__ demureness

__ vanity
__ smugness
__ egotist
__ boastful
__ bluster
__ bully
__ arrogance
__ snobbery
__ presumptuous
__ imperious
__ insolence
__ brazenness
__ impudence
__ disrepute
__ disgrace
__ stigma
__ reputation
__ esteem
__ dear
__ honor
__ prestige
__ distinction
__ honors
__ awards
__ laurels
__ bravery
__ cowardice
__ valor
__ medal
__ title
__ honorific
__ academic degree
__ the people
__ the masses
__ rabble
__ peasant
__ wonder
__ amazement
__ awe
__ prodigy
__ phenomenon

5B

__ sociability
__ gregariousness
__ conviviality
__ fellowship
__ party
__ seclusion
__ hospitality
__ welcome
__ greetings
__ host
__ guest
__ visitor
__ banishment
__ exile
__ blacklist
__ intimate
__ cordial
__ devote
__ dedicate
__ befriend
__ introduce
__ enmity
__ grudge
__ spite

__ romance
__ infatuation
__ sweetheart
__ admirer
__ lovemaking
__ kiss
__ wooing
__ flirtation
__ philander
__ copulate
__ proposal
__ married
__ wedding
__ honeymoon
__ bride
__ bridegroom
__ harem
__ bigamist
__ celibacy

__ courtesy
__ graciousness
__ gallantry
__ suavity
__ polite
__ brotherhood
__ malice
__ rancor
__ virulence
__ cruelty

__ benefactor
__ savior
__ barbarian
__ witch
__ pity
__ mercy
__ ruthless
__ console
__ forgive
__ congratulate
__ gratitude

__ ill humored
__ scowl
__ frown
__ sulk
__ angry
__ resentment
__ jealous
__ suspicious
__ envy
__ retaliate
__ revenge

5C

__ ethics
__ morality
__ immorality
__ conscience
__ right
__ wrong
__ proper
__ decent
__ privilege
__ human rights
__ civil rights
__ merit
__ earn
__ imposition
__ usurp
__ duty
__ necessary
__ unnecessary
__ demand
__ inflict

__ respect
__ disrespect
__ reverence
__ offend
__ insult
__ contempt
__ scorn
__ snub
__ ridicule
__ derision
__ sarcasm
__ irony
__ cynicism
__ satire
__ burlesque
__ lampoon
__ parody
__ caricature
__ sneer
__ invective
__ jest

__ farce
__ humor
__ levity
__ fantasy
__ incredulity
__ applause
__ popularity
__ compliment
__ flatter

__ blame
__ rebuke
__ scold
__ nag
__ slander
__ libel
__ abuse
__ profanity
__ threat
__ deceit
__ infidelity
__ treachery
__ corruption
__ selfish
__ justice
__ injustice
__ fairness
__ impartial
__ honesty
__ trustworthy
__ virtue
__ loyal

__ vice
__ evil
__ misconduct
__ sin
__ atrocity
__ wretch
__ rascal
__ chastity
__ virginity
__ dissolute

__ wanton
__ lewd
__ seduction
__ adultery
__ prostitution
__ pimp
__ brothel
__ debauchery
__ paramour
__ sexy
__ lustful
__ smut
__ fornication
__ immodest
__ risque
__ pornographic
__ ribald
__ scatological

__ ascetic
__ intemperance
__ gluttony
__ fasting
__ intoxication
__ champaign
__ toast
__ cocktails
__ tavern
__ pub
__ brewery
__ distillery
__ sobriety
__ atonement
__ whip
__ redress
__ apology
__ excuse
__ penance

5D

__ religion
__ cult
__ sect

__ denomination
__ theism
__ polytheism
__ monotheism
__ pantheism
__ agnosticism
__ atheism
__ christianity
__ judaism
__ islam
__ buddhism
__ confucianism
__ shintoism
__ taoism
__ scripture
__ bible
__ koran
__ vedas
__ torah
__ revelation
__ prophecy
__ miracle
__ prophets
__ evangelists
__ apostles
__ disciples
__ theology
__ divinity

__ doctrine
__ dogma
__ orthodoxy
__ faith
__ fundamentalism
__ heterodoxy
__ heresy
__ fallacy
__ infidel
__ pagan
__ nonbeliever
__ bigot
__ deity
__ god

__ spirit
__ soul
__ mother nature
__ ghost
__ creator
__ demigods
__ fairy
__ folklore
__ angels
__ saints
__ demons
__ devil
__ goblin
__ werewolf
__ heaven
__ paradise
__ hell
__ purgatory
__ resurrection
__ reincarnation
__ holiness
__ consecration
__ profaneness

__ secular
__ temporal
__ piety
__ impiety
__ zeal
__ fanaticism
__ believer
__ devotee
__ sacrilege
__ blasphemy
__ desecration
__ irreligious
__ skeptic
__ humanism
__ iconoclasm
__ worship
__ paean
__ psalm
__ pray

— supplication
— invocation
— grace
— benediction
— blessing
— propitiation
— offering
— sacrifice
— immolation
— services
— liturgy

— idolatry
— fetishism
— occultism
— mysticism
— theosophy
— supernaturalism
— transcendentalism
— psychics
— parapsychology
— spiritualism
— ectoplasm
— clairvoyance
— telepathy
— extrasensory
— divination
— sorcery
— magic
— witchcraft
— voodooism
— exorcism
— trance
— incantation
— talisman
— religions, various

— priesthood
— ministry
— cleric
— monasticism
— ordination
— clergy

— chaplain
— preacher
— imam
— mullah
— rabbi
— monk
— nun
— high priest
— pope
— cardinal
— archbishop
— bishop
— guru
— bonze
— lama
— laity
— congregation
— parish
— ritual
— baptism
— anointing
— eucharist
— mass
— vestments
— temple
— church
— mosque
— pagoda
— shrine
— cathedral
— abbey
— convent
— altar
— pulpit
— lectern
— pew

6A

— space
— measure
— void
— range
— roominess

— region
— territory
— place
— quarter
— neighborhood
— province
— patch
— state
— township
— city
— town
— village
— diocese

— country
— republic
— commonwealth
— kingdom
— empire
— principality
— colony
— the country
— wasteland
— frontier
— pastoral
— agrarian
— metropolis
— municipality
— suburb
— capital
— county seat
— block
— square

— location
— position
— orientation
— establishment
— elsewhere

— presence
— ubiquity
— attendance

— pervade
— appear
— disappear
— resident
— nonresident
— uninhabited
— habitation
— tenancy
— population
— dwell

— settler
— pioneer
— container
— bottles
— casks
— cases
— box
— basins
— baskets
— bags
— luggage
— pans
— ladles
— bucket
— cupboards
— contents
— components
— ingredients
— parts
— inventory
— load
— filling
— substance
— material

6B

— bigness
— dimensions
— proportions
— huge
— plumpness
— giant

__ littleness
__ shortness
__ scantiness
__ runt
__ miniature
__ development
__ expansion
__ extension
__ enlargement
__ spread
__ distention
__ compression
__ shrinking
__ squeezing
__ shriveling
__ withering
__ pucker
__ pinch

__ linear measures
__ area measures
__ volume measures
__ survey
__ instrumentation
__ gauge
__ criterion
__ pattern
__ geodesy
__ assay
__ weigh
__ metrical
__ remoteness
__ beyond
__ vicinity
__ encounter
__ tangency
__ graze
__ convenient
__ neighboring
__ interval
__ clearance
__ crack
__ gulf

__ breach
__ stretch
__ succinctness
__ lowness
__ abbreviation
__ condensation
__ curtailment
__ abridge

__ radius
__ wide
__ narrow
__ tapering
__ bottleneck
__ leanness
__ tallness
__ stature
__ tower
__ steeple
__ base
__ deepness
__ hole
__ cavity
__ chasm
__ underground
__ underwater
__ shallowness
__ superficiality
__ climax
__ underside
__ underneath
__ nadir
__ ground
__ floor
__ foundation

__ verticalness
__ erectness
__ perpendicularity
__ steep
__ horizontalness
__ levelness
__ flatness
__ recumbency

__ horizon
__ skyline
__ raze
__ pendency
__ sag
__ dangle
__ drooping
__ support
__ aid
__ sustaining
__ bracket
__ brace
__ buttress
__ beam
__ truss
__ footing
__ pillar
__ scaffold
__ platform
__ trestle
__ sawhorse
__ rostrum
__ shaft
__ pole
__ bar
__ rod
__ staff
__ cane
__ rafter

__ zigzag
__ bent
__ stagger
__ crooked
__ leaning
__ slope
__ bias
__ bend
__ twist
__ turn
__ skew
__ swerve
__ inversion

__ transposition
__ overturn
__ upset
__ somersault
__ intersection
__ crossroad
__ crosswalk
__ network
__ webbing
__ netting
__ mesh
__ wickerwork
__ crisscross
__ rood
__ cross
__ saltire
__ ankh
__ maltese cross
__ swastika
__ crosswise
__ traverse
__ weaving
__ lacing
__ twining
__ braiding
__ interweaving
__ wreath
__ warp
__ woof
__ weft
__ loom
__ shuttle
__ treadle

6C

__ fringe
__ outdoors
__ inland
__ midland
__ headquarters
__ concentric
__ layer
__ veneer

__ coating
__ patina
__ slice
__ slab
__ ply
__ covering
__ veiling
__ lid
__ roof
__ umbrella
__ crust
__ shell
__ hull
__ wrapper
__ bandage
__ envelope
__ crate
__ package
__ plaster
__ electroplate

__ environment
__ environs
__ circumstances
__ context
__ situation
__ setting
__ background
__ elements
__ envelopment
__ patent
__ copyright
__ trademark
__ restrict
__ restrain
__ register
__ terminal
__ profile
__ border
__ brink
__ yard
__ pen
__ fence

__ rail

__ injection
__ insertion
__ intermediary
__ partition
__ buffer
__ bumper
__ intrusion
__ interference
__ confrontation
__ antipodal
__ prow
__ onwards
__ askance
__ port
__ starboard
__ leeward
__ windward
__ beside
__ side by side

__ structure
__ arch
__ construction
__ frame
__ form
__ symmetry
__ asymmetry
__ grimace
__ garble
__ directness
__ line, linear
__ angle, angularity
__ triangle
__ curve
__ flexure
__ bow, hair
__ parabolic
__ circle
__ ring
__ circumference
__ round

__ loop
__ oval
__ ellipse
__ curly
__ wavy
__ convolution
__ winding
__ meander
__ coil
__ spiral
__ helix
__ sphere
__ ball
__ globe
__ bead
__ cylinder
__ cone
__ convexity
__ concavity
__ ridge
__ swelling
__ protuberance
__ extrusion
__ bulge
__ hump
__ pit
__ digger
__ hollowness
__ crater
__ dent
__ tunnel
__ burrow
__ dimple
__ recess
__ niche

__ sharpness
__ dullness
__ point
__ hone
__ keen
__ barbed
__ smooth

__ rough
__ sleekness
__ shine
__ slippery
__ notch
__ gash
__ groove
__ trench
__ trough
__ ditch
__ rut
__ fold
__ tuck
__ wrinkle
__ crease
__ open
__ shut
__ gap
__ puncture
__ blockage
__ plug

6D

__ motion
__ inertness
__ velocity
__ acceleration
__ deceleration
__ rapidity
__ slowness
__ walk
__ run
__ dash
__ gallop
__ crawl
__ plod
__ step
__ jump
__ spring
__ skip
__ impel
__ kick
__ impact

__ thrust
__ momentum
__ push
__ crush
__ poke
__ jostle
__ collision
__ bump
__ bounce
__ hit
__ miss
__ tap
__ reaction
__ reflex
__ throwing
__ toss
__ salvo
__ projectile
__ shot
__ pulling
__ traction
__ tug
__ jerk
__ leverage
__ pry
__ fulcrum
__ axis
__ pivot
__ crowbar
__ tackle
__ windlass
__ capstan
__ winch
__ attraction
__ repulsion
__ magnet

__ way
__ aim
__ heading
__ course (route)
__ north
__ south
__ east
__ west
__ through
__ deviation
__ variation
__ wandering
__ deflection
__ refraction
__ diffraction
__ scatter
__ shift
__ divert
__ preceding
__ trailing
__ lag
__ promotion
__ demotion
__ ongoing
__ setback
__ reverse
__ retract
__ convergence
__ divergence
__ focal
__ arrival
__ departure
__ destination
__ reach

__ entry
__ exit
__ intake
__ outlet
__ penetration
__ influx
__ immigration
__ emigration
__ emergence
__ emission
__ leak
__ exude
__ overpass
__ infestation
__ infringement
__ overshoot
__ success
__ failure
__ raise
__ lower
__ soaring
__ diving
__ climb
__ descend
__ stairs
__ ladder
__ elevator
__ escalator
__ ramp
__ drop
__ lift
__ stand
__ kneel
__ squat
__ sit
__ lie

__ excursion
__ detour
__ revolution
__ wheels
__ roll
__ vibration
__ fluctuation
__ pulse
__ swing
__ shake
__ disturbance
__ transport
__ cart
__ trucking
__ freight
__ shipment
__ bearer
__ porter
__ import
__ export
__ dray
__ wheelbarrow
__ pipe
__ funnel
__ express
__ post
__ bring
__ remove
__ in transit
__ vehicle
__ station
__ wagon
__ carriage
__ wheelchair
__ unicycle
__ bicycle
__ tricycle
__ motorcycle
__ pram
__ automobile
__ bus
__ taxicab
__ stagecoach
__ train
__ coach
__ box car
__ wagon-lits
__ dining car
__ streetcar
__ tractor
__ trailer
__ semitrailer
__ sled
__ snowmobile
__ ice skates
__ roller skates
__ skis
__ snowshoes
__ hovercraft
__ scooter
__ forklift

__ travel

__ tourism
__ itinerary
__ journey
__ trip
__ ride
__ drive
__ passenger
__ commuter
__ migrant
__ sailing
__ radar
__ sonar
__ loran
__ swimming
__ pilot
__ boat
__ sextant
__ latitude
__ longitude
__ wake
__ submarine
__ anchor
__ ballast
__ oar
__ paddle
__ knot
__ fathom
__ sailor
__ ship
__ vessel
__ raft
__ rigging
__ mast
__ sail
__ aviate
__ take off
__ flight
__ landing
__ airport
__ runway
__ jet propulsion
__ mach number
__ parachute
__ aircraft
__ helicopter
__ hydroplane
__ blimp
__ dirigible
__ balloon
__ glider
__ kite
__ rocketry
__ space travel
__ astronautics
__ space probe

7A

__ physics
__ nucleonics
__ science
__ thermodynamics
__ element
__ molecule
__ atom
__ nucleus
__ neutron
__ positron
__ proton
__ electron
__ ion
__ anion
__ muon
__ isotope
__ fission
__ fusion
__ critical mass
__ reactor
__ quark
__ radiation
__ cosmic ray
__ half-life
__ uranium
__ plutonium
__ radium
__ geiger counter
__ curie
__ roentgen
__ chemicals
__ reagent
__ acid
__ alkali
__ molecular weight
__ valence
__ atomic number

__ temperature
__ degree farenheit
__ degree celsius
__ degree kelvin
__ heat
__ fire
__ flame
__ ignition
__ spark
__ scintillation
__ coal
__ ember
__ cinder
__ ash
__ fireworks
__ calorie
__ BTU
__ engine
__ smoke
__ fiery

__ stove
__ furnace
__ oven
__ heating
__ boiling
__ melting
__ kindling
__ cauterizing
__ incineration
__ burn
__ scald
__ arson
__ fireplace
__ andiron
__ blowtorch
__ slag
__ coke
__ charcoal
__ soot

__ reheated
__ seared
__ galley
__ bakery
__ fuel
__ peat
__ gasoline
__ alcohol
__ kerosene
__ gas
__ propane
__ firewood
__ bagasse
__ match
__ tinder
__ fuse
__ extinguishing
__ firefighter
__ fireproofing

__ chill
__ shivers
__ freeze
__ thaw
__ frost
__ icicle
__ floe
__ iceberg
__ glacier
__ sleet
__ hail
__ hoarfrost
__ ice
__ snow
__ slush
__ refrigerate
__ arctic
__ cryogenics

__ air conditioning
__ cold storage
__ coolant
__ dry ice
__ freon
__ liquid air

7B

__ light
__ glow
__ incandescence
__ brilliance
__ splendor
__ ray
__ glitter
__ sparkle
__ daylight
__ sunlight
__ moonlight
__ starlight
__ fluorescence
__ phosphorescence
__ halo
__ rainbow
__ aurora
__ lightning
__ thunder
__ iridescence
__ photon
__ quantum
__ candle
__ prisms
__ lenses
__ lasers

__ twinkling
__ flickering
__ lit
__ lamp
__ torch
__ flare
__ traffic light
__ firefly
__ chandelier
__ wick
__ lantern
__ flashlight
__ flashbulb
__ beacon
__ lighthouse
__ stroboscope
__ fluorescent tube
__ sun glasses
__ eyeshade
__ filter
__ blinds
__ shadow
__ shade
__ blackout
__ screen
__ curtain
__ awning
__ transparency
__ opacity
__ clearness
__ translucence

__ electric current
__ amperes
__ voltage
__ electric resistance
__ ohms
__ conduction
__ reactance
__ impedance
__ capacitance
__ conductor
__ condenser
__ electric charge
__ battery
__ circuit
__ electric shock
__ magnetism
__ polarity
__ wattage
__ electrolysis
__ generator
__ motor
__ insulate
__ ground
__ meters
__ wire
__ electronics
__ vacuum tube
__ transistor
__ computer chip
__ frequency
__ band width
__ modulation
__ amplification
__ broadcasting
__ microphone
__ speaker
__ transmitter
__ receiver
__ antennas
__ audio
__ video
__ stereo
__ digital
__ analog
__ oscilloscope

__ mechanics
__ statics
__ dynamics
__ hydraulics
__ pneumatics
__ tools
__ instrument
__ apparatus
__ device
__ scissors
__ hand tool
__ machine tool
__ machinery
__ machine
__ mechanism
__ gear
__ transmission
__ clutch
__ brake
__ mechanic
__ machinist
__ hammer
__ saw
__ shovel
__ spade
__ trowel
__ plane
__ drill
__ wrench

__ mills
__ welders
__ dies
__ presses
__ lathes
__ shapers
__ pumps
__ automatic
__ control
__ feedback
__ remote control
__ servomechanism
__ control panel
__ computer
__ computer memory
__ storage
__ input
__ output
__ program
__ printout
__ friction
__ rubbing
__ abrasion
__ attrition
__ erosion
__ scraping
__ scuff
__ buff
__ burnish

__ polish
__ sanding
__ grinding
__ rasping
__ grating
__ fastening
__ pin
__ nail
__ rivet
__ screw
__ button
__ zipper
__ velcro
__ chain
__ link
__ clamp
__ latch
__ adhere
__ glue
__ rubber cement
__ paste

7C

__ texture
__ surface
__ grain
__ nap
__ weight
__ burden
__ oppressive
__ gravity
__ mass
__ gram
__ pound
__ ounce
__ ton
__ carat
__ lightness
__ buoyancy
__ levitate
__ volatility
__ leaven
__ ferment
__ yeast

__ indivisibility
__ coagulation
__ curdling
__ precipitation
__ clot
__ gel
__ tenuous

__ hard
__ soft
__ stubborn
__ temper
__ tough
__ petrify
__ stiff
__ yielding

__ elastic
__ rubber
__ springs
__ unbreakable
__ strong
__ feeble
__ fragility
__ powder
__ dust
__ crumb
__ meal
__ grate
__ shred
__ mash

__ color
__ stain
__ dye
__ paint
__ blond
__ brunette
__ redhead
__ fading
__ paleness
__ gray
__ bleached
__ white
__ albino
__ black
__ brown
__ red
__ purple
__ orange
__ yellow
__ green
__ blue
__ variegation
__ speckle

7D

__ metals
__ ore
__ alloy
__ amalgam
__ casting
__ ingot
__ mine
__ aluminum
__ brass
__ copper
__ iron
__ steel
__ gold
__ silver
__ platinum
__ mercury
__ lead
__ nickel
__ tin
__ zinc
__ bronze
__ chromium
__ pewter
__ solder
__ phosphorus
__ potassium
__ sodium
__ wood
__ fiber
__ paper
__ cloth
__ plastic
__ glass
__ ceramic

__ fluid
__ sap
__ viscosity
__ emulsion
__ mud
__ solubility
__ solution
__ solvent
__ naphtha
__ turpentine

__ helium
__ hydrogen
__ oxygen
__ nitrogen
__ carbon dioxide
__ carbon monoxide
__ neon
__ poison gas
__ laughing gas

__ lubricants
__ grease
__ graphite
__ mineral oils
__ fuel oils
__ vegetable oils
__ animal fats
__ glycerol esters
__ waxes
__ resins
__ gums

8A

__ matter

__ cosmos
__ universe
__ world
__ nature
__ heavens
__ sky
__ ether
__ outer space
__ stars
__ comets
__ pole star
__ constellation
__ galaxy
__ nebula
__ milky way
__ planet
__ earth
__ moon
__ satellite
__ sun
__ meteor
__ asteroid
__ mercury
__ venus
__ mars
__ jupiter
__ uranus
__ neptune
__ saturn
__ pluto

__ orbit
__ zodiac
__ ecliptic
__ observatory
__ planetarium
__ telescope
__ spectrum
__ astronomy
__ stargazing
__ astrology
__ extraterrestrial

__ raw materials
__ bricks
__ mortar
__ timber
__ board
__ lumber
__ fabric
__ paper
__ synthetics
__ wood
__ plastics

8B

__ inorganic matter
__ quarry
__ minerals
__ rock
__ stone
__ sand
__ gravel
__ pebble
__ boulder
__ basalt
__ chalk
__ flint
__ gneiss
__ granite
__ lava
__ marble
__ quartz
__ slate
__ sandstone
__ limestone
__ gem
__ diamond
__ ruby
__ emerald
__ amethyst
__ opal
__ coral
__ garnet
__ jade
__ lapis lazuli

__ onyx
__ chrysolite
__ sapphire
__ topaz
__ turquoise
__ zircon

__ land
__ soil
__ shore
__ geology
__ geography
__ alluvial
__ littoral
__ clay
__ silt
__ loess
__ marl
__ continent
__ mainland
__ africa
__ asia
__ europe
__ antarctica
__ south america
__ north america
__ australia
__ peninsula
__ island
__ plain
__ prairie
__ steppe
__ tundra
__ pampas
__ plateau
__ veld
__ moor
__ heath
__ mountain
__ mesa

__ moist
__ humidity
__ dew

__ spray
__ sprinkle
__ splash
__ flooding
__ irrigation
__ soaking
__ saturate
__ submerge
__ rain
__ mist
__ rainstorm
__ thunderstorm
__ wet
__ dry
__ thirst
__ stream
__ brook
__ tributary
__ river
__ current
__ torrent
__ deluge
__ trickle
__ drip
__ seep
__ rapids
__ waterfall
__ whirlpool
__ tide
__ wave
__ swell
__ surf

__ channel
__ aqueduct
__ canal
__ gutter
__ drain
__ hose
__ nozzle
__ valve
__ faucet
__ floodgate

_ sluice
_ weir
_ dam
_ lock
_ hydrant
_ vent
_ ventilator
_ chimney
_ flue
_ ocean
_ sea
_ water
_ maritime
_ lake
_ pool
_ pond
_ puddle
_ lagoon
_ reservoir
_ well
_ cistern
_ oasis
_ inlet
_ gulf
_ bay
_ fjord
_ estuary
_ straight
_ sound
_ bight
_ shallows
_ reefs
_ tidal flats
_ marsh
_ morass
_ bog
_ mire
_ quagmire

_ vapor
_ fume
_ reek
_ steam
_ gases
_ evaporation
_ ventilate
_ air
_ atmosphere
_ weather
_ climate
_ meteorology
_ forecast
_ barometer
_ wind
_ draft
_ storm
_ breeze
_ gale
_ hurricane
_ blizzard
_ cyclone
_ tornado
_ vane
_ fan
_ cloud
_ fog
_ cumulus
_ nimbus
_ haze
_ drizzle
_ cirrus
_ overcast
_ bubble
_ foam
_ lather

8C

_ organic matter
_ bio-degradable
_ flora
_ fauna
_ organism
_ cell
_ protoplasm
_ chromosome
_ gene
_ DNA
_ RNA
_ gamete
_ germ
_ sperm
_ spore
_ yolk
_ albumen

_ biology
_ bacteriology
_ biochemistry
_ physiology
_ anatomy
_ botany
_ life
_ lifeless
_ live, to live
_ die, to die

_ birth
_ death
_ bereavement
_ obituary
_ corpse
_ cadaver
_ carrion
_ autopsy
_ postmortem
_ inquest
_ expire
_ drown
_ mortal
_ perishable

_ killing
_ murder
_ assassination
_ suicide
_ asphyxiation
_ strangulation
_ fatality
_ homicide
_ burial
_ cremation
_ embalmment
_ last rites
_ wake
_ funeral
_ mortician
_ morgue
_ coffin
_ hearse
_ urn
_ cemetery
_ tomb
_ epitaph

## 8D FLORA

To some degree this section (flora) and the following section 9A (fauna) will be taxonomic. It is not intended that every single plant or creature be listed herein but even listing all of the best known ones would be beyond the space available without resorting to compounding using it linkages, affixes and POTENTS. Sex is indicated by affixing [glyph] or [glyph]; hermaphroditism by [glyph]; castration by [glyph] and spaying by [glyph]; colt, cub, kitten et al by [glyph] (child); wild (feral) by [glyph] tame (domesticated) by [glyph]; etc. Complete dendritic taxonomies with plenty of room for species yet to be discovered is possible using words of six or more letters and in which both of the first two letters are vowels. (see appendix, p. 150).

_ plants
_ weed
_ legume
_ herb
_ moss
_ wort
_ algae
_ seaweed
_ fungus
_ mold

__ lichen
__ meadow
__ lawn
__ pasture
__ shrubbery
__ tree
__ forest
__ jungle
__ grove
__ undergrowth

__ foliage
__ leaf
__ frond
__ blade
__ needle
__ petal
__ thorn
__ branch
__ twig
__ sprout
__ stem
__ trunk

__ root
__ rhizome
__ tuber
__ bulb
__ seed
__ bud
__ flower
__ nut
__ berry
__ kernel
__ verdant
__ perennial
__ annual
__ ferns

__ grass
__ grain
__ shrubs
__ vines

__ agriculture
__ farming
__ horticulture
__ garden
__ cultivation
__ sowing
__ hoeing
__ plow
__ harrow
__ harvest
__ reap
__ pick
__ gleaning

## 9A FAUNA

__ microfauna
__ zoology
__ protozoa
__ parazoa
__ metazoa
__ chordata
__ vertebrate
__ invertebrate
__ mammal
__ marsupial
__ primate
__ humans
__ biped
__ quadruped
__ ungulate
__ ruminant
__ creature
__ vermin
__ leech
__ worm
__ insect
__ beetle
__ spider
__ scorpion
__ tick
__ fly
__ bee
__ hornet
__ mosquito
__ moth
__ butterfly
__ ant
__ termite
__ locust
__ grasshopper
__ cricket
__ louse
__ flea
__ roach
__ reptile
__ lizard
__ alligator
__ turtle
__ snake
__ amphibian
__ frog
__ toad
__ bird

__ fowl
__ poultry
__ chicken
__ goose
__ duck
__ turkey
__ sea-life
__ coral
__ plankton
__ shrimp
__ fishes
__ salmon
__ minnow
__ whale
__ porpoise
__ dolphin
__ otter

__ deer
__ elk
__ moose
__ reindeer
__ antelope
__ buffalo
__ camel
__ giraffe
__ bear
__ elephant

__ canines
__ fox
__ wolf
__ coyote
__ hyena
__ dog
__ felines
__ cat
__ lion
__ tiger
__ leopard
__ rodent
__ rat
__ mouse
__ raccoon
__ opossum
__ skunk
__ hare
__ rabbit

__ horse
__ steed
__ colt
__ pony
__ ass
__ donkey
__ burro
__ mule
__ monkey
__ ape
__ gibbon
__ chimp
__ orang
__ gorilla
__ baboon
__ lemur
__ tarsier
__ animal husbandry

__ breeding
__ stock
__ pedigree
__ brood
__ rancher
__ herd
__ cattle
__ bovine
__ steer
__ ox
__ heifer
__ sheep
__ goat
__ swine
__ race
__ ethnicity
__ caucasian
__ mongoloid
__ indian
__ arabian
__ semitic
__ nilotic
__ slavic
__ nordic
__ melanesian
__ aborigine
__ bushman
__ pygmy

9B

__ cook
__ fry
__ deep-fry
__ saute
__ broil
__ bake
__ roast
__ barbecue
__ smoke
__ microwave
__ stir
__ blend
__ whip
__ fold
__ grind
__ chop
__ eating
__ feeding
__ chewing
__ bite
__ suckle
__ swallow
__ consume
__ drink
__ meal
__ breakfast
__ lunch
__ tea time
__ dinner
__ supper
__ picnic
__ feast
__ banquet
__ portion
__ menu
__ chop-sticks
__ knife
__ fork
__ spoon
__ plate
__ bowl
__ cup
__ platter
__ napkin
__ glass
__ pot
__ pan
__ skillet
__ wok
__ kettle

__ carnivore
__ cannibal
__ vegetarian
__ nourish
__ restaurant
__ course (food)
__ entre
__ desert
__ reservation
__ tip
__ ambience
__ cafeteria
__ tray
__ cafe
__ food
__ edible
__ drinkable
__ groceries
__ soup
__ broth
__ salad
__ slaw
__ stew
__ meat
__ sausages
__ eggs
__ beef
__ veal
__ mutton
__ lamb
__ pork
__ ham
__ bacon
__ steak
__ seafood
__ fish
__ shellfish
__ eel
__ roe

__ stuffing
__ cereal
__ pancakes
__ doughnuts
__ bread
__ toast
__ biscuit
__ rolls
__ pasta
__ dumplings
__ pastry
__ rice
__ wheat
__ rye
__ corn
__ oats
__ barley
__ millet
__ potato
__ vegetables
__ cabbage
__ celery
__ lettuce
__ carrot
__ beet
__ peanuts
__ avocado
__ bok choy
__ soybeans
__ yams
__ onion
__ garlic
__ leek
__ peppers
__ squashes
__ cucumbers
__ radishes
__ spinach
__ fruit
__ dates
__ figs
__ coconuts
__ oranges
__ lemons
__ tomato
__ bananas
__ apples
__ pears
__ peaches
__ apricots
__ melons

__ berries
__ grapes
__ cherries
__ nuts
__ olives
__ pimento
__ pomegranate
__ sugar
__ candy
__ jelly
__ pudding
__ ice cream
__ sherbet
__ cake
__ cookies
__ chocolate
__ butter
__ oleo
__ cheese
__ ghee
__ yogurt
__ sour cream
__ tofu
__ lard

__ water
__ juice
__ milk
__ coffee
__ tea
__ beverages
__ wine
__ beer
__ liquor
__ digestibility
__ nutrient
__ vitamin
__ carbohydrate
__ starch
__ protein
__ fats
__ enzyme
__ metabolism

9C

__ clean
__ dirty
__ sanitation
__ hygiene
__ sterilization
__ prophylactic
__ aseptic
__ pasteurization
__ cauterize
__ fumigation
__ delousing
__ washing
__ laundering
__ scrub
__ bath
__ shower
__ bathtub
__ sink
__ cleanser
__ soap
__ detergent
__ shampoo
__ mouthwash
__ toothpaste
__ purge
__ diuretic
__ swab
__ mop
__ scour
__ comb
__ wholesomeness
__ beneficial
__ harmful
__ health
__ immunity
__ resistance
__ antigen
__ well
__ sick
__ hearty
__ squalor
__ pollution

__ slime
__ toxicity
__ noxious
__ malignant

__ disease
__ disability
__ symptoms
__ pathology
__ syndrome
__ infection
__ contagion
__ virus
__ epidemic
__ plague
__ pestilence
__ seizure
__ stroke
__ convulsion
__ epilepsy
__ fever
__ prostration
__ inflammation
__ arthritis
__ gout
__ rheumatism
__ colitis
__ hepatitis
__ laryngitis
__ cholera
__ chicken pox
__ small pox
__ leprosy
__ influenza
__ malaria
__ asthma
__ mononucleosis
__ measles
__ tonsillitis
__ rabies
__ tetanus
__ conjunctivitis
__ anemia

__ common cold
__ pneumonia
__ emphysema
__ tuberculosis
__ venereal disease
__ syphilis
__ gonorrhea
__ angina
__ heart attack
__ jaundice
__ cirrhosis
__ headache
__ shock
__ ulcer
__ indigestion
__ constipation
__ diarrhea
__ nausea
__ allergy
__ eczema
__ acne
__ rash

__ lesion
__ tumor
__ cancer
__ gangrene
__ pathogen
__ microbe
__ bacteria
__ invalid
__ patient
__ cripple
__ afflict
__ cure
__ medicine
__ drug
__ dose
__ potion
__ pill
__ capsule
__ tonic
__ stimulant

__ balm
__ lotion
__ salve
__ ointment
__ unguent
__ liniment
__ medicate
__ sedative
__ tranquilizer
__ analgesic
__ sleeping pill
__ narcotic
__ opiate
__ hallucinogen
__ anesthetic
__ laxative
__ disinfectant
__ contraceptive
__ antacid
__ antidote
__ antitoxin
__ antibody
__ vaccine
__ wound dressing

__ surgery
__ dentistry
__ therapy
__ midwife
__ osteopath
__ chiropractor
__ doctor
__ physician
__ intern
__ veterinary
__ nurse
__ hospital
__ ambulance
__ radiology
__ X-ray
__ diagnosis
__ transfusion
__ operation
__ amputation
__ transplant
__ clinic
__ pharmacy
__ nursing home
__ ward
__ spa
__ medical
__ psychology
__ psychotherapy
__ psychiatry
__ psychosomatic
__ psychoanalysis
__ introvert
__ extrovert
__ neurotic
__ psychopath
__ psychotic
__ neurosis
__ inhibition
__ psyche
__ ego

__ cyst
__ rind
__ pelt
__ bark
__ hymen
__ mane
__ braid
__ pigtail
__ whiskers
__ wig
__ hairstyle
__ haircut
__ fluff
__ hairy
__ evacuation
__ vomiting
__ retching
__ hiccup
__ flatulence
__ defecation
__ dysentery
__ dung
__ festering
__ menstruation
__ spit
__ drool
__ innards
__ guts
__ bowel
__ sphincter
__ buttocks
__ physique
__ gasp
__ sniff
__ smell
__ cough
__ breath
__ spasm
__ inhalation
__ exhalation
__ puff
__ sneeze
__ resuscitation

9D

__ body
__ torso
__ back
__ chest
__ abdomen
__ skeleton
__ musculature
__ circulatory system
__ nervous system
__ lymph system
__ skin
__ head
__ face
__ neck
__ waist
__ hips
__ rump
__ arms
__ legs
__ lap
__ skull
__ mandible
__ spine
__ vertebra
__ rib
__ sternum
__ clavicle
__ scapula
__ humerus
__ ulna
__ radius
__ wrist bones
__ hand bones
__ pelvis
__ femur
__ knee cap
__ tibia
__ fibula
__ ankle bones
__ foot bones
__ shoulder
__ arm pit
__ upper arm
__ biceps
__ elbow
__ crazy bone
__ fore arm
__ wrist
__ hand
__ fist
__ palm
__ heel of the hand
__ knuckle
__ finger
__ thumb
__ index finger
__ middle finger
__ forefinger
__ little finger
__ finger nail
__ crotch

__ thigh
__ knee
__ lower leg
__ calf
__ shin
__ ankle
__ foot
__ heel
__ ball
__ arch
__ achilles tendon
__ sole
__ toe
__ big toe
__ little toe
__ pate
__ brow
__ hair
__ hair line
__ temple
__ eye brow
__ eye
__ nose
__ ear
__ cheek
__ mouth
__ lip
__ mustache
__ chin
__ beard
__ eye lid
__ eye lash
__ tear duct
__ eyeball
__ pupil
__ iris
__ lens
__ cornea
__ uvea
__ retina
__ optic nerve
__ ear lobe
__ outer ear
__ middle ear
__ inner ear
__ ear drum
__ hammer
__ anvil
__ ossicles
__ labyrinth
__ cochlea
__ auditory nerve
__ eustachian tube
__ ear wax
__ nostril
__ olfactory bulb
__ cilia
__ sinus
__ tongue
__ gums
__ hard palate
__ soft palate
__ tooth
__ incisor
__ canine
__ bicuspid
__ molar
__ taste bud
__ salivary gland
__ throat
__ tonsil
__ pharynx
__ larynx
__ esophagus
__ epiglottis
__ trachea
__ vocal chord
__ thyroid gland
__ thorax
__ lung
__ bronchi
__ diaphragm
__ heart
__ ventricle
__ valve
__ aorta
__ vena cava
__ artery
__ vein
__ capillary
__ blood
__ lymph
__ platelet
__ plasma
__ breast
__ nipple
__ alimentary canal
__ cardia
__ duodenum
__ stomach
__ small intestine
__ large intestine
__ colon
__ appendix
__ rectum
__ anus
__ kidney
__ bladder
__ urethra
__ liver
__ gall bladder
__ pancreas
__ spleen
__ viscera
__ navel
__ brain
__ frontal lobe
__ temporal lobe
__ cerebellum
__ brain stem
__ pituitary
__ hypothalamus
__ cortex
__ medulla oblongata
__ spinal chord
__ autonomous nervous system
__ nerve
__ neuron
__ synapse
__ epidermis
__ dermis
__ subcutaneous tissue
__ pore
__ sweat gland
__ follicle
__ freckle
__ birth mark
__ mole
__ wart
__ blister
__ callus
__ pimple
__ blackhead
__ burn
__ boil
__ scar
__ tattoo
__ wound
__ scab
__ penis
__ glans
__ foreskin
__ testicle
__ scrotum
__ seminal vesicle
__ prostate
__ vas deferens
__ erection
__ ejaculation
__ semen
__ pubic hair
__ intercourse
__ mound of venus
__ orgasm
__ labia
__ clitoris
__ vulva
__ vagina
__ cervix
__ uterus
__ fallopian tube
__ ovary

__ ovum
__ umbilical cord
__ placenta
__ embryo
__ fetus
__ mitosis
__ meiosis
__ miscarriage
__ abortion
__ secretion
__ excretion
__ hormone
__ endocrine
__ bile
__ saliva
__ mucous
__ urine
__ feces
__ sweat
__ tear
__ sputum
__ phlegm
__ marrow
__ bones
__ cartilage
__ ligament
__ tendon
__ muscle
__ fat
__ flesh
__ tissue
__ nails
__ right
__ left
__ right handed
__ left handed
__ physical
__ craw
__ gullet
__ tusk
__ snout
__ muzzle
__ antler

__ horn
__ trunk
__ tail
__ wing
__ fin
__ fluke
__ flipper
__ talon
__ paw
__ claw
__ pad
__ hoof
__ hide
__ fur
__ fleece
__ feather
__ quill
__ down
__ fuzz
__ plume
__ scale
__ udder
__ pouch
__ gill
__ blow hole
__ carcass

10A

__ sensation
__ sense
__ sensibility
__ sensitivity
__ insensitivity
__ susceptible
__ receptive
__ aware
__ conscious
__ unconscious
__ numb
__ faint
__ stupor
__ stunned
__ pain

__ distress
__ hurt
__ pang
__ twinge
__ sting
__ ache
__ agony
__ anguish
__ torment
__ torture
__ inflamed
__ tender
__ sore
__ raw
__ throbbing

__ rub
__ touch
__ caress
__ manipulate
__ stroke
__ pet
__ lick
__ tactile
__ brush
__ massage
__ tingle
__ prickle
__ itch
__ gooseflesh
__ sex
__ sexuality
__ sexual preference
__ heterosexuality
__ bisexuality
__ homosexuality
__ lesbianism
__ sadism
__ masochism
__ incest
__ sodomy
__ masturbate
__ aphrodisiac

__ taste
__ savor
__ unsavoriness
__ flavor
__ tang
__ zest
__ gusto
__ seasoning
__ condiment
__ spice
__ salt
__ pepper
__ sweet
__ sour
__ honey
__ nectar
__ cloying
__ inedible
__ tasteless

__ bitter
__ tartness
__ dryness
__ vinegar
__ pickle
__ pungency
__ piquancy
__ saltiness
__ rank
__ gamey
__ acrid

__ tobacco
__ cigar
__ cigarette
__ pipe
__ chewing tobacco
__ snuff
__ nicotine
__ smoking
__ stink
__ fetidness
__ mustiness

__ odorous
__ odorless
__ scent
__ sniff
__ fragrance
__ perfume
__ aroma
__ bouquet
__ incense
__ sachet

10B

__ vision
__ sight
__ eyesight
__ watching
__ viewing
__ notice
__ glance
__ gaze
__ stare
__ wink
__ behold
__ witness
__ glare
__ defective vision
__ astigmatism
__ nearsighted
__ farsighted
__ squint
__ cross-eyed
__ tunnel vision
__ blindness
__ blind spot
__ day blindness
__ night blindness
__ color blindness
__ braille
__ blindfolded

__ spectator
__ sight-seeing
__ optical instruments
__ spectacles
__ contact lenses
__ field glasses
__ opera glasses
__ binoculars
__ mirror
__ optics
__ optometry
__ oculist
__ ophthalmologist
__ microscope
__ spectroscopes
__ visibility
__ invisibility
__ distinct
__ indistinct
__ conspicuous
__ inconspicuous
__ apparent
__ hidden
__ blurred
__ phantom

__ hearing
__ audience
__ interview
__ conference
__ eavesdrop
__ earshot
__ sound
__ hearing aid
__ megaphone
__ otology
__ deafness
__ sound
__ acoustics
__ sonics
__ decibel
__ headset
__ phonograph
__ public address system
__ bull horn
__ tape rec.
__ digital recording

__ quiet
__ mute
__ dumb
__ muffle
__ gag
__ soundproofing
__ inaudible
__ tacit
__ implicit
__ thud
__ patter
__ whisper
__ murmur
__ undertone
__ humming
__ rustle
__ sigh
__ mutter
__ moan
__ whine
__ loud
__ noise
__ blast
__ racket
__ noisemaker
__ resonance
__ sonority
__ rumble
__ echo

__ ring
__ tinkle
__ repeated sounds
__ staccato
__ beat
__ clicking
__ ticking
__ rattle
__ detonation
__ boom
__ pop
__ burst
__ hissing
__ shrillness
__ hoarseness
__ scream
__ squeal
__ squawk
__ calling
__ crying
__ yelling
__ cheering
__ shouting
__ animal sounds

10C

__ clothing
__ pocket
__ sewing
__ needle
__ sewing machine
__ stitch
__ seam
__ baste
__ buttonhole
__ collar
__ lapel
__ pleat
__ crochet
__ embroider
__ hemstitch
__ needlepoint
__ dress
__ frock
__ costume
__ wardrobe
__ suit
__ uniform
__ mufti
__ cloak
__ coat
__ jacket
__ overcoat
__ topcoat
__ waistcoat

__ vest
__ shirt
__ skirt
__ apron
__ trousers
__ belt
__ diaper
__ negligee
__ nightwear
__ underwear
__ lingerie
__ corset
__ girdle
__ brassiere
__ loincloth
__ millinery
__ cap
__ hat
__ kerchief
__ veil
__ footwear
__ shoes
__ boots
__ sandals
__ socks
__ stocking
__ bathing suit
__ children's wear
__ tailoring
__ sweaters
__ pants
__ bathrobe
__ kimono
__ gloves
__ leggings

__ thread
__ strand
__ cord
__ string
__ twine
__ knot
__ rope
__ hawser
__ cable
__ ribbon
__ tape
__ cotton
__ canvas
__ silk
__ wool
__ linen
__ rayon
__ nylon
__ dacron
__ polyester
__ leather
__ felt
__ yarn
__ undress
__ molt
__ shedding
__ baldness
__ peel
__ strip
__ husk
__ flake
__ nudity
__ barefoot

__ house
__ home
__ household
__ hearth
__ building
__ homestead
__ mansion
__ villa
__ chateau
__ palace
__ bungalow
__ cabin
__ shack
__ shed
__ tent
__ apartment
__ inn
__ hotel
__ motel
__ dormitory
__ mobile home
__ motor home
__ greenhouse
__ barn
__ stable
__ doghouse
__ coop
__ aviary
__ nest
__ den
__ resort
__ cave
__ camp
__ barracks
__ house boat

__ room
__ cell
__ hallway
__ living room
__ bedroom
__ dining room
__ playroom
__ natatorium
__ kitchen
__ pantry
__ storeroom
__ closet
__ attic
__ basement
__ corridor
__ vestibule
__ threshold
__ porch
__ balcony
__ floor
__ ceiling
__ wall
__ door
__ window
__ transom
__ bathroom
__ garage
__ carport

__ furniture
__ chest
__ drawer
__ seat
__ table
__ chair
__ counter
__ shelf
__ refrigerator
__ freezer
__ couch
__ bed
__ bunk
__ bedding
__ blanket
__ bedspread
__ quilt
__ mattress
__ pillows
__ sheet
__ pillowcase
__ rug
__ carpet
__ mat
__ upholstery
__ cushions
__ armchair
__ sofas
__ daybed
__ bassinet
__ crib
__ cot
__ cradle
__ hammock
__ pallet
__ water bed

10Dcvc

__ doer; one who does the action
__ recipient, object of the action
__ initiator of
__ creator of something
__ destroyer of
__ device for
__ maker of the device that does the action
__ caretaker of the device
__ operator of a device that does the action
__ practitioner of
__ artist in
__ artisan in or of, -smith
__ artiste (professional performer)
__ manager, executive
__ one connected with or belonging to
__ intern, apprentice
__ amateur, dilettante
__ study of something
__ facts regarding something; conceptual
__ purpose, use, application of
__ user of, consumer
__ maker of
__ industry, trade in something
__ vendor of
__ fancier, lover of
__ fear, dread of
__ place where the action occurs
__ place where something is made
__ place where something is stored or sold
__ place where something is used
__ teacher of
__ student of
__ promoter of
__ possessor of
__ player, participant
__ enthusiast, fan of
__ heavy
__ light
__ dense
__ thin
__ rich in
__ poor in
__ open
__ closed
__ original
__ copy of
__ genuine
__ fake
__ subtle
__ obvious
__ overt
__ secret
__ true
__ false
__ actual
__ virtual
__ real
__ unreal
__ natural
__ artificial
__ torrid
__ frigid
__ hot
__ cold
__ warm
__ cool
__ liquid
__ viscous
__ thin
__ molten
__ solid
__ vaporous, ephemeral
__ logical
__ illogical
__ orderly
__ chaotic
__ stationary, fixed
__ portable
__ rich
__ poor
__ light
__ dark
__ bright
__ dim
__ intense
__ mild
__ re-; see again
__ ex-; former
__ de-; out of
__ vice-; substitute
__ -ic;-al; pertaining to
__ -ish; like
__ -ern;-ese; of or relating to
__ -ed; of that nature, characteristic
__ -ly; similar in manner
__ -ful; tending, able to
__ -tude; state, quality
__ -ant; -ent; agency
__ -parous; bearing
__ -mony; result; abstract condition
__ -fy, -ify; to make, form into
__ -facient; making, causing
__ -ade; denotes action or product
__ -escent; beginning to be
__ -ice; state, characteristic
__ -ar, -ary, in the nature of
__ -ness; quality
__ -hood; state, condition
__ -esque, style
__ -ate; result of action
__ -ance, -ence
__ -ity; condition
__ -osity; excessive condition
__ -en; appearance, made of
__ -ory; having the effect of
__ -worthy
__ -able; capable of
__ uni-; mono-; single
__ bi-; dual
__ tri-; triple
__ multi-; many
__ ambi-; both
__ -ility; makes abstract nouns from adjectives
__ function
__ mentor
__ protege
__ relative to
__ -cracy
__ -crat
__ peace
__ war
__ patriotic
__ speaker, auditor, reader, writer of

10Dcvv

__ amount
__ abounding
__ rare
__ sufficient
__ lacking
__ much
__ little
__ superfluous, beyond need
__ devoid of
__ more
__ less
__ most
__ least
__ semi, hemi, demi
__ usual
__ unusual
__ limited
__ infinite
__ exceeding
__ short of
__ exactly
__ approximately
__ maximum
__ minimum
__ hyper
__ hypo
__ superior
__ inferior
__ surpassing, out-

— falling short
— succeeding
— failing
— variety, misc-
— uniformity
— throughout
— about
— almost
— macro
— micro
— ultra
— infra
— sorted
— mixed
— homogeneous
— heterogeneous
— equal
— unequal
— completely
— partially
— both
— including
— excluding
— capacity
— volume
— full, -ous
— empty
— degree
— scale
— still
— though
— match
— grand
— very
— glory
— heroic
— craven
— remarkable
— nice
— awful
— extreme
— major
— minor

— better
— worse
— best
— worst
— increase
— decrease
— expand
— contract
— grow
— diminish
— intensify
— weaken
— simple
— complex
— pure
— impure
— easy
— difficult
— plain
— ornate
— unite
— splinter
— connect
— disconnect
— repetition
— free
— fixed
— tight
— loose
— intact
— broken
— cut
— separate
— bit
— in
— out
— quite

— factor
— element
— detail
— whole
— part

— harmony
— discord
— form
— arrangement
— disarrangement
— sort
— shuffle
— grade
— first
— last
— finished
— unfinished
— continuity
— discontinuity
— change
— contain
— common
— uncommon
— general
— specific
— special
— quality
— expert
— list
— unit
— individual
— only
— guide
— pair
— copy
— half
— split
— meeting
— group
— band

DIMENSIONS

— length
— width
— sideways
— area
— height
— depth

— thick
— thin
— cubic
— diameter
— radians
— perimeter
— arc
— degree
— minute
— second
— distance
— AU, astronomical unit
— LY, lightyear
— MLY, million lightyears
— BLY, billion lightyears

DIRECTION

— near
— far
— abutting
— apart
— contiguous
— noncontiguous
— direction
— toward
— away from
— forward
— backward
— go over
— go under
— go through
— go around
— -ways
— -wise
— into
— out of
— upward
— downward
— rotation
— spin
— parallel to
— diverging from
— across

_ crossing
_ leaving
_ returning
_ approaching
_ receding
_ leading
_ following
_ inward
_ outward
_ rising
_ falling
_ clockwise
_ counterclockwise
_ diagonally
_ athwart
_ this side of
_ that side of
_ ahead
_ behind
_ atop
_ beneath
_ over
_ under
_ up
_ down

LOCATION

_ inside of
_ outside of
_ here
_ there
_ in situ
_ on
_ off
_ enclose
_ source; -head
_ terminus
_ foremost
_ hindmost
_ front
_ back
_ top
_ bottom
_ side
_ corner
_ edge
_ interior
_ exterior
_ above
_ below
_ high
_ low
_ inner
_ outer
_ between
_ among
_ alongside
_ middle, centered
_ surrounding
_ around, peripheral

SHAPE

_ large
_ small
_ straight
_ bowed
_ rectangle
_ square
_ multifaceted
_ pyramid
_ cube
_ ovate, solid
_ cruciform
_ crescent
_ stellate
_ -form
_ plane

Pages 105 through 146 are the index to the preliminary vocabulary. The computer sorting program gives precedence to punctuation and Arabic numerals. Starred entries indicate duplication of the English equivalent; not of the ⊦⅃Γ2ₓ word. Many English words have several meanings, but ⊦⅃Γ2ₓ words have only one which is determined by its first two letters.

If the vocabulary equivalents in the previous section (pages 67 to 103) had been given in some language other than English the index would then be in that language providing, of course, that the computer program and the printer are able to handle that language. The same is true for the spreadsheets.

-able; capable of
-ade; denotes action or product
-ance, -ence
-ant; -ent; agency
-ar, -ary, in the nature of
-ate; result of action
-cracy
-crat
-ed; of that nature, characteristic
-en; appearance, made of
-ern;-ese; of or relating to
-escent; beginning to be
-esque, style
-facient; making, causing
-form
-ful; tending, able to
-fy, -ify; to make, form into
-hood; state, condition
-ic;-al; pertaining to
-ice; state, characteristic
-ility; makes abstract nouns from adjectives
-ish; like
-ity; condition
-ly; similar in manner
-mate; play, team etc.
-mony; result; abstract condition
-ness; quality
-ory; having the effect of
-osity; excessive condition
-parous; bearing
-tude; state, quality
-ways
-wise
-worthy
1st bracket
1st person
1st sub-quote
2nd bracket
2nd person
2nd sub-quote, or 'a set-off' if not in a standing quotation
3rd bracket
3rd person (definite forms)
3rd person indefinite
'sounds like', 'rhymes with'
a la
a
abandon
abbey
abbreviation
abdication, abandon
abdomen
abet
able
aborigine
abortion
abounding
about
above
abrasion
abridge
absent
abstain
abuse
abutting
academic degree
academy
acceleration
accent
accept
accession
accessory
accident
accomplice
according to
accordion
account
accuse
ache
achievement
achilles tendon
acid
acne
acoustics
acquaintance
acquisition
acquittal
acrid
across
act
★ act
active
actor
actual
ad infinitum
ad nauseam
adamant
add
addiction
address
adequate
adhere
adjective
adjustment
administration
admiral
admirer
admit
adopted
adore

adult
adultery
advance
advantageous
adventure
adverb
Advertisement
advice
advisability
advocate
aesthetics
affix
afflict
africa
after
afternoon
again
against
age
agent
agility
agitation
agnosticism
agony
agrarian
agree
agriculture
ahead
aid
aide
aim
air conditioning
air force
air lane
air
aircraft
airport
aka
alarm
albino
albumen
alcohol
alderman
algae
algebra
alibi
alien
alimentary canal
alkali
all the best to you
all
allegation
allegiance
allergy
alley
alliance
alligator
alloy
alluvial
almost
alongside
alphabet
altar
alternately
alto
aluminum
alumnus
always
amalgam
amateur, dilettante
amazement
ambassador
ambi-; both
ambience
ambiguity
ambition
ambulance
AMENITIES 2
AMENITIES 3
AMENITIES 4
amethyst
ammunition
amnesty
among
amount
amperes
amphibian
amplification
amputation
amusement
analgesic
analog
analogy
analysis
anarchy
anatomy
ancestor
anchor
and, for pairing
and
⋆ and
and/or
⋆ and/or
andiron
anemia
anesthetic
angels
angina
angle, angularity
angry
anguish
animal fats
animal husbandry
animal sounds
animals', bulls', etc.
animals', cows', etc.
animations
anion
ankh
ankle bones
ankle
annihilation
anniversary
annoy
annual
annuity
annul
anointing
answer
ant
antacid
antarctica
antelope
antennas
anthem
anthology
antibody
anticipate
antidote
antigen
antipodal
antitoxin
antler
antonym
anus
anvil
anxiety
any

aorta
apart from
apart
apartment
ape
aphrodisiac
apology
apostles
apparatus
apparent
appeal
appear
appeasement
appendix
appetite
applause
apples
appliances
appointment
approaching
appropriate
approval
approximately
apricots
apron
aqueduct
arabian
arbitrary, uncategorized, (expands meaning by rote)
arc
arch
★ arch
archbishop
architecture
archives
arctic
area measures
area
arena
argument
aria
aristocracy
arithmetic
arm pit
armchair
armistice
armor
armory
arms
army
aroma
around, peripheral
arrangement
★ arrangement
arrest
arrival
arrogance
arrow
arson
art
artery
arthritis
article
articulate
artifact
artifice
artificial
artillery
artisan in or of, -smith
artist in
artiste (professional performer)
as in
as it were
as
ascetic
aseptic
ash
asia
askance
asleep
asphyxiation
ass
assassination
assay
assembly
assessment
assets
assignment
associate
assumption
assure
asterisk; with numerals for footnotes or with single letters for instructions; also an aside
asteroid
asthma
astigmatism
astronautics
astrology
astronomy
astute
asymmetry
asynchronous
at
atheism
athletics
athwart
atlas
atmosphere
atom
atomic number
atonement
atop
atrocity
attache
attack
attainder
attempt
attendance
attention
attic
attorney
attraction
attribution, not an exact quotation
attrition
AU, astronomical unit
auction
audience
audio
auditing
auditory nerve
aunt
aurora
austerity
australia
author
authority
autobiography
automatic
automobile
autonomous nervous system
autopsy
autumn
available
average
aviary
aviate
avocado

bi-; dual
bias
bible
bibliography
biceps
bicuspid
bicycle
big toe
bigamist
bight
bigness
bigot
bile
bill
billion years ago
binary
binding
binoculars
bio-degradable
biochemistry
biography
biology
biped
bird
birth mark
birth
birthday
biscuit
bisexuality
bishop
bit
bite
bitter
black
blackhead
blacklist
blackmail
blackout
bladder
blade
★ blade
blame
blanket
blasphemy
blast
bleached
blemish
blend
★ blend
blessing
blight
blimp
blind spot
blindfolded
blindness
blinds
blissful
blister
blizzard
block
blockage
blond
blood
blow hole
blow
blowtorch
blue
bluff
blurred
bluster
BLY, billion lightyears
board
boastful
boat
body
bodyguard
bog
boil
boiling
bok choy
bold
bomb
bombard
bon chance
bonds
bones
bonus
bonze
book
bookkeeping
bookstore
boom
boor
boots
border
bore
borrowing
botany
both
bottleneck
bottles
bottom
boulder
bounce
bouquet
bovine
bow, hair
bow
★ bow
bowed
bowel
bowl
box car
box
boy
brace
bracket
braid
braiding
braille
brain stem
brain
brake
branch
brand
brass
brassiere
bravery
brazenness
breach
bread
breakfast
breast
breath
breeding
breeze
brewery
bribery
bricks
bride
bridegroom
bridge
brigade
bright
brilliance
bring
brink
broadcasting

broil
broken
broker
bronchi
bronze
brood
brook
broth
brothel
brother
brotherhood
brow
brown
bruise
brunette
brush
brutal
BTU
bubble
bucket
bud
buddhism
budgeting
buff
buffalo
buffer
bugle
build
building
bulb
bulge
bull horn
bullet
bulletin
bully
bump
bumper
bungalow
bungle
bunk
bunker
buoyancy
burden
bureau
bureaucracy
burglary
burial
burlesque
burn
★ burn
burnish
burro
burrow
burst
bus
bushman
business company
business
busy
but
★ but
butter
butterfly
buttocks
button
buttonhole
buttress
buyer
by permission
by-product
c.f.
cabaret
cabbage
cabin
cabinet secretary
cabinet
cable
cadaver
cafe
cafeteria
cake
calculating
calculus
calendar
calf
calligraphy
calling
callous
callus
calm
calorie
camel
cameo
camera
camp
campaign
can
canal
cancer
candidate
candle
candy
cane
canine
canines
cannibal
canvas
cap
capacitance
capacity
capillary
capital
capitalism
capitol
capstan
capsule
captain
capture
carat
carbohydrate
carbon dioxide
carbon monoxide
carcass
card
cardia
cardinal number
cardinal
care
carelessness
caress
caretaker of the device
caricature
carillon
carnival
carnivore
carpet
carport
carriage
carrion
carrot
cart
cartel
cartilage
cartoon
cartridge
carve
cases
cashier

construction
consul
consume
contact lenses
contact
contagion
contain
container
contemporary
contempt
contentment
contents
context
contiguous
continent
continue
continuity
contradiction
contraband
contraceptive
contract
★ contract
contrary
contrast
contribute
control panel
control
convenient
convent
convention
convergence
conversation
convexity
conveyance
conviction
conviviality
convolution
convulsion
cook
cookies
cool
coolant
coop
cooperation
copper
copulate
copy of
copy
copyright
coral
★ coral
cord
cordial
corn
cornea
corner
cornet
corporal
corporation
corpse
correct
correlate
corridor
corruption
corset
cortex
cosecant
cosine
cosmic ray
cosmos
costume
cot
cotangent
cotton
couch
cough
could
council
counter
counterattack
counterclockwise
counterpoint
counting
country
county seat
course (food)
course (route)
course of study
court case
court hearing
court house
courtesy, honor m/f
courtesy
cousin
cousine
cousins
cover
covering
cowardice
★ cowardice
coyness
coyote
cozy
crack
cradle
craft
crash
crate
crater
craven
craw
crawl
crazy bone
crease
create
creator of something
creator
creature
credit
★ credit
cremation
crescent
crib
cricket
crime
cripple
crisscross
criterion
critical mass
criticism
crochet
crockery
crooked
croon
crop
cross-eyed
cross
crossing
crossroad
crosswalk
crosswise
crotch
crowbar
crown
cruciform
crude
cruelty
crumb

crush
crust
crying
cryogenics
cube of
cube root of
cube
cubic
cucumbers
cult
cultivated
cultivation
culture
cum
cumulus
cunning
cup
cupboards
curdling
cure
curie
curly
currency
current
curse
curtailment
curtain
curve
cushions
custodian
custody
custom
customer
cut
cuz m/f
cyclone
cylinder
cymbals
cynicism
cyst
dacron
dam
damage
damnable
dance
danger
dangle
dark
dash
data
dates
dating
daughter
dawn
day blindness
day
daybed
daylight
de-; out of
dead
deafness
deal
dean
dear
death
debase
debate
debauchery
debentures
debit
debt
decade
deceit
deceleration
decent
deception
decibel
decimal
decision
declare
decode
decoration
decrease
decree
dedicate
deed
⋆ deed
deep-fry
deepness
deer
deface
default
defeat
defecation
defect
defection
defective vision
defendant
defense
defiance
definitely
definition
deflection
deform
defy
degree celsius
degree farenheit
degree kelvin
degree
⋆ degree
deity
delay
delegates
delicate
delightful
delivery
delousing
deluge
delusion
demand
demigods
demobilize
democracy
demonstrate
demons
demoral(ize)
demotion
demur
demureness
den
denial
denomination
dense
dent
dentistry
departments
departure
dependence
deplore
deploy
deposit
depositions
deprecate
depreciate
depression
depth
deputy
derelict

derision
dermis
descend
descendent
describe
desecration
desert
design
desire
desk
despair
desperation
despicable
destination
destiny
destitution
destroyer of
destruction
detail
detective
detergent
deterrent
detest
detonation
detour
develop
development
★ development
deviant
deviation
device for
device
devil
devoid of
devote
devotee
devotion
dew
diagnosis
diagonally
diagram
dialect
diameter
diamond
diaper
diaphragm
diarrhea
diary
dictator
dictionary
did
die, to die
dies
diet
difference
different
difficult
difficulty
diffraction
digestibility
digger
digital recording
digital
dignified
dignity
dilemma
diligence
dim
dimensions
diminish
dimple
dining car
dining room
dinner
diocese
diploma
diplomat
direction
★ direction
directness
directory
dirigible
dirty
disability
disable
disagree
disappear
disappoint
disarmament
disarrangement
disaster
disbelief, incredulity
discard
disciples
discipline
disclosure
discomfort
disconnect
discontinuity
discord
discount
discourage
discover
discretion
discussion
disease
disgrace
disguised
disgusting
disinfectant
dislike
dismantle
dismiss
dismissal
display
disprove
disrepute
disrespect
dissent
dissolute
distance
distention
distillery
distinct
distinction
distort
distraction
distress
distribution
district
disturbance
ditch
ditto
diuretic
divergence
diverging from
diverse
divert
divide
dividends
divination
diving
divinity
division
★ division
divorced m/f
divulge
DNA

do
dock
doctor
doctrine
document
documentary
doer; one who does the action
dog
doghouse
dogma
doll
dolphin
dominance
dominant
donkey
doom
door
doorkeeper
dormitory
dose
doubt
doughnuts
down
★ down
downfall
downward
dowry
draft
drain
drama
drawback
drawer
drawing
dray
dread
dress
drill
★ drill
drink
drinkable
drip
drive
drizzle
drool
drooping
drop
drown
drudge
drug
drum
dry goods
dry ice
dry
dryness
duck
duke
dullness
★ dullness
dumb
dumplings
dung
duodenum
duress
during
dusk
dust
duty
dwell
dye
dynamics
dysentery
e.g.
each
eager
ear drum
ear lobe
ear wax
ear
early
earn
earnings
earshot
earth
ease
east
easter
easy
eat
eating
eavesdrop
echo
eclipse
ecliptic
ecstacy
ectoplasm
eczema
edge
edible
edict
edit
edition
editor
editorial
education
eel
effect
effective
eggs
ego
egotist
eh?
either
either/or
ejaculation
elastic
elbow
elder
electioneering
electorate
electric charge
electric current
electric resistance
electric shock
electroplate
electrolysis
electron
electronic keyboard
electronics
elegance
element
★ element
elements
elephant
elevator
eligibility
elk
ellipse
ellipsis
elsewhere
embalmment
embargo
embarrass
ember
emblem
embossment
embroider
embryo
emerald

explore
explosion
export
express
expression
extender
extension
exterior
extinct
extinguishing
extortion
extrasensory
extraterrestrial
extreme
extrovert
extrusion
exude
exult
eye brow
eye lash
eye lid
eye
eyeball
eyeshade
eyesight
fabric
face
fact
factor
factory
facts regarding something; conceptual
faculty
fading
failing
failure
faint
fair
fairness
fairy
faith
fake
fall
fallacy
falling short
falling
fallopian tube
false
familiar
family chief
family name
family
fan
fanaticism
fancier, lover of
fantasy
far
farce
farming
farsighted
fascination
fashion
fast
fastening
fastidious
fasting
fat
fatality
fate
father
fathom
fats
faucet
faultless
fauna
favor
fax
fear, dread of
fear
feast
feather
feature
feces
federal
fee
feeble
feedback
feeding
feel
felines
fellowship
felony
felt
female animal, e.g. hen.
female ego
females, ewes, etc.
feminine
femur
fence
ferment
ferns
fertile
fertilizer
fervor
festering
fetidness
fetishism
fetter
fetus
fever
few
fiance
fiber
fibula
fickleness
fiction
field glasses
field
fiery
fife
fight
figs
figuratively
figure
filibuster
filling
film
filter
fin
final statement
finale
finance
find
fine arts
fine
finger nail
finger
finished
fire
firefighter
firefly
fireplace
fireproofing
firewood
fireworks
firmness
first
fish

★ fish
fishes
fission
fist
fitness
fix, repair
fixed
fjord
flag
flake
flame
flare
flashbulb
flashlight
flat
flatness
flats
flatter
flatulence
flavor
flea
flee
fleece
fleet
fleeting
flesh
flexibility
flexure
flickering
flight
flint
flipper
flirtation
floe
floodgate
flooding
floor show
floor
★ floor
flora
flower
fluctuation
flue
fluent
fluff
fluid
fluke
fluorescence
fluorescent tube
flute
fly
foam
focal
fog
fold
★ fold
foliage
folk arts
folk music
folklore
folkway
follicle
follower, disciple
following core is dominant, used between cores and after prefixes
following
font
food
fool
foolish
foot bones
foot
footing
footwear
for the purpose of
for, substitution
for
forbearing
forbid
force
★ force
fore arm
forecast
foreclosure
forefinger
foremost
forenoon
foresight
foreskin
forest
forever
forgery
forget
forgive
fork
forklift
forlorn
form
★ form
formality
FORMS OF ADDRESS 1
FORMS OF ADDRESS 2
FORMS OF ADDRESS 3
formula
fornication
fortification
fortnight
fortunate
forum
forward
foul
foundation
★ foundation
foundry
fowl
fox
fraction
fraction; per; divided by, in math
fragility
fragrance
frailty
frame
franchise
fraternity
fraud
fray
freckle
free lance
free person
free will
free
freedom
freeze
freezer
freight
french horn
frenzy
freon
frequency
frequent
fresh
friction
friend
frigid
fringe
frock
frog

helix
hell
hello, are you there?
hello
help
hemstitch
hepatitis
her, animal
her, she
her
herb
herd
here goes
here
heredity
heresy
hero
heroic
herself, animal
herself
hesitation
heterosexuality
heterodoxy
heterogeneous
hiatus
hibernate
hiccup
hidden
hide
hideous
hierarchy
high priest
high school
high-schooler
high
hijacking
him, he
himself, animal
himself
hindmost
hindrance
hips
his, animal
his
hissing
history
hit
hoarfrost
hoarseness
hoeing
hold
hole
holiday
holiness
hollowness
holy days
home
homely
homesickness
homestead
homicide
homosexuality
homogeneous
hone
honesty
honey
honeymoon
honor
honorific
honors
hoof
hook
hope
horizon
horizontalness
hormone
horn
★ horn
hornet
horse
horsepower
horticulture
hose
hospital
hospitality
host
hostage
hostility
hot
hotel
hour
house boat
house
★ house
household
housewares
hovercraft
how
hug
huge
hull
hum
human rights
humanism
humans
humerus
humidity
humility
humming
humor
humoring
hump
hunger
hunt
hurdy-gurdy
hurricane
hurt
husband
husk
hydrant
hydraulics
hydrogen
hydroplane
hyena
hygiene
hymen
hymn
hyper
hypo
hypocrisy
hypothalamus
I, me
i.e.
ibid
ice cream
ice skates
ice
iceberg
icicle
iconoclasm
idea
ideal
idealism
identification
idiom
idle
idolatry
if, conditional

if?
ignition
ignorance
ignore
ill humored
illegal
illegibility
illicit
illogical
illusion
illustrate
illustration
image
imagination
imagine
imam
immigration
immodest
immolation
immorality
immunity
imp
impact
impartial
impassive
impatient
impeachment
impedance
impel
imperious
impiety
implicit
imply
import
important
imposition
impossibility
impregnable
imprison
improper
improvise
impudence
impulsive
impure
in a like manner
in situ
in transit
in trust
in-law coparent
in
inaction
inaudible
incandescence
incantation
incense
incest
incineration
incisor
including
income
incompetent
inconspicuous
increase
incredible
incredulity
incurable
indecency
indeed
indenture
independence
index finger
index
indian
indicate
indictment
indifferent
indigestion
indistinct
individual
indivisibility
induction
indulgence
industrial plant
industry, trade in something
inedible
ineffective
inertness
inevitable
infantry
infatuation
infection
infer
inferior
infestation
infidel
infidelity
infinite
infinitive
inflamed
inflammation
inflection
inflict
influence
influenza
influx
infra
infraction
infringement
ingenious
ingot
ingredients
inhalation
inheritance
inhibition
initiative
initiator of
injection
injunction
injury
injustice
ink
inland
inlet
inn
innards
inner ear
inner
inorganic matter
input
inquest
inquiry
insect
insensitivity
insertion
inside of
insolence
inspection
inspector
inspiration
instinctive
instrument
instrumentation
insulate
insult
insurance policy
insurance
insurgency
insurrection

intact
intake
intangible
intellect
intelligence
intelligible
intemperance
intense
intensify
intent
intention
intermediate
interpretation
intercom
intercourse
interest
★ interest
interference
interior
intermediary
intermission
intermittent
intern, apprentice
intern
interruption
intersection
interval
interview
interweaving
intimate
intimidation
into
intolerant
intone
intoxication
introduce
introvert

intrusion
intuit
intuitive
invalid
invasion
invective
invention
inventory
inversion
invertebrate
investment
invisibility
invite
invocation
invoice
involve
inward
ion
iridescence
iris
iron
irony
irregularity
irrelevant
irreligious
irrigation
islam
island
isolation
isotope
it (animal)
★ it (animal)
it (inanimate tangible)
★ it (inanimate tangible)
it (intangible)
it, thing (intangible)
itch

item
itinerary
its, animal
itself, animal
itself
jacket
jade
jaundice
jealous
jelly
jerk
jest
jet propulsion
jewel
jinx
job
join
joke
jostle
journey
journeyman
joyful
judaism
judge
judicial
judiciary
juice
jump
jungle
junior high sch.
junk
junta
jupiter
jurisdiction
juror
justice
kazoo

keen
keep
kerchief
kernel
kerosene
kettle
key
★ key
kick
kidney
killing
kiln
kimono
kind
★ kind
kindergarten
kindling
king
kingdom
kiss
kitchen
kite
knee cap
knee
kneel
knife
knight
knot
★ knot
know
knowledge
knuckle
koran
label
labia
labor union
labor

laboratory
labyrinth
lacing
lacking
lad
ladder
ladles
lag
lagoon
laity
lake
lama
lamb
lament
lamp
lampoon
land
landing
landlord
language
lantern
lap
lapel
lapis lazuli
lard
large intestine
large
laryngitis
larynx
lasers
lass
last rites
last
lasting
latch
late
later
lather
lathes
latitude
laugh
laughing gas
laundering
laurels
lava
lavish
law
lawless
lawn
laxative
layer
lazy
lead
★ lead
leading
leaf
leak
leaning
leanness
learning
lease
least
leather
leaven
leaving
lectern
lecture
ledger
leech
leek
leeward
left handed
left
legacy
legal tender
legal
leggings
legibility
legislature
legitimacy
legs
legume
leisure
lemons
lemur
lending
length
leniency
lens
lenses
leopard
leprosy
lesbianism
lesion
less than
less
lesson
let
lethargic
letter
★ letter
lettuce
levelness
leverage
levitate
levity
lewd
liability
liar
libel
liberal arts
liberalism
library
libretto
license
lichen
lick
lid
lie
lien
lieutenant
life
lifeless
lift
ligament
light
★ light
★ light
lighthouse
lightness
lightning
like
★ like
limestone
limited
line, linear
line
linear measures
linen
lingerie
linguistic group
linguistics
liniment
link
links cores of equal importance; minus in math; as a dash with full spaces fore and aft.
lion
lip

liquid air
liquid
liquidate
liquor
lisp
list
listen
lit
lithography
little finger
little toe
little
littleness
littoral
liturgy
live, to live
lively
liver
living room
living
lizard
load
★ load
loathsome
lobby
local
location
lock
★ lock
lockout
locust
lodgings
loess
logical
logo
loincloth
longitude

look
lookout
loom
loop
loose
looting
loran
lordship
lore
lose
loss
lotion
loud
louse
love
lovemaking
lover
low
lower leg
lower
lowness
loyal
lubricants
luck
luggage
lullaby
lumber
lunch
lung
lurk
lustful
luxury
LY, lightyear
lying
lymph system
lymph
mach number

machine shop
machine tool
machine
machinery
machinist
macro
magazine
magic
magistrate
magnet
magnetism
mail
mailbox
mainland
maintain
majesty
major
★ major
★ major
make
maker of the device that does the action
maker of
makeshift
malaria
male animal, e.g. cock.
male ego
males, rams, etc.
malice
malignant
maltese cross
mammal
man's
man
manager, executive
mandate
mandible

mandolin
mane
manipulate
manners
manpower
mansion
many
map
mar
marble
march
margin
marines
maritime
mark
market
marl
married
marrow
mars
marsh
marshal
marsupial
masculine
mash
mask
masochism
mass
★ mass
massage
mast
master
masterpiece
masturbate
mat
match
★ match

material
materialism
maternal
mathematics
matriarch
matter
mattress
mature
maximum
may
maybe
mayor
me, I
meadow
meal
★ meal
mean
meander
meaning
means
meanwhile
measles
measure
meat
mechanic
mechanics
mechanism
medal
median
mediation
medical
medicate
medicine
mediocrity
medium
medulla oblongata
meekness
meeting
megaphone
meiosis
melancholy
melanesian
melodrama
melody
melons
melting
membership
memorize
men's
men
menstruation
mentor
menu
mercenary
merchandising
mercury
★ mercury
mercy
merit
mesa
mesh
mess
messenger
metabolism
metals
metanym
metaphysics
metazoa
meteor
meteorology
meter
meters
meticulousness
metrical
metronome
metropolis
micro
microbe
microfauna
microphone
microscope
microsecond
microwave
mid-life; prime
midday
middle ear
middle finger
middle, centered
middleman
midland
midnight
midwife
might
migrant
mil. draft
Mil. police
mild
military
militia
milk
milky way
mill
millennium
millet
millinery
million years ago
millisecond
mills
mimic
mind
mine, my
mine
★ mine
mineral oils
minerals
miniature
minimum
minister
ministry
minnow
minor
★ minor
★ minor
minus
minute
★ minute
miracle
mire
mirror
misbehave
miscarriage
mischief
misconduct
misdemeanor
miserable
misery
misfortune
mislead
miss
missile
mist
misunderstanding
mitosis
mixed
MLY, million lightyears
moan
mobile home
mobilize

★ **negative**
**neglect**
**negligee**
**negotiate**
**neichevo**
**neighborhood**
**neighboring**
**neither**
**neon**
**nephew**
**nephew/niece**
**neptune**
**nerve**
**nervous system**
**nervous**
**nest**
**net**
**netting**
**network**
**neuron**
**neurosis**
**neurotic**
**neutrality**
**neutron**
**never**
★ **never**
**new year's day**
**new year's eve**
**new**
**newborn**
**news article**
**news**
**newsletter**
**newspaper**
**nice**
**niche**
**nickel**
**nicotine**
**niece**
**night blindness**
**night**
**nightwear**
**nihilism**
**nilotic**
**nimbus**
**nipple**
**nitrogen**
**no, non, not**
**nobility**
**noise**
**noisemaker**
**nominate**
**nonbeliever**
**nonchalance**
**noncom**
**noncontiguous**
**none**
**nonentity**
**nonpartisan**
**nonpayment**
**nonresident**
**nonsense**
**nonviolence**
**noon**
**nordic**
**norm**
**normal**
**north america**
**north**
**nose**
**nostril**
**not equal to**
**notary**
**notch**
**note**
**notice**
★ **notice**
**noun**
**nourish**
**novel**
**now**
**noxious**
**nozzle**
**nucleonics**
**nucleus**
**nudity**
**numb**
**number**
**numeral**
**nun**
**nurse maid**
**nurse**
**nursing home**
**nurture**
**nut**
**nutrient**
**nuts**
**nylon**
**oar**
**oasis**
**oath**
**oats**
**obituary**
**object**
**objection**
**oboe**
**obscene**
**observation**
**observatory**
**obsolescent**
**obstinacy**
**obvious**
**occasion**
**occasional**
**occultism**
**occupancy**
**occur**
**ocean**
**octave**
**oculist**
**odd**
★ **odd**
**odds**
**odorless**
**odorous**
**of, made of; (can stand alone)**
**of**
**off**
**offend**
**offensive**
**offer**
**offering**
**office**
**officer**
**official of**
**official**
**offspring**
**often**
**ohms**
**oils**
**ointment**
**OK**
**old**
**oleo**
**olfactory bulb**
**olives**
**omen**
**ominous**

on
one (a person)
one connected with or belonging to
one's own, animal
one's own
★ one's own
one's
★ one's
one
oneself (ego?)
oneself
ongoing
onion
only
onwards
onyx
op.cit.
opacity
opal
open
★ open
opera glasses
opera
operation
★ operation
operator of a device that does the action
ophthalmologist
opiate
opinion
opossum
opponent
opposite
opposition
oppressive
optic nerve
optical instruments
optics
optimism
optometry
or
★ or
oral
orang
orange
oranges
orate
orbit
orchestra
order
orderly
ordinal number
ordinance
ordination
ore
organ
organic matter
organism
organization
orgasm
orientation
origin
original
ornament
ornate
orphan m/f
orthodoxy
oscilloscope
ossicles
ostentation
osteopath
other
otology
otter
ought
ounce
our
ours
ourselves
out of
out
outdoors
outer ear
outer space
outer
outlet
outline
outpost
output
outrageous
outside of
outward
oval
ovary
ovate, solid
oven
over and out
over to you
over
overact
overcast
overcoat
overdo
overnight
overpass
overrule
overshoot
overt
overthrow
overture
overturn
ovum
owing
owner
ox
oxygen
pace
pacifist
package
pad
paddle
paean
pagan
page
pagoda
paid
pain
paint
painting
pair
pairing 'and'; plus in mathematics
palace
paleness
pallet
palm
pampas
pamphlet
pan
pancakes
pancreas
panel
pang
panic
pans
pantheism
pantry
pants
paper

★ paper
parapsychology
parabolic
parachute
paradise
paragraph
parallel to
paramour
paraphrase
parazoa
parcel
parent
parenthesis; ellipsis when empty
parish
park
parliament
parody
parole
part in play
part
partially
participle
partition
partner
partnership
parts
party
★ party
passage
passenger
passion
passport
password
past
pasta
paste
pasteurization
pastoral
pastry
pasture
patch
pate
patent
paternal
path
pathogen
pathology
patient
★ patient
patina
patriarch
patrician
patriotic
patrol
patron
patronage
patter
pattern
pauper
pavement
paw
payment
peace
★ peace
peaches
peanuts
pears
peasant
peat
pebble
pedigree
peel
peerless
pelt
pelvis
pen
★ pen
penalty
penance
pencil
pendency
penetration
peninsula
penis
penitence
pension
people
peoples'
pepper
peppers
per se
percentage
perception
perennial
perfection
performance
perfume
perhaps
perimeter
period
periodic
periodical
perishable
perjury
permanent
permission
perpendicularity
perpetual
perseverance
persist
persistent
person 1,2,3
person
★ person
perspective
persuasion
pertain to
pervade
perversity
pessimism
pesticide
pestilence
pet
petal
petition
petrify
petty officer
petty
pew
pewter
phantom
pharmacy
pharynx
phase
phenomenon
philander
philology
philosophy
phlegm
phoneme
phonograph
phosphorescence
phosphorus
photography
photon
phrase
physical

physician
physics
physiology
physique
piano
piccolo
pick
picket
pickle
picnic
picture
piety
pigtail
pill
pillar
pillowcase
pillows
pilot
pimento
pimp
pimple
pin
pinch
pioneer
pipe
★ pipe
piquancy
pit
pitch pipe
pitch
pituitary
pity
pivot
place name
place where something is made
place where something is stored or sold
place where something is used
place where the action occurs
place
placenta
plagiarism
plague
plain
★ plain
plaintiff
plane
★ plane
planet
planetarium
plankton
plants
plasma
plaster
plastic
plastics
plate
plateau
platelet
platform
★ platform
platinum
platoon
platter
play
★ play
player, participant
playground
playroom
plea
pleadings
pleasant
please
★ please
pleasure
★ pleasure
pleat
plebeian
plebiscite
plectrum
pledge
plod
plot
plow
plug
plume
plumpness
plural-possessive-reflexive
plural-possessive
plural-reflexive
plural
plus or minus
plus
pluto
plutonium
ply
pneumatics
pneumonia
pocket
poetry
point
poison gas
poison
poke
polarity
pole star
pole
police
policy
polish
polite
politics
polls
pollution
polyester
polyphony
polytheism
pomegranate
pomp
pond
pony
pool
poor in
poor
pop
pope
popularity
population
porcelain
porch
pore
pork
pornographic
porpoise
port
portable
porter
portion
portraiture
position
positive
positron
posse
possessive-reflexive
possessive
possessor of
possible
post office

post-graduate
post
postage stamp
postcard
poster
postman
postmortem
pot
potassium
potato
potent
potion
pottery
pouch
poultry
pound
powder
power plant
power
powers of ten, both positive and negative
§
practical
practitioner of
prairie
praise
pram
pray
prayer
preacher
preceding core is dominant, used between cores and before suffixes
-
preceding
precept
precinct
precipitation
precursor
predawn
predicate
prediction
preference
prefix
prehistoric
premature
premier
premium
prenatal
preparation
preposition
preschooler
presence
present
presentation
preservation
president
press
presses
pressure
prestige
presume
presumptuous
prevent
prey
price index
price
prickle
pride
priesthood
primate
primer
primitive
prince
principal
principality
principle
print
printout
prisms
prison
prisoner of war
pristine
private
privilege
pro
probability
probable
problem
process
proclamation
prodigy
produce
product
★ product
production
productive
profaneness
profanity
professional
professor
profile
profit
program
progress
prohibition
projectile
projector
prominence
promise
promoter of
promotion
pronoun
pronunciation
proof
prop
propaganda
propane
proper
property
prophecy
prophets
prophylactic
propitiation
proportions
proposal
proposition
prose
prosecutor
prospect
prosperity
prostate
prostitution
prostration
protect
protege
protein
protest
proton
protoplasm
protozoa
protuberance
prove
proverb
province
provincial group
provoke
prow
pry
psalm
psyche
psychiatry

psychics
psychoanalysis
psychotherapy
psychology
psychopath
psychosomatic
psychotic
pub
pubic hair
public address system
public
publication
publicity
publish
pucker
pudding
puddle
puff
pulling
pulpit
pulse
pumps
punctuation
puncture
pungency
punishment
pupil
puppet
pure
purgatory
purge
purple
purpose, use, application of
purpose
purse
pursue
push
put
puzzle
pygmy
pyramid
q.v.
quadruped
quagmire
quality
quantum
quarantine
quark
quarrel
quarry
quarter
★ quarter
quartz
quest
question
★ question
quick
quiet
quill
quilt
quit
quite
quotient
rabbi
rabbit
rabble
rabies
raccoon
race
racket
racketeering
radar
radians
radiation
radicalism
radio
radiology
radishes
radium
radius
★ radius
raft
rafter
rage
rail
railroad
rain
rainbow
rainstorm
raise
★ raise
ramadan
ramp
ramshackle
rancher
rancor
random
range
rank
rapacity
rape
rapidity
rapids
rapport
rare
rascal
rash
★ rash
rasping
rat
rate
rating
ratio
rationality
rattle
raw materials
raw
rawness
ray
rayon
raze
re-; see again
reach
reactance
reaction
reactionary
reactor
reading
ready
reagent
real estate
real
reap
rearguard
rearing
reason
rebel
rebuke
recall
receding
receipt
receipts
receiver
recent
receptive
recess
recession
recipient, object of the action

reckless
recompense
record
recreation
recruitment
rectangle
rector
rectum
recumbency
recurrent
red tape
red
redhead
redress
reduction
reed
reefs
reek
referee
referendum
refinement
reflex
reflexive
reform
reformatory
refraction
refresh
refrigerator
refrigerate
refuse
regent
regiment
region
register
regret
regularity
regulation

rehabilitation
rehearse
reheated
reimbursement
reincarnation
reindeer
reject
rejoicing
relationship
relationship
relative by blood
relative by marriage
relative to
relax
relaxation
release
relentless
relevant
reliable
relic
relief
★ relief
religion
religions, various
reluctance
remain
remainder
remark
remarkable
remember
remind
remote control
remoteness
remove
renewal
renounce
rental

repair
repeal
repeated sounds
repertory
repetition
reply
report
repossession
representatives
reprieve
reptile
republic
repulsion
reputation
request
require
rescue
research
resentment
reservation
reserves
reservoir
resident
resins
resistance
resonance
resort
respect
respite
responsible
rest
restaurant
restore
restrain
restrict
resurrection
resuscitation

retail
retaliate
retching
retina
retired
retirement
retract
retreat
retrieval
returning
revelation
revenge
reverence
reverse
revival
revolt
revolution
★ revolution
reward
rheumatism
rhizome
rhyme
rhythm
rib
ribald
ribbon
rice
rich in
rich
riddle
ride
ridge
ridicule
rifle
rigging
right handed
right

scold
scooter
score
★ score
scorn
scorpion
scour
scout
scowl
scramble
scraping
scream
screen
screw
script
scripture
scrotum
scrub
scuff
sculpture
sea lane
sea-life
sea
seafood
seam
search
seared
season
seasoning
seat
seaweed
secant
seclusion
second
★ second
secrecy
secret
secretary
secretion
sect
secular
securities
security
sedative
seduction
see above
see below
see
seed
seem
seep
seizure
seldom
selection
self-reliance
selfish
seller
semen
semi, hemi, demi
semicolon
seminal vesicle
semitic
semitrailer
senate
send
senile
sensation
sense
★ sense
sensibility
sensitivity
sentiment
sentinel
separate
separated, m/f
sequel
sequence
serfdom
sergeant
seriousness
servant
services
servility
servomechanism
session
setback
setting
settlement
settler
sewing machine
sewing
sex
sextant
sexual preference
sexuality
sexy
shabby
shack
shackle
shade
shadow
shaft
shake
shall
shallowness
shallows
shame
shampoo
shapers
sharing
sharp
sharpness
shatter
she, her
shed
shedding
sheep
sheet
shelf
shell
★ shell
shellfish
shelter
sherbet
sheriff
shield
shift
shin
shine
shintoism
ship
shipment
shirt
shivers
shock
★ shock
shocking
shoes
shoot
shop
shore
short of
shortness
shot
should
shoulder
shouting
shovel

solstice
solubility
solution
solvency
solvent
some
somebody
somersault
son
sonar
song
sonics
sonority
sooner
soot
soprano
sorcery
sore
sorry
sort
sorted
soul
sound
★ sound
★ sound
soundproofing
soundness
soup
sour cream
sour
source
source; -head
south america
south
sowing
soybeans
spa
space probe
space travel
space
spade
spark
sparkle
spasm
speaker, auditor, reader, writer of
speaker
spear
special import; followed by other marks to indicate jest, sarcasm, fantasy, etc.
special
specific
speckle
spectacles
spectator
spectroscopes
spectrum
speculate
speech
spell
spend
sperm
sphere
sphincter
spice
spider
spin
spinach
spinal chord
spine
spiral
spirit
spiritualism
spit
spite
splash
spleen
splendor
splinter
split
spokesman
sponsorship
spontaneity
spoon
spore
sport
sports
spouse
spray
spread
spring
★ spring
springs
sprinkle
sprout
sputum
spy
spying
squad
squalor
square
★ square
squashes
squat
squawk
squeal
squeezing
squint
stable
staccato
staff
★ staff
★ staff
stage
stagecoach
stagecraft
stagger
stain
stairs
stake
stale
stamp
stand
star
starboard
starch
stare
stargazing
starlight
stars
start
startle
state
statement
statics
station
stationary, fixed
statistics
statuary
stature
statute
steady
steak
steam
steed
steel
steep
steeple

steer
stellate
stem
step-
step
steppe
stereo
sterilization
sternness
sternum
stew
steward
sticker
sticks
stiff
stifle
stigma
still
stimulant
stimulate
sting
stinginess
stink
stipend
stipulation
stir
stitch
stock
stocking
stocks
stomach
stone age
stone
stop
⋆ stop
storage
store
storeroom
storm
story
stove
strafe
straight
⋆ straight
strand
strange
strangulation
strategy
stream
street
streetcar
strength
stress
stretch
strictness
strike
string
strip
strive
stroboscope
stroke
⋆ stroke
strong
structure
struggle
strum
stubborn
student of
student
studio
study of something
study
stuffing
stunned
stupid
stupor
stutter
style
suavity
subcutaneous tissue
subject
submarine
submerge
submission
submissive
subscriber
subsidy
substance
subtle
subtract
suburb
succeeding
success
succinctness
such
suckle
suddenness
sue
suffer
sufficient
suffix
suffrage
sugar
suggestion
suicide
suit
⋆ suit
sulk
summer
summons
sun glasses
sun
sunlight
supermarket
supernaturalism
superb
superficiality
superfluous, beyond need
superior
superstition
supper
supplication
supply
support
supposedly
surety
surf
surface
surfeit
surgery
surpassing, out-
surprise
surrender
surrogate
surrounding
survey
surviving spouse
susceptible
suspense
suspicious
sustaining
swab
swallow
swastika
sweat gland
sweat
sweaters
sweatshop

★ themselves
then
theology
theory
theosophy
therapy
there
thermodynamics
these
they or them, animals
they, them
thick
thigh
thin
★ thin
★ thin
thing's
thing
★ thing
★ thing
things'
things
think
thirst
this side of
this
thorax
thorn
those
though
thread
threat
threshold
thrift
thrill
throat
throbbing
throne
through
throughout
throwing
thrust
thud
thumb
thunder
thunderstorm
thyroid gland
tibia
tick
ticket
ticking
tidal flats
tide
tiger
tight
till
timber
time
★ time
timer
times
timidity
tin
tinder
tingle
tinkle
tip
tired
tissue
title
to
toad
toast
★ toast
tobacco
today
toe
tofu
together
token
tolerant
tomato
tomb
tomorrow
ton
tone
tongue
tonic
tonight
tonsil
tonsillitis
tools
tooth
toothpaste
top
topaz
topcoat
topic
torah
torch
torment
tornado
torrent
torrid
torso
torture
toss
total
touch
tough
tourism
toward
tower
town meeting
town
township
toxicity
toys
trachea
traction
tractor
trade school
trade
trademark
traffic light
tragedy
trailer
trailing
train
trance
tranquilizer
transmission
transcendentalism
transfer
transfusion
transgression
transient
transistor
translation
translucence
transmitter
transom
transparency
transplant
transport
transposition
travel
traverse

tray
treachery
treadle
treason
treasurer
treatment
treaty
tree
trench
trespass
trestle
tri-; triple
triangle
★ triangle
tribe, clan
tribunal
tributary
trick
trickle
tricycle
trigonometry
trill
trip
trombone
troop
trophy
trouble
trough
trousers
trowel
truce
trucking
true quotation of speech or writing
true
trumpet
trunk
★ trunk
truss
trust
trustworthy
truth
try
tuba
tuber
tuberculosis
tuck
tug
tumor
tundra
tuning fork
tunnel vision
tunnel
turkey
turn off
turn on
turn
turpentine
turquoise
turtle
tusk
twig
twine
twinge
twining
twinkling
twist
typewriter
typography
ubiquity
udder
ugly
ulcer
ulna
ultra
umbilical cord
umbrella
un-, de-
unable
unbreakable
uncle, aunt
uncle
uncommon
unconcern
unconscious
uncooked
uncouth
under
underground
undergrowth
underneath
underside
understand
understudy
undertone
underwater
underwear
undress
unequal
unfinished
unguent
ungulate
uni-; mono-; single
unicycle
uniform
uniformity
uninhabited
unit
★ unit
unite
universe
university
unlike
unnecessary
unproductive
unreal
unruly
unsafe
unsavoriness
unusual
up
upholstery
upper arm
upset
upward
uranium
uranus
urethra
urge
urgency
urine
urn
us, we
use
★ use
user of, consumer
usual
usurp
uterus
uvea
vacate
vacation
vaccine
vacuum tube
vagina
valence
valid
valor

watch
★ watch
watching
watchman
water bed
water colors
water
★ water
waterfall
wattage
wave
wavy
waxes
way
★ way
we, us
weaken
weakness
wealth
wean
weapons
weather
weaving
webbing
wedding
weed
week
weekend
weeping
weft
weigh
weight
weir
welcome
★ welcome
★ welcome
welders
welfare
well
★ well
★ well
werewolf
west
wet
whale
what
wheat
wheelbarrow
wheelchair
wheels
when
where
wherewithal
which
while
whim
whine
whip
★ whip
whirlpool
whiskers
whisper
whistle
★ whistle
white
who
whole
wholesale
wholesomeness
whose
why
wick
wickerwork
wide
widow
widower
width
wife
wig
wild
will
willingness
winch
wind
winding
windlass
window
windward
wine
wing
wings
wink
winner
winter
wire
wise
witch
witchcraft
with, (can stand alone)
with
withering
without
witness
wits
wok
wolf
woman's
woman
women's
women
wonder
wonderful
wood
★ wood
woodwind
woof
wooing
wool
word-processor
word
work
★ work
world
worm
worry
worse
worship
worst
wort
worthless
worthy
would
wound dressing
wound
wrapper
wreath
wreck
wrench
wretch
wrights
wrinkle
wrist bones
wrist
writ
writing
wrong
X-ray
yams

yard

★ yard

yarn

year

yeast

yelling

yellow

yes

yesterday

yet

★ yet

★ yet

yield

yielding

yogurt

yolk

you

young

your (pl.) own

your own

your

yours

yourself

yourselves

youse? (slang) English has no distinctive plural form for you

zeal

zest

zigzag

zinc

zip code

zipper

zircon

zodiac

zoology

Active participation in ⊦JΓ2x will take several forms. Most urgently needed is vocabulary improvement as noted in several places in the text and critical evaluation both pro and con. All such participation must be made as a contribution to the Hankes Foundation with all copyright rights, if any, assigned to that Foundation under its existing and subsequent copyrights. This is essential in order to keep control of ⊦JΓ2x as a viable universal communication system. In due course an ⊦JΓ2x governing board will be established to put control on an international basis. It could be that you or your associates may come to serve on that board or its committees.

Financial contributions are welcome. The Foundation is tax exempt in the United States. Similar status should be obtained in other countries for affiliated organizations. If you have available office space and facilities and can get volunteer assistance you might want to consider establishing a local activities center. Retirees, administrators, teachers, engineers, anyone with vision and initiative would find satisfaction in the work. We need leaders and innovators, because there is no present organization for guidance. A newsletter would be useful. Is there some group out there that might take on that task? Carefully constructed experiments to test the validity of the system, probe its weaknesses and seek improvements should be conducted and reported. Educational materials will be needed. Opportunities for publication must be provided for ⊦JΓ2x writers. Publicity, public relations, legal and governmental aspects should be consolidated.

Some publishers are being contacted. If you are interested and capable of a major undertaking of vast economic potential please contact the Foundation directly.

This appendix discusses a variety of other projects some of which are peripheral to ⊦JΓ2x but depend upon it to some degree. The special VV and CC vocabularies are totally ⊦JΓ2x while the hardware items may be adaptations of existing devices. The Foundation expects to derive some benefit from these adaptations.

Ownership of the copyrights is divided into four equal parts. One quarter belongs to the Camilla Publishing Company, the original (1982) publisher. I have kept one quarter to my self during my lifetime and to my estate for five years thereafter. This quarter then passes to the Foundation. The other two quarters I have already assigned to the Foundation under the terms of our contract to create and propagate ⊦JΓ2x. Under these arrangements it is hoped that the Foundation will be able to derive sufficient revenue on an international basis from all ⊦JΓ2x publications and related items to promote and maintain the integrity of ⊦JΓ2x and to expand its usefulness. The Foundation is empowered to assign no more than a total of one of these quarter interests to other entities for significant major contributions such as a complete translation and publication in any particular language, with such concession of interest covering just the subject work and only those items directly connected to it. Such concession of interest shall not apply to any other publications or to concessions granted to other persons or entities. The symbols and content of this book and its predecessor are fully covered under the international copyright conventions and by U.S. design patent 269,281 (1983). Additional patent protection is being sought.

There are multitudes of desk-top computers that fall into 3 principal groups; IBM, Mac, and the versatile Amiga. I chose the Amiga 4 years ago because it was the most adaptable to my ⊦JΓ2x work. Now that we have achieved the programming success that permitted us to create this book, the other manufacturers may decide to extend themselves. As it stands I have TeX programs for all aspects of ⊦JΓ2x but only for the Amiga. I can furnish two 3 1/2" discs for $25.00 (to cover our costs) to linguistic researchers and/or institutions who agree to maintain the international integrity of the language, to honor the copyrights and other rights of the Hankes Foundation and to cooperate with other such developers and researchers.

These discs contain the data base and the special programs, but not the TeX program itself. That is copyrighted software which you may get from a local dealer or directly from Radical Eye Software, Box 2081, Stanford, CA 94309. You will want AmigaTeX version 3.1 (July 1991 or later) plus a driver for your printer. If you have a Mac. or IBM and are already a TeX user you can enter our data but you may need adaptive programming to manipulate it. TeX has an international clientele so help may be nearby. Computer expertise is not necessary for participation. Intelligence, experience, ingenuity and insight together with pen and paper still give the best results. TeX is a proprietary program but I place our modifications in the public domain asking in return that any improvements be posted to us for evaluation and further dissemination; and that the two stroke numeric key pad entry system be given the same considerations and be known as "ElmEntry". ElmEntry the computer program is placed in the public domain but the two stroke computer entry system is a unique concept of my own and I shall seek patent rights for it on behalf of the Hankes Foundation. This ElmEntry concept produces a one handed keyboard, one fourth the width of the present standard, which can also incorporate 'ball' or mouse functions. Any revenues derived from ElmEntry® will accrue solely to the Foundation.

To obtain the discs please send information regarding your interests, qualifications, affiliations, type of computer or other equipment or facilities.

Computer operation by vocal commands using the ˥ family.

Direct machine dictation and transcription with audio feed-back of what the device understood the speaker to have said. All in ⊧JΓ2x of course.

Page scanners.
1. To input ⊧JΓ2x to computers.
2. To vocalize ⊧JΓ2x material being read.
3. To read hand written ⊧JΓ2x material.

Braille adaptation is readily accomplished. ⊧JΓ2x needs three of the six braille dots for the bars; two for the dots; and one for V/C. So another raised symbol must be devised to signal punctuation, numerals and aliens. Perhaps an upper short vertical bar for numbers and a lower bar for punctuation and aliens.

Portable or small keyboards using ten key numerical or five key binary (simultaneous key stroke) format plus auxiliary keys.
1. For ⊧JΓ2x and computer functions.
2. For private communication.
3. For people having limited visual, auditory, or tactile capabilities.

Rapid hand signaling using the five-finger binary codes.
1. Line of sight for the deaf.
2. Hands-on for those both blind and deaf.

Educational material.
1. Printed material.
2. Audio cassettes.
3. VCR presentations.

Computer program compatibility.
1. Amiga to IBM.
2. Amiga to Apple or Mac.
3. Other computers and/or programs.

Some of these possibilities have been discussed with expert consultants and contractors who could bring them to fruition at certain costs. Neither I nor the Hankes Foundation have funds for these projects right now and anyhow some of them must await further development and stabilization of the project. If we were to receive 2,000 cash contributions of $15.00 each we could produce audio tapes and distribute them to our benefactors, schools and libraries. It would take about eight months. To produce a creditable Video-tape we would need 2,000 contributions of $100.00 each and that project would take about fifteen months from the time that enough money was in hand. Both projects are designed to be multi-lingual through the use of voice-over techniques. An amateur, but adequate, audio tape is provided with this book.

This book has been concerned with VC and CV three letter words. Yet to come are the special vocabularies. These vocabularies are not needed for a utility language but would be for a high level one. Words that begin VV are associated with specific fields of human activity. The VV words are to be arranged into five general classes each with four broad divisions. This is done with the first letter. The second letter (also a vowel) provides twenty more breakdowns. The result is that the first two letters permit us to list up to four hundred fields of activity. Since the actual cataloging of each individual field doesn't begin until the third letter, which can be either V or C, these words are sure to be more than three letters long. The fourth and succeeding characters may also be numerals, aliens or in extreme cases, with some loss of machine scanning and dictational qualities, other alphabets or symbols. It was for this eventuality that the extender POTENT **E** was created. When **E** appears before any letter it adds its name (*hoi*) to that letter and that letter keeps its place in the hierarchy but a half step behind. **Each VV and CC vocabulary is a major undertaking. These notes are merely suggestions.**

The CC words are divided as follows:

˥C, ˙˥C, .˥C, and :˥C are reserved for vocal control of computers. There isn't much reason for these words to be more than three letters long because there are 3200 words available in this group. Indeed, it's best that they always be triads because the computer will be more comfortable and can use letter count as a sort of parity check.

˥CC or ˥CV Input...

˙˥CC or ˙˥CV Internal...

.˥CC or .˥CV Output...

:˥CC or :˥CV Other...

⊣C, ˙⊣C, .⊣C, AND :⊣C are used to describe and define devices and things, tangible or intangible, animate or inanimate, by size, means of control, power. function and area of utility. This is for the generic identification of new items. The basic ID lies in the first three letters. These words can be longer than three letters and the subsequent characters may be numerals or aliens or other alphabets because the words in this category are names of a controlled nature. The plus sign (+) indicates that there may be additional characters appended.

⊣CC+ or ⊣CV+ inanimate tangible...

˙⊣CC+ or ˙⊣CV+ inanimate intangible...

.⊣CC+ or .⊣CV+ animate tangible...

:⊣CC+ or :⊣CV+ animate intangible...

Global physical features are the counterpart to global locations and they may often be used together to give names to rivers, seamounts, cities etc.

]CV or ]CC Land: Mountains, mesas, islands.

˙]CV or ˙]CC Water: Seamounts, bays, straits, currents, rivers, lakes.

.]CV or .]CC Sky: Heavenly bodies, weather, atmosphere.

:]CV or :]CC Manmade: Cities, canals, roads, mines.

*The* ⊣C *family is not yet assigned.*

The globe is divided into 4 spherical segments starting at 180° east longitude. Proceeding eastwards the 90° segments will be designated ┘ ˙┘ .┘ and :┘. The second 20 C letters divide each 90° segment into 4.5° segments. The third letter is the latitudinal designation. V is used in the northern hemisphere and C in the southern. The latitudinal divisions are bands 4.5° wide. The boxes formed by this lattice are all of the same height but taper in width from about 300 miles at the equator to zero at the poles. The 3rd letter is assigned in order reading upwards from the equator in the north 'V' and downwards in the south 'C'. Further subdivision of each rhomboid will follow the same pattern with the starting point always being the eastern corner closest to the equator. Thus ┘┐┌ is an area about 300 miles square whose eastern edge is 150° east longitude and just north of the equator. To the west is :┘]┌; to the south is ┘┐┐; and diagonally southwest of it is :┘]┐. Smaller divisions are achieved in steps by the use of numbers from 00 to 99 arranged in a 10x10 lattice. Each box in that lattice can be subdivided in turn with a second series of numbers 00 to 99. The first series gives 30x30mi. areas and the second 3x3mi. This global lattice can be used as a universal address code for mail and phone. The extender POTENT E can be used as a corrective for closely related areas that are split by a major dividing line as is eastern Australia or the west coast of the United States. Nomenclature for large divisions starts with monad ┘ (or ˙┐ .┐ and :┐) to indicate an entire global quarter. ┘0 is its northern half, and ┘9 its southern. Then ┘1, ┘2, ┘3, ┘4 are successive 22.5° northern bands and ┘5, ┘6, ┘7, and ┘8 southern. ┘┐, ┘┤, ┘ㅋ, ┘┘, and ┘] produce similar results. The numbers always begin at the equator. The map shows a rather fortuitous situation as regards the global divisions. If the international dateline were to coincide with the ┘ starting line, the first two letters of global location could divide the world into 20 or 80 equal time zones, instead of the present 24 giving simultaneous general indication of time difference for the various sectors.

The present numeric keypad has 18 keys that are easily covered by one hand. A computer could be operated by a 6x5 keyboard no bigger than the present-day mouse, in fact all input functions, including the ball, could be incorporated into a single assembly which could be desk based, carried in a pocket or fitted to the hand somewhat like a glove. Considering the remarkable speed that experienced 10-key adding machine operators achieve, the fact that ⊧JΓ2x characters require two strokes does not mean that entry would be slow. Another positive factor is the ease of learning because of the logical nature of the two number codes. It is possible to arrange the program so that the letters appear after the second stroke without pressing 'enter', but for a single finger hunt and peck novice, which I continue to be, errors are too frequent. Computer fonts have a maximum of 256 possible characters. A 4x4 ElmEntry configuration covers that and if a two position toggle were to be added another 256 codes would be available. Some control functions like space, delete, backspace, caps, enter and return require dedicated keys; add another for the decimal point and the total is 22. If we use a 6x5 layout together with a ball and four toggles on the sides of the assembly (one to shift from a right-handed to a left-handed accommodation, one for 1st or 2nd sets of 256, one for single stroke entry for doing extensive numerics and one for two stroke with or without enter) we would have a one hand operating system that would be no more difficult to learn than the present two handed touch-typing. The units have separate viewing screens for operator and addressee. (fig.2, p.155)

An entry system devoted to ⊧JΓ2x exclusively is even simpler. The keyboard procedures and the hand signaling system for handicapped people follow the same pattern so that by learning one you've learned the other. ⊧JΓ2x has a dual binary basis (page 1) consisting of three bars and two dots. The three bars become the three middle fingers of either hand and the dots are the thumb and pinkie. In this system all five fingers are in use simultaneously (chording), each being either *on* or *off*. The operation is similar to a stenotype machine. For the handicapped four distinct hand positions; say, up for Vs: down for Cs; rotated, thumb up, for punctuation; and thumb down for numerals and aliens. This system was selected without testing because it is so much like the system that must be used with a hand held ⊧JΓ2x keyboard (fig.1, p.155). There are many other possibilities such as the ones described in my earlier book where the hand was held against the chest. The decision rests with the users and I expect various associations of handicapped people to get together to pick the one best suited to their needs. Page 154 shows four different hand positions for V, C, punctuation, and aliens and numbers.

The addition of vocal capabilities to these devices would give handicapped persons a useful range of speech. The Amiga can do this now but it is not portable. Not only can computers like the Amiga speak, but their voices can be adjusted over a range of frequencies and rates. Perhaps, in the future, other qualities such as anger, incredulity or tenderness can be introduced to make the reading more effective. Our language has a punctuational series that gives the reader instructions or asides to set the tone of the action or scene. The development of optical scanners and vocal input and output devices for ⊧JΓ2x may be greatly expedited by limiting and standardizing the ⊧JΓ2x parameters.

For high speed touch-typing of standard and ⊦⌋⌈2x characters. It incorporates features for accounting and ⊦⌋⌈2x vocal output and can include a mouse or ball, all or some of the usual computer keyboard items and left/right configuration. As a portable unit with a small display window it can serve the needs of the handicapped by offering vocal, tactile and visual input or output in various combinations to suit the needs of the user. Key size may vary but location must be fixed. The **bold-face** lower case letters in fig.3, p.155 are just to identify the keys for discussion.

This is a multi-mode system. In two-stroke (ts) it can be set to operate with or without 'enter'. The **defg** keys make a standard adding machine when switched to single-stroke (ss). The sixteen keys enclosed by the heavy border give 256 ts combinations. **cv** is marked Lc1 for lower-case 1, and **cw** is marked Lc2. **cx** and **cy** are marked Uc1 and Uc2 for upper-case. These four keys are the initial stroke for all standard alphabets. **cv** plus any of the other 16 shaded keys gives a letter; **cv/dv** is a; **cv/ev** is b; in regular order to **cv/fy** as o. Then **cw/dv** is p; **cw/ev** is q; etc. to **cw/fx** which is z. Inputs beginning with **cx** (Uc1) or **cy** (Uc2) produce the same letters but in the upper-case. This system provides for 31 letters, so most alphabets can be accommodated.

Back-space is **cv** in ss mode and **cv/cv** in ts; each additional depression of cv is another back-space; holding it down after an initial activation gives continuous back-spacing. **cw, cx,** and **cy** function in the same way for delete, return and dash. The cursor controls are at the top and the spacer bar is at the bottom so that it can be actuated by the heel of the hand. At the left, provision is made for 20 (or more) 'functional' keys. The 'functional' keys are not a part of the touch-typing system, so they can be small. Full size keys are .75in. square to preserve the established key-board 'feel' but three sizes, small; medium and standard could be economically provided. On either or both sides imbedded toggles are provided for left or right configuration, ss or st, with or without 'enter', vocal output or input, plus other computer controls as needed. The keys in the shaded area, numbered 0 to 9 are used for ⊦⌋⌈2x entry in ts mode and for arithmetic in ss mode. In ss mode the period . and the comma , are achieved with one stoke and in ts mode those keys are depressed twice. The various special items should always carry the same ts codes regardless of the font design so that operators don't have to consult a different chart for each font.

The two long dotted outlines in fig.3 are smooth concave channels for the thumb and pinkie to slide in so that the other three fingers are always properly positioned above the keys and so that the weight of the hand is not carried by the arm, wrist and elbow. Carpal tunnel syndrome should be reduced or eliminated. Professional typists should train in both left and right hand operation in order to reduce strain by switching back and forth on a frequent basis. The full-size keyboard is less than a hand-span wide so it can be placed along either side of the screen at various heights and angles for greatest individual comfort, keeping table space free for the work in hand. Some situations might require a remote screen or one imbedded in the table surface with the key-board to the left or right. For inveterate one-finger typists an optional screen can be placed where shown or just above the cursor keys. The TEX backslash key **cu** is included for the ⊦⌋⌈2x programming presently available.

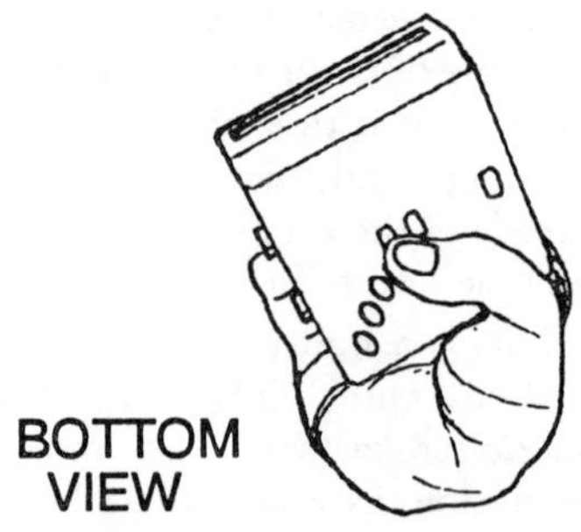


The proposed 5 button 'chording' communicator is based on the dual binaries of dots and bars. Thumb and pinkie are upper and lower dots and the other three fingers function as bars. The unit is held to the hand by an elastic harness, leaving all five fingers free to operate the keys in a chording mode. The bottom view shows the thumb at the upper-dot key, in range of the functional toggle keys.

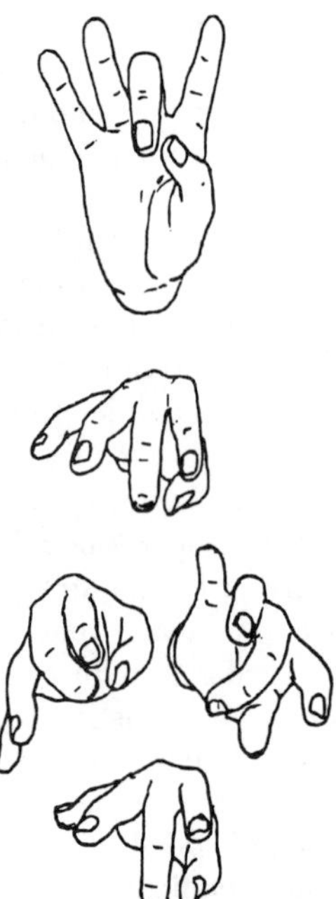

Hand signals can take many forms but in ⊧⅃Γ2ₓ they all equate the fingers to the dots and bars.

In the illustrations the thumb and pinkie represent the dots and the other three fingers, the bars. They show upper dot (thumb) and binary bar two (middle finger) to be active, indicating ⊧ or ⫤ depending on the general inclination of the hand.

There is no doubt about the ability of people to achieve phenominal speeds with accuracy for signing and reading such signals. It is up to the organized institutions for the deaf, blind and mute to establish the best solution for visual, auditory and tactile communication.

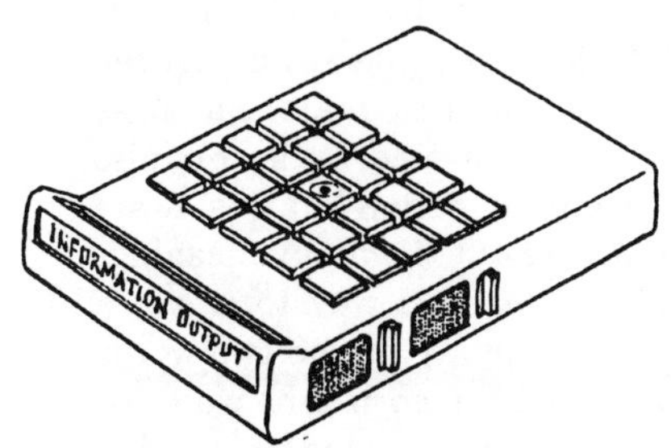


Proposed as a small hand held communicator, primarily for ⊦⅃Γ2ₓ users. May have visual output for both operator and addressee, and audio input and output as well. This unit is held by the thumb and pinkie and operated by the other three fingers in ts or ss mode. Has many of the functions of its big brother, shown below.

## MONOMANUS CONTROL

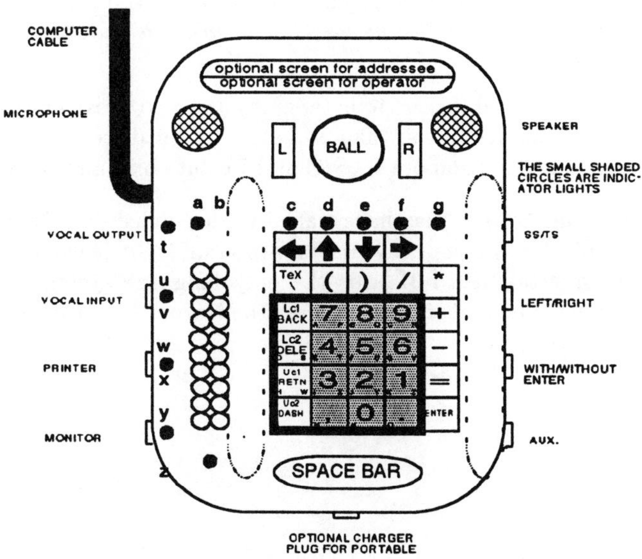


The monomanus (ryhmes with monogamous) control or keyboard is a full function touch-typing computer data-input device designed around an expanded ElmEntry concept. It is regarded as expanded because it may have multi-macro functional capabilities for massive programs like TeX, or for summoning up and sorting out huge character assemblages such as Mandarin Chinese. Patent applications have been filed for this and the other devices. The cooperation of manufacturers is solicited.

BASIC ENGLISH (C. K. Ogden) which was designed between 1926 and 1930 received a strong boost from Winston Churchill and Franklin Roosevelt in Sept. 1943 but the war stymied its growth. It was probably the spark that set me on the road to ⊧┘Γ2ₓ. I first became aware of it when at age 16 my first major purchase was the newly issued 14th ed. of the Britannica. I was impressed by its premise that only 850 English words were enough for general communication but was aware of the fact that you had to know a lot of English to separate out the many meanings of most of the 850 words. Anyway over the years I sought for a way to create a vocabulary in which each word had only one meaning (synonym) and no two words had the same sound (homonym). The answer was to tag and categorize the words so that they couldn't stray. The Orthological Institute graciously granted permission to reprint their word list in "Enterprises of Great Pith and Moment" ©1982. In 1991 after many attempts to contact them I finally received the following dated November 21, 1991 from the British Information Services. In part;-

*"I have checked to see wether there is a new address for the Orthological institute, but unfortunately it seems the organization is no longer in existence.*

*You refer in your letter to 'BASIC English'; I am not sure exactly what you mean by this; is it something formulated by the Orthological Institute?"*

Sic transit... From enthusiastic acceptance by the two most powerful figures in history to a feeble inquiry in less than 50 years. I later discovered that Mr. Mark Haymon has continued to promote BASIC and I salute him and his work.

But the quest goes on. BASIC may have waned while English itself blossomed because it's a matter of "in for a penny, in for a pound". To learn English at any level is a major undertaking. ⊧┘Γ2ₓ is the only language system that can materially reduce learning time and then only when the learner's ideative processes are sufficiently developed.

One of the finest speeches ever was delivered by Abraham Lincoln at Gettysburgh in 1863. It is often cited for succinctness and literary beauty. As my own personal favorite I am using here to emphasize the utilitarian nature of in its present stage of development.

> "Fourscore and seven years ago our fathers brought forth on this continent a new nation, conceived in liberty and dedicated to the proposition that all men are created equal.
>
> "Now we are engaged in a great civil war, testing whether that nation or any nation so conceived and so dedicated can long endure. We are met on a great battlefield of that war. We have have come to dedicate a portion of that field, as a final resting-place for those who here gave their lives that that nation might live. It is altogether fitting and proper that we should do this.
>
> "But, in a larger sense, we can not dedicate—we can not consecrate—we can not hallow—this ground. The brave men, living and dead, who struggled here, have consecrated it, far above our poor power to add or detract. The world will little note, nor long remember, what we say here, but it can never forget what they did here. It is for us the living, rather, to be dedicated here to the unfinished work which they who fought here have thus far so nobly advanced. It is rather for us to be here dedicated to the great task remaining before us—that from these honored dead we take increased devotion to that cause for which they gave the last full measure of devotion—that we here highly resolve that these dead shall not have died in vain—that this nation, under God, shall have a new birth of freedom—and that government of the people, by the people, for the people, shall not perish from the earth."

In (with a running English commentary), this might be something like—

In (the year ) '76 our ancestors (both sexes) created a new nation

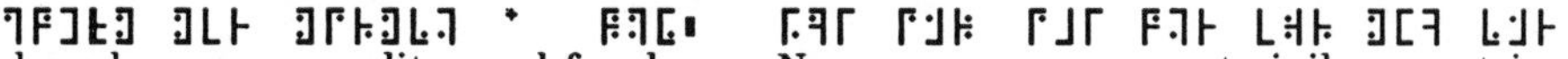
based on equality and freedom. Now as a great civil war tries

their concepts we meet here to consecrate this battlefield although they who

fought and died here have done so with their very own blood and souls.

May their valor and sacrifice, inspire and compel us to continue the struggle

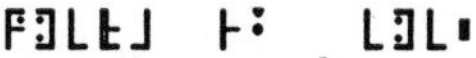
to preserve our democracy.

Or by itself—

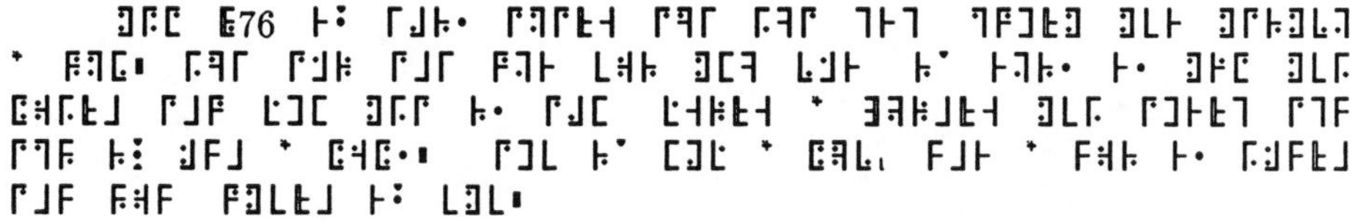

Roget's International Thesaurus™ Fourth Edition
Revised by Robert L. Chapman
Published by Thomas Y. Crowell, New York and Harper and Row, London and Sydney. copyright 1977 by Harper & Row, Publishers, Inc.

Basic English; C. K. Ogden, The Orthological Institute, London, England. See Encyclopædia Britannica 14th ed. vol.3, p.170.

A Spoken Word Count; Lyle V. Jones and Joseph M. Wepman copyright 1966 Language Research Associates Chicago, IL

The American Heritage Word Frequency Book; John B. Carrol, Peter Davies, and Barry Richman. Houghton Mifflin Company, Boston, MA. American Heritage Publishing Co., Inc., New York

The Flash Card Vocabulary Builder; Snowden Arthur copyright 1951 Lexicon Press Washington D.C.

Suffixes and Other Word-Final Elements of English copyright 1982.
Prefixes and Other Word-Final Elements of English copyright 1984.
Both by Laurence Urdang.
Both published and copyrighted by Gale Research Company, Detroit Michigan.

The South Asia Hankes Foundation; Calcutta, India. Established to permit Indian nationals and businesses to make financial contributions for ⊦⅃Γ2ₓ projects in India.

| | | | | | | | | | |
|---|---|---|---|---|---|---|---|---|---|
| 01 Ay | 02 Ee | 03 I | 04 Aw | 05 Ow | 06 OO | 07 Oi | 08 kern ← Fuh | 09 alien ‿ Shuh | 00 space → Suh |
| 11 wAy | 12 wEe | 13 wYe | 14 wAw | 15 wOw | 16 woo | 17 wOi | 18 Saw | 19 Sow | 10 See |
| 21 Ah | 22 Eh | 23 Ih | 24 I | 25 Oh | 26 who | 27 hOi | 28 Swaw | 29 Swow | 20 Swee |
| 31 wAh | 32 wEh | 33 wIh | 34 wI | 35 wOe | 36 you | 37 yOi | 38 CHwah | 39 CHwih | 30 Sweefee |
| 41 K | 42 T | 43 P | 44 M | 45 L | 46 D | 47 N | 48 SI | 49 Soh | 40 Seh |
| 51 sK | 52 sT | 53 sP | 54 sM | 55 sL | 56 sD | 57 sN | | | 50 Seefeh |
| 61 King | 62 Ting | 63 Ping | 64 Ming | 65 Ling | 66 Ding | 67 Ning | | | 60 Sweefeh |
| 71 sKing | 72 sTing | 73 sPing | 74 sMing | 75 sLing | 76 sDing | 77 sNing | 78 SwI | 79 Swoe | 70 Sweh |
| 81 Say | 82 Sway | 83 Swayfay | 84 Sah | 85 Sayfah | 86 Swayfah | 87 Swah | 88 CHay | 89 CHway | 80 CHah |
| 91 Sigh | 92 Swye | 93 Swyefie | 94 Sih | 95 Sighfih | 96 Swyefih | 97 Swih | 98 CHigh | 99 CHwye | 90 CHih |

See is the decimal point     Soi is the comma for pointing off 1,000's     \chuh is 1/2 kern

| | | | | | | |
|---|---|---|---|---|---|---|
| 01 | 02 | 03 | 04 | 05 | 06 ōō | 07 oi |
| 11 | 12 | 13 | 14 | 15 | 16 | 17 |
| 21 R | 22 Uh | 23 H | 24 | 25 | 26 | 27 |
| 31 Rr | 32 W | 33 Yih | 34 F | 35 V | 36 Yoo | 37 |
| 41 G | 42 J | 43 Z | 44 | 45 | 46 B | 47 N |
| 51 | 52 | 53 | 54 | 55 | 56 | 57 |
| 61 Ch | 62 Th | 63 | 64 | 65 | 66 | 67 |
| 71 S | 72 Sh | 73 | 74 | 75 | 76 | 77 Ñ |

UNITS
1 *Gay*
2 *Ghee*
3 *Guy*
4 *Gaw*
5 *Gow*
6 *Gah*
7 *Geh*
8 *Gih*
9 *Gă*
0 *Go*

DECADES
10 *Jay* etc.

HIGHER ORDERS
1,000 *Zay* etc.

*SwawFaw*   *SwowFow*   *CHwayVay*   *CHwyeVigh*
*SawFa*   *SowFoh*   *CHayVah*   *CHighVih*
*SwawFa*   *SwowFoh*   *CHwayVah*   *CHwyeVih*



LAGNIAPPE — (a little extra)   These pages are included for your convenience. You may cut out, fold on the dash line and paste back to back to make a handy pocket size reference.


| | | | | | | | | | |
|---|---|---|---|---|---|---|---|---|---|
| 01 Ay | 02 Ee | 03 I | 04 Aw | 05 Ow | 06 OO | 07 Oi | 08 kern ← Fuh | 09 alien ‿ Shuh | 00 space → Suh |
| 11 wAy | 12 wEe | 13 wYe | 14 wAw | 15 wOw | 16 woo | 17 wOi | 18 Saw | 19 Sow | 10 See |
| 21 Ah | 22 Eh | 23 Ih | 24 I | 25 Oh | 26 who | 27 hOi | 28 Swaw | 29 Swow | 20 Swee |
| 31 wAh | 32 wEh | 33 wIh | 34 wI | 35 wOe | 36 you | 37 yOi | 38 CHwah | 39 CHwih | 30 Sweefee |
| 41 K | 42 T | 43 P | 44 M | 45 L | 46 D | 47 N | 48 SI | 49 Soh | 40 Seh |
| 51 sK | 52 sT | 53 sP | 54 sM | 55 sL | 56 sD | 57 sN | | | 50 Seefeh |
| 61 King | 62 Ting | 63 Ping | 64 Ming | 65 Ling | 66 Ding | 67 Ning | | | 60 Sweefeh |
| 71 sKing | 72 sTing | 73 sPing | 74 sMing | 75 sLing | 76 sDing | 77 sNing | 78 SwI | 79 Swoe | 70 Sweh |
| 81 Say | 82 Sway | 83 Swayfay | 84 Sah | 85 Sayfah | 86 Swayfah | 87 Swah | 88 CHay | 89 CHway | 80 CHah |
| 91 Sigh | 92 Swye | 93 Swyefie | 94 Sih | 95 Sighfih | 96 Swyefih | 97 Swih | 98 CHigh | 99 CHwye | 90 CHih |

See is the decimal point     Soi is the comma for pointing off 1,000's     \chuh is 1/2 kern

| | | | | | | |
|---|---|---|---|---|---|---|
| 01 | 02 | 03 | 04 | 05 | 06 ōō | 07 oi |
| 11 | 12 | 13 | 14 | 15 | 16 | 17 |
| 21 R | 22 Uh | 23 H | 24 | 25 | 26 | 27 |
| 31 Rr | 32 W | 33 Yih | 34 F | 35 V | 36 Yoo | 37 |
| 41 G | 42 J | 43 Z | 44 | 45 | 46 B | 47 N |
| 51 | 52 | 53 | 54 | 55 | 56 | 57 |
| 61 Ch | 62 Th | 63 | 64 | 65 | 66 | 67 |
| 71 S | 72 Sh | 73 | 74 | 75 | 76 | 77 Ñ |

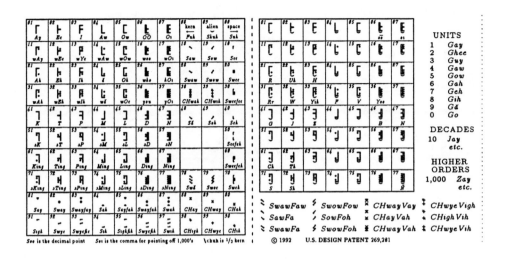

UNITS
1 *Gay*
2 *Ghee*
3 *Guy*
4 *Gaw*
5 *Gow*
6 *Gah*
7 *Geh*
8 *Gih*
9 *Gă*
0 *Go*

DECADES
10 *Jay* etc.

HIGHER ORDERS
1,000 *Zay* etc.

*SwawFaw*   *SwowFow*   *CHwayVay*   *CHwyeVigh*
*SawFa*   *SowFoh*   *CHayVah*   *CHighVih*
*SwawFa*   *SwowFoh*   *CHwayVah*   *CHwyeVih*

© 1992     U.S. DESIGN PATENT 269,281

| 01 Ay | 02 Ee | 03 I | 04 Aw | 05 Ow | 06 OO | 07 Oi | 08 kern ⟵ Fuh | 09 alien Shuh | 00 space ⟶ Suh |
|---|---|---|---|---|---|---|---|---|---|
| 11 wAy | 12 wEe | 13 wYe | 14 wAw | 15 wOw | 16 woo | 17 wOi | 18 Saw | 19 Sow | 10 See |
| 21 Ah | 22 Eh | 23 Ih | 24 ă | 25 Oh | 26 who | 27 hOi | 28 Swaw | 29 Swow | 20 Swee |
| 31 wAh | 32 wEh | 33 wIh | 34 wă | 35 wOe | 36 you | 37 yOi | 38 CHwah | 39 CHwih | 30 Sweefee |
| 41 K | 42 T | 43 P | 44 M | 45 L | 46 D | 47 N | 48 Să | 49 Soh | 40 Seh |
| 51 sK | 52 sT | 53 sP | 54 sM | 55 sL | 56 sD | 57 sN | | | 50 Seefeh |
| 61 King | 62 Ting | 63 Ping | 64 Ming | 65 Ling | 66 Ding | 67 Ning | | | 60 Sweefeh |
| 71 sKing | 72 sTing | 73 sPing | 74 sMing | 75 sLing | 76 sDing | 77 sNing | 78 Swă | 79 Swoe | 70 Sweh |
| 81 Say | 82 Sway | 83 Swayfay | 84 Sah | 85 Sayfah | 86 Swayfah | 87 Swah | 88 CHay | 89 CHway | 80 CHah |
| 91 Sigh | 92 Swye | 93 Swyefie | 94 Sih | 95 Sighfih | 96 Swyefih | 97 Swih | 98 CHigh | 99 CHwye | 90 CHih |

*Soo* is the decimal point *Soi* is the comma for pointing off 1,000's \chuh is 1/2 kern

| 01 | 02 | 03 | 04 | 05 | 06 ōō | 07 oi |
|---|---|---|---|---|---|---|
| 11 | 12 | 13 | 14 | 15 | 16 | 17 |
| 21 R | 22 Uh | 23 H | 24 | 25 | 26 | 27 |
| 31 Rr | 32 W | 33 Yih | 34 F | 35 V | 36 Yoo | 37 |
| 41 G | 42 J | 43 Z | 44 | 45 | 46 B | 47 N |
| 51 | 52 | 53 | 54 | 55 | 56 | 57 |
| 61 Ch | 62 Th | 63 | 64 | 65 | 66 | 67 |
| 71 S | 72 Sh | 73 | 74 | 75 | 76 | 77 Ñ |

UNITS

1 *Gay*
2 *Ghee*
3 *Guy*
4 *Gaw*
5 *Gow*
6 *Gah*
7 *Geh*
8 *Gih*
9 *Gă*
0 *Go*

DECADES

10 *Jay* *etc.*

HIGHER ORDERS

1,000 *Zay* *etc.*

| | | | |
|---|---|---|---|
| *SwawFaw* | *SwowFow* | *CHwayVay* | *CHwyeVigh* |
| *SawFa* | *SowFoh* | *CHayVah* | *CHighVih* |
| *SwawFa* | *SwowFoh* | *CHwayVah* | *CHwyeVih* |

A UNIVERSAL 2ND LANGUAGE  U.S. DESIGN PATENT 269,281

LAGNIAPPE — This page is designed to be cut out and pasted to a card or hung in some convenient place as a quick reference. It can also be folded at the dotted line and the back sides pasted together to make a portable reference. The next page has two wallet size sets that are designed to be folded and pasted so that you can always have one with you.

PageStream is a proprietary computer program of the Soft-Logi Publishing Corporation (11131South Towne Sq. Suite F, St. Louis, M 63123). Our modifications were made by Richard Landry under th direction of the Hankes Foundation. The modifications have to do wi ElmEntry and the ⊦JΓ2x font. We place those program modifications in th public domain but still subject to the rights of Soft-Logik. PageStream an extremely useful program but lacks the analytical capabilities of Amig TeX. Some of the ornamental capabilities of the PS program a illustrated. These variants are not machine scanable.